CELTIC SPIRIT

CELTIC SPIRITUAL VERSE

Poems of the
Western Highlanders

From the Gaelic

G.R.D. McLEAN

Published in Great Britain in 2002 by
Society for Promoting Christian Knowledge
Holy Trinity Church
Marylebone Road
London NW1 4DU

Originally published in 1961 by SPCK under the title
Poems of the Western Highlanders

British Library Cataloguing-in-Publication Data

A catalogue record for this book is available from the British Library

ISBN 0-281-05544-0

1 3 5 7 9 10 8 6 4 2

Typeset by WestKey Ltd., Falmouth, Cornwall
Printed in Great Britain by Creative Print and Design (Wales), Ebbw Vale

CONTENTS

vi

Flannan Isles

Butt of Lewis
Ness

Bragair

LEWIS

Bernera

Callernish
Stornoway

Scarp

HARRIS
Clisham

Taransay

Scalpay

Shiant Islands

Pabbay
Sound
Boreray

Ensay

Berneray

Roaul

NORTH UIST

Lochmaddy

Monach Islands

Balivanich

BENBECULA

The Minch

SKYE

Stilligarry

Stoneybridge

Benbore

SOUTH UIST

Loch Boisdale

Sound of Eriskay

ERISKAY

Eoligarry

of Barra

Hellisay

BARRA

Castlebay

Vatersay

Sandray

Pabbay
Mingulay
Berneray

THE OUTER HEBRIDES

xxii

INTRODUCTION

THIS WORK is the result of some ten years or so of labour and study. A chance meeting and a chance word in Inverness during the closing stages of the 1939 war led the writer to the originals from which this book has sprung. It was in the year 1900 that the late Dr Alexander Carmichael published his two volumes of *Carmina Gadelica* in Edinburgh in a limited edition. It made a great stir in the world of Celtic scholarship—"hymns and incantations . . . orally collected in the Highlands and Islands of Scotland". He set down the Gaelic text with a line by line translation on the opposite page—the work of most of his lifetime, long periods of which were spent among the people who retained this spoken literature. In 1928, sixteen years after his death, his daughter Elizabeth Catherine, the wife of Professor W. J. Watson of Edinburgh University, published a second and cheaper edition. In 1940 and 1941 two further volumes (from his grandfather's notes and papers) were issued by her son, Professor James Carmichael Watson, who held the chair of Celtic at Edinburgh University; before he could proceed further he lost his life in the Mediterranean in 1942 while serving with the Royal Navy. But a fifth volume was published in 1954, edited by Mr Angus Matheson of Glasgow University, with the material unexhausted still.

It is the poems of the first four volumes which have here been done into verse for English readers, the translations of Dr Carmichael and his grandson being followed fairly closely. The additional material entailed rearrangement from the first volumes of the work. When all was done—with copious notes —it was found to consist of over seven hundred poems and fragments. Exigencies of space led to revision and cutting, and the removal of the bulk of the notes, and also of prose liturgical versions of many of the prayers. But there are still 535 poems. The grouping of all similar poems, while convenient

xxiii

for comparison, produced an impression of too great mass and too little variety; in the interest of general readability further section-breaking was imperative.

The visitor to the Highlands of Scotland, whether he goes by road, by railway, or by sea, is at once struck by the majestic range of the hills and mountains. To travel from Glasgow by Loch Lomond through Glen Coe and the Great Glen, to go from Stirling to Loch Awe and the Pass of Brander, to take the North Road or the Highland Railway from Perth by Killiecrankie to Inverness and beyond, is to pass through a stretch of country unrivalled in Europe. To one who has never before done so, the first sight is breathtaking. In the same way the archipelagoes of the Hebrides are something not to be forgotten.

These poems have some of this about them; they unfold the secrets of the people of the hills and islands to the eye. Where known, the place in which a poem was recited is given; most come from the Outer Isles—the sandy, treeless, marshy, rocky, furthest Hebrides—for it was there that Dr Carmichael was living during some years of his collecting.

Some of the poems have clearly an ancient origin; distinctly pre-Christian elements may be traced in them. Since all the material in the first volumes was transcribed from the 'sixties up to the close of the last century from persons almost invariably advanced in years, none of it can now be less than one hundred and fifty years old; and most must go back at the least to before 1745 and the break-up of the Highlands. Dr Carmichael's own claim is that the bulk goes back with tolerable exactness a further hundred years to the first half of the seventeenth century. So far the pedigree is reliable. But it is clear that much older elements are present. The nearest parallel is provided by the late Dr Douglas Hyde, the former President of Eire, who published his work *The Religious Songs of Connacht* in two volumes in Dublin in 1906 as the tailpiece to *The Songs of Connacht*. The occasional striking identities of language in the Scottish and Irish works have sometimes been noted—Dr Hyde himself drew attention to them and quoted the *Carmina Gadelica*. These set a fascinating possibility of date; yet no conclusion can be established. The general inferiority of the Irish material is, however, apparent normally, a much greater medieval or Roman Catholic veneer—indeed smothering—having taken place.

But whatever the date, in bulk the *Carmina Gadelica* poems represent what Dr D. J. Macleod described as "the biggest sum of literature in any Western European language handed down by word of mouth". The wonderful thing is that they recreate a whole life and civilization that is now past, while the religion they breathe has largely become merged in more formalized expression. They present a pastoral and sea-going race, with its celebrations, its "guisers" or carollers, its customs, its seed-time and its harvest; its games, its difficulties, its scourges, prejudices, and fears; its simple but deep faith, coming sometimes near to a pantheism of earth, living creature, and element.

"Gaelic oral literature", wrote Dr Carmichael, "has been disappearing during the last three centuries. It is now becoming meagre in quantity, inferior in quality, and greatly isolated." But he does also say: "Although in decay, these poems are in verse of high order, with metre, rhythm, assonance, alliteration, and every quality to please the ear and to instruct the mind." Professor Watson says much the same thing: "It is as literature, and noble literature, that these poems make their highest appeal; and he is little to be envied in whom it wakens no response. They have beauties and graces which are at once apparent, and others they yield only to a faithful lover."

Dr Carmichael laments that he was unable to convey "the simple dignity, the charming grace, and the passionate devotion of the original". Nor was it possible for him to reproduce fully the features he enumerated above; nor is it possible to render them adequately in any translation. But there does remain a verbal quality which corresponds to the disciplined repetitions of developed Celtic art—oral repetitions of an exactness that parallels the scholar's exactness of text in a manuscript.

Fortunately something of their musical quality has been expressed in the great collection of material edited and published as the *Songs of the Hebrides* by the late Mrs Marjorie Kennedy-Fraser and the Reverend Dr Kenneth Macleod. Their work on a more local scale has been amplified considerably by

Miss Margaret Fay Shaw (Mrs J. L. Campbell) in her *Folksongs and Folklore of South Uist*. It is therefore possible to know of the sound of this poetry. But, except musically, the *Carmina Gadelica* go far beyond these works.

They are offered therefore mainly for the original purpose for which the bulk of them was composed, namely their values of religious expression. They have an especial worth in their nearness in spirit and tradition to the early Christian religion of North Britain, and in their wonderful mirror of the faith of a people who were of necessity individualists, and whose church was nature. Learned by heart and passed on from generation to generation, these are the prayers and hymns of the nomadic Christian missionaries, similar to those heard by the first converts of the Saxon Church in Northumbria and Mercia.

They have a particular quality; it is their New Testament character. References to the Old Testament are but few (to be numbered on the hand, and they influenced for the most part by Bishop Carswell's Gaelic Prayer Book). For this element is entirely filled by the Celt's own previous background, by his druids, his circles and cairns, his plants and moon-worship, his fairies and sprites, his experiences in his daily struggles and tasks amidst his natural surroundings. Unrefined like Judaism by contacts with busy civilizations and the influences of Hellenism, this may seem to obtrude the primitive too greatly; but at least it avoids successfully some of the Old Testament excursions that from time to time have marked the development of Christianity.

It is easy to see the later traces both of Romanism (very prominent, though very Highland) and of Protestantism. The late Frank Adam, the modern historiographer of the Highlands, held the view that the clans, with notable exceptions like the Campbells, adhered in spirit to the Celtic Church and inclined to a modified Romanism and to Episcopalianism rather than to the uncompromising Calvinism of the Kirk. The intoning also of these poems was that of the Celtic Church, similar to and dissimilar from Gregorian chanting. All that has survived has survived the Roman Church, the Reformation, the Risings, the Disruption, the emigrations, the evictions, the schools, and the ages of reason and science. But it is still possible to discern the spirit of that Columban church in these poems to which even now they are a more durable monument than the stones and crosses of Iona which they (or something very like them) inspired.

The unique feature here is that for the most part the poems are private; they reveal what is not usually revealed to strangers and outsiders. This fact, of itself, commands a respect. They do not include the heroic and public literature of the *ceilidh* which owes so much to Campbell of Islay and to Hector Maclean, and which first won for the Highlands their place in European folklore.

It is hardly too much to say that these poems are virtually unknown in England. Perhaps Macpherson's Ossian ultimately created too suspicious a reaction; perhaps the excesses of Celtic twilight and revivalism and their connection with strident nationalisms have made people wary. Whatever the reason, the average cultured person in England has no knowledge of them. The *Carmina Gadelica* was indeed catalogued by the appropriate United Nations body as one of those Gaelic works inadequately rendered into English. For the original volumes, splendid as they are, intrinsically are works of Gaelic scholarship.

A traditional rhymed verse has been chosen to present these poems in English; above all this is traditional poetry. Fidelity to the original has been a primary aim, and sometimes also to its metre. The work entailed achieving a rough self-taught Gaelic, for first attempts through translation only, under an impulsion of Keats' "On first looking into Chapman's Homer", were both unsatisfactory and inaccurate.

Study of the poems reveals certain things. Two great religious conceptions, peculiar to the Celtic Church, the one a theme, the one a practice, are discovered. There is upon occasion an almost word-for-word identity between Highland and Western Irish versions of evening prayers—survivals only upon the fringes or within the recesses of the Celtic world—which perpetuates a striking and original sacramental contribution. This is the remarkable "lying-down" theme, an extension of the Communion and Eucharist of the Last Supper to cover the hospitality afforded by God and Christ and the Holy Spirit to life's traveller or pilgrim; God is regarded both in himself and in his Three Persons as a Chief and *Ard Righ*, with personal ties to his people. It is after the manner of a chieftain, of a hero, or of a prince of royal feasting—a link with the world of the saga and the heaven of the nobles, and a more full version of the Communion and Agape of the Son of God. There is an immanence here; it is quite without parallel in English Christianity.

The second contribution is the ministry of the soul-friend, also without parallel. The diminution of the *anam-chara*, soul-friend, into confessor is Irish rather than Highland. In the Hebrides especially the soul-friend remained lay, although he had a priestly function. His task was to sing the "soul-peace" slowly over a dying person, leading the other watchers; he made the sign of the cross with his right thumb over the lips of the stricken one. Afterwards the soul-friend retained a place of special affection in the family.

One of the notable features of later Highland life was its Jacobitism. It will be observed that there is a fondness for such incidents as the Flight into Egypt that is out of proportion. Of course the identification was never made; but there was, it must be suspected, a mental approximation of similarity between the romantic son of the king over the water who was rejected by his own people, and the Messiah who "came unto his own". This fugitive parallel more than anything else serves to explain the fascinating ascendancy of the House of Stewart over the Highland imagination.

The Highlander from rude experience was unaccustomed to look for security. He did look for protection, and of various sorts. He liked his spells and charms, his talismans, those minor Acropolis-presences or Jerusalem-citadels that serve to focus the tenacity of strong, simple people. These were for the unpredictable or imponderable and awful dangers of life and war. And then he was deeply aware of the day-to-day perils of dangerous living, which his so often was. Here the shield of God was very real to him; here the little ritual of encompassment (*caim*) gave comfort and assurance; here the "good spirits"—the saints and the angels—were called in to aid. And then he was sufficiently a man of God to be conscious of the abysses of mortal jeopardy into which his soul could fall. Here self-dedication and prayer were his strong allies.

If protection prayers are defensive, good wishes attack the dangers of life without and within. The animal life, the elements, the hazards, the teeming seas are miraculously converted into immense sources of spiritual power—the wildness, almost savagery, of this western world harnessed under God to the life of man.

By far the greatest number of prayers are connected in some way with healing. The range of ailment and cure displayed is impressive, even if impossible of a testing acceptable to this generation. They are of particular interest in showing a complete subordination of the creature to the divine will and power. But nowhere is the difference in emphasis between two civilizations more apparent than in the prominence given to the eye. For the Highlander regarded the eye as the main physical link between the outer and the inner world, and as the means of connection (moving both ways) between the two. The very terms indicate a strangeness—some of it seeming ghostly or eerie, some of it fanciful or archaic, some of it penetrating and powerful but not easily intelligible, some of it simply different. This is the world of the "sight" and the "two sights", of the "evil eye" and of the "mote", of the damaged eye made healthy.

The notes of the true countryman are best seen in the cattle poems; for cattle were part of the family, from the widow's one cow to the herds of Macneill of Barra. The great cattle-fairs (Muir of Ord, Crieff, Falkirk, and so on) played a large part in the economy of all but the most remote isles of the Highlands. Chiefs and apostles were assumed to be absorbed in the interest of such things. It was St Columba's Franciscan attitude to animal life which left its mark here and in veterinary skill. But it was the tacksman who at one time supplied the integrating factor and was the source of the virtues in Highland agricultural life. (If he "be banished, who will be left to impart knowledge, or impress civility?" asked Dr Johnson.)

But everything in Highland life was orientated to God—even the tartan and kilt was apparently of ecclesiastical origin. The priest, when celebrating the Christian mysteries, was permitted a garment or vestment of eight colours—one more than the *Ard Righ* or High King; thereafter six colours for great chiefs and less down the scale, all depending on some fifty or sixty roots, plants, flowers, lichens, juices, trees, and barks, and combinations of these, which made the wonderful range of vegetable dyes used.

Law too was largely ecclesiastical in origin—it stemmed from "the four chief laws of Ireland", the law of Patrick against the slaying of clerics, the law of Darí against cattle-stealing, the law of Adamnan against the slaying of women, the law of Sunday against travelling then. Even in fighting (and over a number of centuries the Highlands are not without their atrocities, which were recognized as such), the prevailing tradition was of a noble ferocity.

Economically the sea was essential, for the soil was insufficient. Highland sea-power fluctuated, and it diminished earlier than other springs of life—the warning of what was to come. It was never stable. The Celtic Church was compelled to retreat before maritime marauders; nor did Norwegian suzerainty supply a sufficiently constant resin of sustenance, with the result that the defeat at Largs became ultimately inevitable. The period of independence under the Lords of the Isles, like the golden age of the Children of Israel, was fitfully glorious. And by degrees the sea-power of the clans, once divided, would be plucked and impaired by more consistent and better supported forces. By the sixteenth century's close the clans were much less able to launch out, and their sea-power was virtually gone. After Culloden there was not a vestige and no maritime ability to retain the Prince in retreat. Whether the Highlander realized that he never fully mastered the sea is doubtful; but the poems show that he understood it and came to terms with it.

Otherworldliness is represented in concrete form by the sun, the moon, the planets, and the stars. They were connected with earlier faiths; they have become loosely interwoven into the Celtic Christian tradition. The sun survives only as an adjunct of the Father's glory (the eye of God); the moon remains, mostly because no theology was attached to her and she does not impinge on the Creeds. The planets and the stars are swallowed up in the angels and saints, the holy ones, the household and company of heaven.

There seems to be no doubt that the Celtic Church was over-liberal in its canonizations, allowing almost any passably able missionary, abbot, or bishop to drift into the status for local, patriotic, or family reasons; dedications become legionary—perhaps originally simply stations or outposts called after the first man in charge—and sainthood was felt to be the natural adjunct to any patron, founder, or progenitor. The Roman Church on the other hand substituted another equally numerous galaxy of distinguished unknowns, and in the process suppressed much of the Celtic identity. The result is that the Celtic saints in their hundreds fail to triumph as completely as they might, and upon occasion give way lamely before a more vigorous and more ancient paganism.

Bird and animal life was minutely observed and interpreted. The tradition was Columban. Plant-life was primarily a marvellously spread world of healing, of colouring for wool, of fodder and uses for stock, of the gifts of God the Creator. The tradition was of St Beatan and of all the Macbeths, Beatons, Bethunes, Livingstones, and others of the healing hand.

Evening prayers are the most interesting of any, partly from the "lying down" theme already mentioned, partly because the ancient origins and forms happen to be the clearest. Archbishop Bernard observed that the structure of the great Lorica of St Patrick "seems to have been followed more or less closely in the composition of later charms of a similar character". Other early examples of loricas or breastplates begin in the same way "with an invocation of the Trinity", and then call upon "saints and angels", finally enumerating in detail "the parts of the human body which might be subject to injury. . . . The opening invocation of the Trinity . . . is undoubtedly a very ancient Celtic form" (Bernard and Atkinson, *The Irish Liber Hymnorum*, ii, pp. 210-11). For it will be noticed that a structure of prayer exists. Openings are made, followed by the necessary special adaptation—a similar opening introduces a prayer of baptism and a prayer of sea-voyaging. It is possible therefore still to utilize this prayer language for many purposes to-day.

The weaknesses revealed are noteworthy, though not requiring emphasis. The lack of poems for Easter, Whitsunday, and many parts of the Church's year is paralleled in medieval England by a similar paucity of carols; the lack of expression of a strong Resurrection hope is more serious. It may be that the defeat over Easter observance left an ineradicable mark upon the Celtic Church; and too naïvely (as St Patrick with the shamrock) it took ready circumstance or existing tradition to convey Christian truth. The story of St Oran was swiftly utilized to symbolize the reality and the certainty of the after-life, doubts and questions being met by the vivid but unsatisfactory tale.

At the last, four hands bore up the soul of a dying person—those of the priest of "happy death" who gave anointing and absolution; those of the mourning-woman (who held an honoured place in each townland); those of the soul-friend who pleaded with the delicacy of a deep humanity and spirit-uality; those of the soul-meeter, St Michael, who overrode all, even St Peter and others of the *Clan an oister*, as he bore "the little draggler" to the solemn "balancing of the beam".

Prayer language is the achievement of these poems; there are many word-contributions, such as "the water of meaning" and "one foot in the boat and one on land". The variations and combinations of the titles ascribed to the Deity are numerous; upon occasion there is confusion of the Three Persons of the Trinity; the same titles are even sometimes accorded outside, to St Mary and St Michael particularly. To the Gael, God is clearly of nature, of humanity, and of the spirit; and in all these aspects he is real, tremendous, near, loving, and within. He is the *De nan dul*, the God of life, the living God, the God of all.

He is revealed through the words and personalities of the many reciters, known and unknown, and through Dr Alexander Carmichael himself, to whom it is not possible to pay adequate tribute and of whom no one speaks or writes but with respect and affection.

One problem raises itself. How was it that such an extraordinarily strong and deep faith should prove inadequate and fail to triumph and survive? A full answer would be hard to give; nor would it be altogether true that it was inadequate or failed. But partially it is true to say that some of its trappings were too vulnerable to the modern onslaught of reason, utilitarianism, scientific knowledge, and economic necessity. The fairies and spirits had to go; with them went much of the religious faith and practice with which they were sometimes confused. And yet it is still a tremendous spiritual achievement, capable even of a revivification in these days of a latter Dispersion.

The numbered poems in this book are those which derive directly from the Gaelic of the *Carmina Gadelica*.

PRELUDE

A prince of men from Erin forth
To expiate too fierce a wrath
On open waves that wash the north
        Launched boat.

A prince of men Columba called
For wolf the gentle dove installed
With holy new intent enthralled
        Afloat.

A prince of men by call impelled
And with him twelve in friendship held
From strifely land of birth expelled
        He sailed.

A prince of men in boat away
Cleaving the heaving waters grey
Met the gale-tossing wind-whine spray
        Nor quailed.

A prince of men o'er ocean's waste
By swells and breaking seas embraced
Where whirlpools, tides and currents raced
        He steered.

A prince of men beweathered weak
By rock and strait and firth and creek
The place of life that was to seek
        He neared.

A prince of men his final goal
An isle white-sanded, green the knoll
With back to Erin, green the whole
        Humped land.

I

A prince of men by turquoise sound
The caves and waves and winds around
The coracle keel upmost downed
            'Neath sand.

A prince of men o'er stranded kyle
To Dutchman's Cap and Staffa's isle
Ben More and far off hills a-mile
            Conned space.

A prince of men from wrath now moved
His face meek kindly humble grooved
Friend to wild men and cattle hooved
            Donned grace.

A prince of men 'neath wattled roof
Taught twelve and more the Spirit's proof
Nor from the clans of men aloof
            He stood.

A prince of men he travelled forth
By love and word engrossed the north
From ocean to the eastern Forth
            For good.

A prince of men but always back
To recreate his saintly lack
Where once the printless ocean track
            Finished.

A prince of men and on the hill
The angels converse would instil
When travelworn his power's fill
            Minished.

A prince of men from o'er the seas
Apostle of the Hebrides
Serene and smiling through the breeze
            Foam-blown.

A prince of men from him the lore
Of Jesus Christ friend of the poor
Of godly love the harvest store
        Home-grown.

A prince of men he midmost stands
From Man to farthest Orkney lands
Where sacred shine Iona's strands
        Shell-strown.

A prince of men Columba bold
Great Shepherd of a Highland fold
Great Saint infusing hearts untold
        Sin-sown.

I. THROUGH THE DAY

The stony low-built clachans stand
Beside the spreading machair-land,
Between the hills and ocean strand,
    Smoke rising up away.

Smoke rising from rekindled peat,
With household sounds of wakened feet,
The prayer accompanies to greet
    The Lord God of the day.

The Lord God blesses all inside,
The keeping-house and farming plied,
From morn till noon, till eventide
    When the fire-shadows play.

When the fire-shadows fainter grow,
The smooring hides the ashes' glow,
But angel-flames on guard below
    Within the clachans stay.

1. *The Kindling* *North Uist*

This morning I will kindle the fire upon my hearth
Before the holy angels who stand about my path,
Both Ariel the lovely and Uriel of grace,
Beneath the sun not frightened by one of human race,
No envy, hatred, malice, no fear upon my face,
But the Holy Son of God the guardian of the place.
   Beneath the sun not frightened by one of human race,
   No envy, hatred, malice, no fear upon my face,
   But the Holy Son of God the guardian of the place.

God, a love-flame kindle in my heart to neighbours all,
To foe, to friend, to kindred, to brave, to knave, to thrall,
O Son of lovely Mary, from lowliest thing on earth,
To the Name that highest is and of the greatest worth,
   O Son of lovely Mary, from lowliest thing on earth,
   To the Name that highest is and of the greatest worth.

2. *The Creed Prayer* *Morar*

O great God of all gods, I believe
That thou art the Father eternal of all life above;
O great God of all gods, I believe
That thou art the Father eternal of goodness and love.

O great God of all gods, I believe
That thou art the Father eternal of each holy one;
O great God of all gods, I believe
That thou art the Father eternal of each lowly one.

O great God of all gods, I believe
That thou art the Father eternal of each clan of men;
O great God of all gods, I believe
That thou art the Father eternal of earth of our ken.

Chief and God of the hosts, I believe
That thou art the creator and maker of heav'n on high,
That thou art the creator and maker of soaring sky,
That thou art the creator of oceans that under lie.

Chief and God of the hosts, I believe
That thou art the creator and warper of my soul's thread,
Thou my body's creator from dust and earth-ashes' bed,
Thou my body's breath-giver and thou my soul's domain bred.

O Father, bless to me my members,
O Father, bless my soul and being,
O Father, bless to me life's embers,
O Father, bless belief and seeing.

Father eternal, Chief of hosts, I believe
That my soul thou with thine own Spirit of healing didst mend,
And thou thy belov'd Son in covenant for me didst send,
And thou the blest blood of thy Son for my soul didst expend.
Father eternal, Chief of all, I believe
That thou at baptising thy Spirit of grace didst extend.

Father eternal, Chief of mankind,
Enwrap my body and soul entwined,
Safeguard me to-night in thy love shrined,
The saints' aid to-night my shelter kind.

For thou hast brought me up from the night
Unto this morning's most gracious light,
Great joy unto my soul to provide,
And excelling good to do beside.

O Jesu Christ, all thanks be to thee
For the many gifts bestowed on me,
For each sea and land, each day, each night,
For each mild, each fresh, each weather bright.

I am giving thee worship with my whole life every hour,
I am giving thee assent with my whole power,
With my fill of tongue's utterance I am giving thee praise,
I am giving thee honour with my whole lays.

I am giving thee reverence with my whole knowledge upcaught,
I am giving thee offering with my whole thought,
I am giving extolling with my whole good intent's flood,
I am giving thee meekness in the Lamb's blood.

I am giving thee loving with my devotion's whole art,
I am giving kneeling with my whole desire,

I am giving thee liking with my whole beating of heart,
  I am giving affection with my sense-fire;
I am giving mine existing with my mind and its whole,
  O God of all gods, I am giving my soul.

  My thought, my deed, my word, and my will,
  My mind, my brain, my state, and my way,
  I beseech thee to keep me from ill,
  To keep from hurt and from harm to-day;
  To keep me from grieving and from plight,
  In thy love's nearness to keep this night.

  O may God shield me, and may God fill,
  O may God watch me, and may God hold;
  O may God bring me where peace is still,
  To the King's land, eternity's fold.

  Praise to the Father, praise to the Son,
  Praise to the Spirit, the Three in One.

3. Petition for Protection

  O holy God of truth who art,
  O loving God of pity's part,
  Encharm me from all spelling made,
  Encharm me from all snaring laid.

  O God of life and tenderness,
  With thy forgiveness do thou bless,
  In each my word of wickedness,
  In each my oath's untruthfulness,
  In each my deed of foolishness,
  And in my speech of emptiness.

  O God of life and tenderness,
  My hiding from the danger bless,
  Of the women of silentness;
  O God of life and tenderness,
  My hiding from the danger bless,
  Of the women of wantonness;
  O God of life and tenderness,
  My hiding from the danger bless,
  Of the women of witchingness;

O God of life and tenderness,
My hiding from the danger bless,
Of the women of lyingness.

Thou wast before my life's first friend,
Thou again at my journey's end;
Thou wast beside to shape my soul,
Father, be at my journey's goal.

Be with me when I rise or lie
In sleep, my dear companions nigh;
Each eve and morn my watchman stand,
Home draw me to the holy land.

4. *Grace before Food*   *Benbecula*

Be with me, O God, at breaking of bread,
And be with me, O God, when I have fed;
Naught come to my body my soul to pain,
O naught able my contrite soul to stain.

5. *Thanks after Food*   *Benbecula*

O God, all thanks be unto thee,
O God, all praise be unto thee,
O God, worship be unto thee,
For all that thou hast given me.

As thou didst give my body life
To earn for me my drink and food,
So grant to me eternal life
To show forth all thy glory good.

Through all my life grant to me grace,
Life grant me at the hour of death;
God with me at my leaving breath,
God with me in deep currents' race.

O God, in the breath's parting sigh,
O, with my soul in currents deep,
Sounding the fords within thy keep,
Crossing the deep floods, God be nigh.

6. *A Journey Prayer* *Benbecula*

This day to me, God, do thou bless,
This very night, God, blessing give;
Thou God of grace, o do thou bless
All days and all the times I live;
   Thou God of grace, o do thou bless
   All days and all the times I live.

God, bless the path I walk above,
God, bless the earth beneath my toes;
God, bless me, give to me thy love,
O God of gods, bless rest, repose;
   God, bless me, give to me thy love,
   O God of gods, bless my repose.

7. *Power of Raven* *South Uist*

Power of raven black be thine,
Power of eagle's back be thine,
   Hound-chase power.
Power of stormy wrack be thine,
Power of moonbeam track be thine,
   Sun's face power.
Power of ocean tack be thine,
Power of land attack be thine,
   Heav'n grace power.

Good of ocean space be thine,
Good of land and place be thine,
   Of heav'n's city.
Every day joy's trace be thine,
No day sorrow's case be thine,
   Honour, pity.
Love of every face be thine,
Pillow-dying grace be thine,
   Saviour, with thee.

8. Over the Pass

> May God be your shield
> On sheer when spins the head,
> Christ keep you afield
> When climbing up you tread,
> Spirit bathing yield
> You at the pass-brow shed.

9. Smooring Blessing   Barra

> I will keep in and smoor the hearth
>   As Mary would smoor the peat;
> Bride and Mary making a path
>   Round floor and fire with their feet,
>   The protection to fall
>   On the household, on all.
>
> Who is out on the grassy lawn?
>   Mary sun-white, her Son there;
> God's angel spake, God's mouth hath sworn;
>   Angels of promise flame-fair
>   Watch the hearth, till white day
>   On the ash-glow doth play.

10. Undressing Prayer

> O thou great God, thy light grant to me,
> O thou great God, thy grace may I see,
> O thou great God, thy felicity,
> And in thy health's well cleanse me pure-white.
>
> O God, lift from me mine anguish sore,
> O God, lift from me what I abhor,
> O God, lift from me vanity's store,
> And lighten my soul in thy love's light.
>
> As I shed off my clothing at night,
> Grant that I shed off my conflict-plight,
> As vapours lift off the hill-crests white,
> Lift thou my soul from the mist of death.

O Jesu Christ, O MacMary One,
O Jesu Christ, O thou Paschal Son,
My body shield in thy shield-cloak spun,
My soul made white in thy white grace-breath.

11. *Night Blessing*

The dwelling, O God, by thee be blest,
And each one who here this night doth rest;
My dear ones, O God, bless thou and keep
In every place where they are asleep;

In the evening that doth fall to-night,
And in every single evening-light;
In the daylight that doth make to-day,
And in every single daylight-ray.

12. *Sleep Blessing*   *South Uist*

Be thy right hand, O God, under my head,
Be thy light, O Spirit, over me shed,
Be the nine angels' cross over me down,
From the soles of my feet to topmost crown,
    From the soles of my feet to topmost crown.

O Jesu offenceless, sore crucified,
By the wicked's decree scourged and tried,
O the many ills in my body done
That I cannot this night count one by one,
    That I cannot this night count one by one!

O thou King of the blood loyal and true,
Exclude me not from thy covenant new,
For my unjust misdeeds make me not pay,
Overlook me not in thy counting day,
    Overlook me not in thy counting day.

Mary's and Michael's cross o'er me in peace,
My soul dwell in truth, from guile my breast cease,
My soul in peace with thee, wilderness Light,
Bold Michael, at one with my soul in flight,
    Amen, be it so, morn, eve, day and night.

To-night I lie down for my rest,
With mild Mary and with her Son,
With my King's Mother, Virgin blest,
Who shieldeth from evils each one.

With evil I will not lie down,
Nor shall evil lie down with me,
But with God I will lie me down,
God himself will lie down with me.

God and Mary and Michael kind
And the cross of nine angels white,
As Three and as One my shield twined,
From my face-brow to foot-tip quite.

I call unto Peter, to Paul,
I call unto Mary, the Son,
Twelve trusty Apostles I call
To keep me from hurt and harm done;
From dying ere my race be run,
    From death to-night ere 'tis out-run!

O God, Mary-Maid glory-crowned,
Jesu, fragrant Virgin's own Son,
From the pains eternal spell-bound
Be we from the fierce smoke-fire won,
    From the pains eternal spell-bound,
    From the fierce and smoking fire won!

II. INFANCY

Thou who wast the Giver of childhood's birth,
Thou who didst deliver me safe to earth,
O thou Life-Fountain true;

Thou who didst bless me with water of grace,
Who didst caress me, limbs, body and face,
Thou by whom my shape grew;

Thou who didst fend me the spirit and gnome,
Thou who didst send me my food and my home,
And with strength didst endue;

Thou who didst guide all my footsteps aright,
Grant I may bide always as in thy sight,
And my spirit renew.

14. Saint Bride the Aid-Woman
Skye and South Uist

There came to me assistance, aid
From Mary white and Bridget maid;
As Anna bore her Mary small,
As Mary bore her Christ for all,
As Eile bore the Baptist John,
No flaw or spot his body on,
In mine unbearing grant me aid,
      Aid me, O Bridget maid.

As Christ of Mary was conceived,
A Perfect Son travail-achieved,
Assist me, mother-fostering,
Conception from the bone to bring;
As thou didst help the Virgin fine,
No gift of gold or corn or kine,
Great is my sickness, grant me aid,
      Aid me, O Bridget maid.

15. The Invitation to the Aid-Mother

Come in, come in, O Bride, O Bride,
And thy welcome shall truly be,
Come, relieve the woman inside,
Give the birth to the Holy Three.

16. The Mothering-Nut of Saint Mary

"Behold, O Mary Mother, behold,
    The woman near to death is she".
"Behold her thyself, O Christ, enfold,
    Since it is of thy mercy free
To give thy rest to the childlike thing,
The woman from her labour to bring.

"Behold her thyself, O Christ, enfold,
    Thou art the King of saving mild,
Deliver the woman from death's hold,
    Do thou sain the innocent child,
Unto the vine-shoot give thou thy rest,
Give peace to the mother labour-blest".

17. *Mothering-Nut Charm*

"See the woman, O Mary mild,
Thy smile of grace above her head;
Freedom give thou unto the child,
And keep the woman from the dead".

"Behold thou her, O Christ so mild,
Since it is the act of thy hand
To give freedom unto the child,
And the woman to cause to stand".

"I do as is thy wish so mild,
Beloved little Mother of sleep;
Freedom I give unto the child,
From the dead the woman I keep".

18. *Lullaby of the Ocean Shore*

Thou art no seal-cub round-headed and blue,
No fledgeling of sea-gull greyish in hue,
  Sleep, my pretty one, Mother loves true;
Thou art no otter-whelp coated and wry,
Nor the lean cow's little calf standing by,
  O sleep, my pretty one, do not cry.

19. *Fairy Lullaby*   Lismore

Lilting on the light foot,
The left foot, the right foot,
Lilting on the light foot,
My dearie trips the floor.

In the cot I set thee,
And myself I pet thee,
Many fain would get thee
Their very own to be.

Lilting on the light foot,
The left foot, the right foot,
Lilting on the light foot,
My dearie trips to door.

18

Shoulder-high I ride thee,
Light and gay beside thee,
'Tis I that would pride me
Beside the flocks with thee.

Lilting on the light foot,
The left foot, the right foot,
Lilting on the light foot,
My dearie trips the more.

Mead and nectar for thee,
Chalice wine I pour thee,
Honey-combs restore thee,
And white milk flowing free.

Lilting on the light foot,
The left foot, the right foot,
Lilting on the light foot,
My dearie trips the floor.

20. *Lullaby of the Swan*   *Benbecula*

O swan white thou,
  Hu hi, ho ho!
Sad thy plight now,
  Hu hi, ho ho!
Sad thy showing,
  Hu hi, ho ho!
Thy blood flowing,
  Hu hi, ho ho!
  Hu hi, ho ho!

O swan white thou,
  Hu hi, ho ho!
From friend-sight now,
  Hu hi, ho ho!
Lady singer,
  Hu hi, ho ho!
Near me linger,
  Hu hi, ho ho!
  Hu hi, ho ho!

Healing joy thou,
  Hu hi, ho ho!

Keep my boy now,
  Hu hi, ho ho!
Shield from dying,
  Hu hi, ho ho!
Health supplying,
  Hu hi, ho ho!
By thy sighing,
  Hu hi, ho ho!
  Hu hi, ho ho!

Pain and sorrow,
  Hu hi, ho ho!
May thy foe know,
  Hu hi, ho ho!
  Hu hi, ho ho!

Thousand blessings,
  Hu hi, ho ho!
Life's caressings,
  Hu hi, ho ho!
Joy and grace thine,
  Hu hi, ho ho!

In each place thine,
  Hu hi, ho ho!
  Hu hi, ho ho!

His be growth, rest,
  Hu hi, ho ho!
Strength and worth best,
  Hu hi, ho ho!
Vict'ry grace his,
  Hu hi, ho ho!
In each place his,
  Hu hi, ho ho!
  Hu hi, ho ho!

Mother Mary,
  Hu hi, ho ho!
Mild-white fairy,
  Hu hi, ho ho!
Fair, caress thee,
  Hu hi, ho ho!
Loving, bless thee,
  Hu hi, ho ho!
Bathe and clean thee,
  Hu hi, ho ho!
Nurse and wean thee,
  Hu hi, ho ho!

Shielding, caring,
  Hu hi, ho ho!
From foe's snaring,
  Hu hi, ho ho!
  Hu hi, ho ho!

Fondly stroke thee,
  Hu hi, ho ho!
Ward and cloak thee,
  Hu hi, ho ho!
Full embracing,
  Hu hi, ho ho!
With all gracing,
  Hu hi, ho ho!
  Hu hi, ho ho!

Mother's eyes thou,
  Hu hi, ho ho!
Her love's eyes now,
  Hu hi, ho ho!
Angels' eyes thou,
  Hu hi, ho ho!
Paradise thou!
  Hu hi, ho ho!
  Hu hi, ho ho!

21. Baby's Bath   Skye and South Uist

A splash for my big darling,
    A splash, and how you grow!
A splash for catawauling,
    A plop, you're greedy so.

Your helping of the treating
    The crowdie and the kail;
Your helping of the eating
    Sweet honey, milk from pail.

Your helping of the boiling
    Whey-whisk and curdle-flow;
Your helping of the spoiling
    With spear and with the bow.

The yellow eggs of Easter
    Your helping as we make;
My treasure-joy, my feaster,
    Your helping as we bake.

With present and with parcel
    Your helping of the dish;
My lovely little castle,
    Your helping treasure-wish.

Your helping of the chasing
    On face of misted ben;
Your helping of the racing
    And ruling hosts of men.

I beg your royal pardon,
    Your helping of a king;
Your helping of the Garden,
    Good peaceful blossoming.

If you grow not at dawning,
    Your growth let evening see;
What does not grow ere morning,
    High noontide's growing be.

The Secret Three's three splashes
    Your full safe-keeping be
From death, eye's evil flashes,
    From every jealousy.

The splash of God the living,
    The splash of Christ of love,
The Spirit splash peace-giving,
    Grace-Trinity above.

22. *The Wings of a Dove*   *Barra*

The little lovely child who dies
Through pains of the beyond will rise
As dove of valour upward flies
Through all the darkness of the skies.

III. CHRISTMAS

The long night dead with the dark and snow
The flake-breath eddyeth to and fro
And Joseph treadeth with Mary slow
  Unto the numbering place.

The messenger's flight unrolls the sky,
The star in his might shining on high,
The seraphim bright carolling nigh,
  And the sun rising to space.

The world aglow, the sea and the land,
The waves arow break white on the sand,
The mountains show a long rose-tipped hand
  For his foot's descending pace.

The Virgin is here upon her knee,
While Saint Bride bows near the Christ to see,
And stable-beams rear protectingly,
  The beasts with wondering face.

The Father's heir, who is King above,
O Jesu fair, who dost come in love
From the pure air of the Holy Dove,
  Bless our giving human race.

As the Egypt-flight is swift for thee,
Pursuing despite fugitive free,
As returning's light is thine to see,
  So to the wayward be grace.

23. The Star-Kindler

The Kindler of the starry fires
Behold, cloud-pillowed like desires,
And all the aery feathered quires
    Are lauding him.

With heavenly music down he came
Forth from the Father of his Name,
While harp and lyre in song acclaim
    Applauding him.

O Christ, thou refuge of my love,
Why lift not I thy fame above?
When saints and angels full enough
    Are songing thee.

O sweet MacMary of all grace,
How glist'ring white thy pure fair face,
How rich the joyful pasture place
    Belonging thee!

O Christ my loved beyond the flood,
O Christ, thou of the Holy Blood,
By day and night outswell my bud
    Of praising thee.

24. A Time there Was

Lochalsh, Kintail and Harris

A time there was ere God's Son's birth,
A great big black morass was the earth,
    No star, no sun, no moon gave light,
No body, no heart, no form's delight.

Forth shone the plain, forth shone the steep,
Forth shone the great grey-green of the deep,
    Forth shone the whole globe's circling girth,
When the Son of God came down to earth.

Then 'twas Mary of grace made say,
The favouring Virgin, wise her way,
    Love unto her when Joseph brought,
To be by her side he often sought.

A pact 'twixt Joseph and the Maid
In order seemly and just was laid,
    Drawn up and sealed by God, a cause
Fit to the Great King of virtues' laws.

    Into God's Temple they did go,
Where the priests within stood in a row;
    As did the Great High King ordain,
Ere they came out they were wed the twain.

    An angel then so soft came he:—
"Why, Joseph, what has come over thee?"
    "Came from the priests my wife to dwell,
My nature tells me it is not well".

    "Now, Joseph, by thy reason stay,
'Tis foolish of thee ill word to say;
    She of thine is a Virgin Maid,
On whom ne'er a hand of man was laid".

    "How to me can there be belief?
The knowing is mine, and to my grief—
    When by her shoulder down I slept
A living child 'neath her girdle leapt".

25. *The First Miracle of Christ*   *Benbecula*

Joseph and Mary they went the two
    To the numbering up so far,
And the birds began to sing and coo
    In the woods where turtle-doves are.

The two on their journey they did fare,
    Till a thick tree-wood they did reach,
In the wood the fruit was hanging there
    And as red as the raspberry each.

For it was then that her time was near,
    And she carried the King of grace,
A wish took her for the fruit so dear
    That grew on the slope of the place.

Then Mary to Joseph word spake she,
    And gentle and rich was her voice,
"O Joseph, give thou the fruit to me
    That I sate the wish of my choice".

And Joseph to Mary word spake he,
    With hard pain his breast was afire,
"I'll give of the fruit, Mary, to thee,
    But o who is thy burden's sire?"

It was the time that the Baby now
    From out of her womb forth he spake,
"Come bend thee down each beautiful bough,
    That my Mother her sating take".

And from the top branch that swayed on high,
    To the branch that did lowest lie,
    They all bent down unto her knee,
And Mary took of the fruit nearby
    In her loved land of prophecy.

Then Joseph to Mary said his part,
    With dire sorrow filling his face,
"It is a-carrying him thou art,
    The King of the glory and grace.
Blessed art thou, O Mary my heart,
    'Mid the women of every place;
Blessed art thou, O Mary my heart,
    'Mid the women of every place".

26. *The Long Night*   *Mingulay of Barra*

This night the long eve, dark it is through,
        Hu ri vi ho hu,
It will be snowing and drifting too,
        Hu ri vi ho hu,
The snow will be white until the day,
        Hu ri vi ho hu,
And the moon white till the morn away,
        Hu ri vi ho hu.

This night the eve-night of great birth done,
        Hu ri vi ho hu,
This night born he, Mary Virgin's Son,
        Hu ri vi ho hu,

This night born he, King of glory's Boy,
Hu ri vi ho hu,
This night born he, the Stem of our joy,
Hu ri vi ho hu,
This night the great bens gleamed with the sun,
Hu ri vi ho hu,
This night sea and shore gleamed as if one,
Hu ri vi ho hu,
This night born Christ, King of greatness, Son,
Hu ri vi ho hu.

Ere 'twas heard of the Glory at hand,
Hu ri vi ho hu,
There was heard the wave upon the strand,
Hu ri vi ho hu,
Ere 'twas heard that his foot reached the land,
Hu ri vi ho hu,
Heard was the angels' glorious song,
Hu ri vi ho hu,
This night the dark night, eve that is long,
Hu ri vi ho hu.

To him there shone the wood and the tree,
To him there shone the mountain and sea,
To him there shone the ground and the plain,
When that his foot on the earth was lain,
Hu ri vi ho hu.

27. Christmas Hail *Lewis*

Ho to the King, ho to the King,
Blessed is he, blessed is he,
Ho to the King, ho to the King,
Blessing and hail unto him be.

Blest is he who hath come so well,
Ho to the King, ho to the King,
Blest be the house and all who dwell,
Ho to the King, ho to the King.

The stock, the stone, each beam and stave,
Ho to the King, ho to the King,
Cover to cloth for God to save,
Ho to the King, and ho we sing.

28

The health of folk therein to be,
Ho to the King, ho to the King,
Blessed is he, blessed is he,
Ho to the King, ho to the King,
Blessed is he, blessed the King,
Ho to the King, ho to the King.

Long life around the house for all,
Ho to the King, ho to the King,
Healthy round the fire and wall,
Ho to the King, ho to the King.

Many a beam the house inside,
A household on the found abide,
Ho to the King, ho to the King,
Blessed is he, blessed the King,
Ho to the King, ho to the King,
Blessed is he of whom we sing.

Ho to the King, ho to the King,
This night the eve of the greatest birth,
Ho to the King, ho to the King,
Blessed is he, blessed the King,
Ho to the King, ho to the King,
His feet's two soles have reached the earth,
Ho to the King, ho to the King,
Blessed is he, blessed the King,
Hail and blessing unto the King.

Born is the Son of Mary Maid,
Ho to the King, ho to the King,
Blessed is he, blessed the King,
Ho to the King, ho to the King,
The mountains high the sun arrayed,
Ho to the King, ho to the King,
Blessed is he, blessed the King.

The earth did shine and shone the land,
Ho to the King, ho to the King,
Blessed is he, blessed the King,
Ho to the King, ho to the King,
Heard was the wave upon the strand,
Ho to the King, ho to the King,
Blessed is he, blessed the King.

Blessed is he, blessing we send,
Ho to the King, ho to the King,

Without beginning, without end,
Blessed the King of whom we sing,
For aye unto infinity,
To all time, to eternity,
To all ages, for evermore,
Blest be the King whom we adore.

28. *Christmas Carol* *Lewis*

Ho to the King! blessed is he!
Ho to the King! blessed is he!
Ho to the King of whom we sing!
   Ho! ro! joy let there be!

This night is the eve of greatest birth,
   Born is the Son of Mary Maid,
The soles of his feet have touched the earth,
   Son of glory above displayed,
   Heaven and earth to him aglow
      As he comes below,
   Ho! ro! joy let there be!

Heavenly joy and peace upon earth,
   Behold his feet have reached the place;
O worship the King, hail the Lamb's birth,
   King of the virtues, Lamb of grace,
   Ocean and earth to him alit
      As he doeth it,
   Ho! ro! joy let there be!

The gleam of distance, the gleam of sand,
   Roar of waves with a tide that sings
To tell us that Christ is born at hand,
   Saving Son of the King of kings,
   Sun on the mountains high ashine
      Reveals him divine,
   Ho! ro! joy let there be!

The earth and the spheres together shine,
   The Lord God opes the starry floor;
Haste, Son of Mary, assistance mine,
   Thou Christ of hope, and joy's wide Door,
   On hills and ranges, golden Sun,
      Behold, it is done!
   Ho! ro! joy let there be!

Ho King! ho King! blessed is he!
Ho King! ho King! o blessed be!
   Ho, hi! blessed le Roy!
   Ho, hi! let there be joy!

To this dwelling prosperous word,
To all that you have seen and heard,
To the floor-flags laid clean and clear,
To the neat stone staves standing here,
  Ho King! ho King! blessed is he!

Bless this house and its contents all,
From rafter, stone and beam to wall,
Cover to cloth to God consigned,
Weal of men within to find,
  Ho King! ho King! blessed is he!

Long life at home be unto you,
Good health about the hearth your due,
Many a tie and house-stake round,
And people dwelling on this found,
  Ho King! ho King! blessed is he!

Offer the Being roof to floor,
From stave to stone, from beam to door,
Both rods and cloth offer again,
To the folk here good health to reign,
  Ho King! ho King! blessed is he!

Ho King! ho King! blessed is he!
Ho King! ho King! o blessed be!
   Ho, hi! blessed le Roy!
   Ho, hi! let there be joy!

Sans a beginning, sans ending,
All hail, le Roy! blessed the King!
Ho, hi, the King everlasting!
To eternal infinity,
Generations for ever be,
   Ho, hi! blessed le Roy!
   Ho, hi! let there be joy!

30. *The Christmas Gift*   *Mingulay of Barra*

A hey the Gift, for the Gift a ho,
Hey the Gift, for the living to go.

On her knee the mild-white Mary Maid,
In her lap the King of glory laid.

The sack and shirt are struck on the side,
The spar is beaten upon the hide.

To tell us that Christ is born it rings,
From salvation's land the King of kings.

I see the hills and I see the strand,
I see the elders hover at hand.

I see the angels on clouds descend,
Coming to us to speak and befriend.

31. *Hey the Gift*   *Scalpay of Harris*

A hey to give, a ho to give,
A hey for the Gift for to live.

Son of the clouds, Son of the dawn,
Son of the sphere and star of morn,
   A hey to give, a ho to give,
   A hey for the Gift for to live.

Son of the rain, of dew to lie,
Son of the firmament and sky,
   A hey to give, a ho to give,
   A hey for the Gift for to live.

Son of the flame, Son of the light,
Son of the earth, the world in sight,
   A hey to give, a ho to give,
   A hey for the Gift for to live.

Son of all nature, Son of heav'n,
Son of the sun, of moon at ev'n,
   A hey to give, a ho to give,
   A hey for the Gift for to live.

Son of Mary the God-look one,
Chief of all news God's only Son,
　　A hey to give, a ho to give,
　　A hey for the Gift for to live.

32. *Christmas Monday*　　　　　　　　*Benbecula*

I am the Gift, and I am the Poor,
I am the Man of this evening's night;
I am the Son of God at the door,
Requesting the Monday gifts aright.

On her knee noble the mild-white Bride,
Noble the King of life at her side,
Son of the moon, and Son of the sun,
Great MacMary the God-looking Maid.
I am at the door, be it undone,
With a cross on each right shoulder laid.

I see the hills, and I see the strand,
The herald angels coming I see,
I see the kind graceful dove at hand,
Coming so gently and friendlily.

33. *The Virgin and Child*
　　　　　　South Uist and Eriskay of Uist

Lo, comes the Virgin, blesséd one,
The Christ so young upon her breast!
O Mary Virgin, O thou Son,
The house and all therein be blest.

Bless ye the table and the food,
Bless corn and flocks and money-store,
Virgin thyself our mother good,
The lean drought-quarter at the door.

Thou than the waxing moon more white
Arising o'er the hilltops' length;
Thou than the summer sun more bright
As he rejoices in his strength.

33

But since the bard is hastening by,
Place in the bag your alms and bless;
God the Son's servant knocking I,
Ope thou for sake of God no less.

34. *The Night of the Star* *Benbecula*

That night when afar
There shone forth the star
For the flock ere dawn
The Shepherd was born;
A hundred the Mary Virgin's charms
As he lay in his Mother's arms.

By her side the Three
Of eternity
In the manger cold
Of the humble fold;
O come and give tithes of all thy wealth
To the Man of Saving and Health.

The Child white as foam
With no single home
Throughout the whole earth,
So lovely his birth;
Driven forth as an exile to dwell,
Holy tender Immanuel.

Three angels of power
Come down at this hour,
O Faith, Hope and Love,
Come down from above;
To the Christ of the people, the King,
Salutation and hail o bring.

For hand give a kiss,
A foot dried be his
With locks of your hair
Like men bent in prayer;
Thou One of the world, thou Jesu Son,
Michael and Mary, ne'er us shun.

35. The Virgin

Behold the Virgin approaching near,
And the Christ so young upon her breast,
Angels low-bowing before them here,
And the King of life saying, "'Tis best".

The Virgin of most glorious hair,
Jesus more white than the snowflake tressed,
The seraphs of song praising them there,
And the King of life saying, "'Tis best".

O Mary Mother of wondrous power,
With thy mighty aid do thou invest,
Bless the meat and the board and the flour,
The ear, the corn and the food be blest.

The Virgin of most glorious mien,
Jesus more white than the snowflake tressed,
She like the moon o'er the mountains seen,
He like the sun on the ranging crest.

36. Christmas Procession South Uist

O God of the moon, God of the sun above,
Who ordained for us the Son of mercy-love,
The gentle-white Mary is upon her knee,
The Christ the King of life at her breast is he.
I am the priest here established in the place,
I am processing the founded stones in grace;
In my sight are dwellings and the far-off strands,
In my sight the angels floating in their bands,
In my sight their graceful curving column fleet
Coming to us landbound in friendship to greet.

37. The Child of Glory

The Baby of joy,
Mary's Baby-boy,
Was born in the stall
    The King of all;
To the waste he came
And suffered our blame;
Who to him are near
    Are counted dear.

He saw with his eye
That in straits we lie;
Heav'n opened in love
    Our head above:
Christ came to our view,
The Spirit so true,
His crown our defence
    Drawing us hence.

O make our hope strong,
Make happiness long,
In might keep us here
    Loyal and near,
Our Lamp thou alight,
With the virgins bright
Who sing the new song
    In glory-throng.

38. Christmas Fishing
Benbecula

The day of light is to us at the morn,
The Christ of our Lady Virgin is born.

In his name I sprinkle the water round
Upon everything in my boatyard found.

O thou King above of virtues and power,
Thy blessing for fishing upon us shower.

I will take the thwart, an oar in my hand,
Row strokes seven-hundred-seven from land.

36

I will cast down my hook a fish to bring,
And the first to bite be my tributing,

In the name of Christ, the elements' King,
For the poor shall have it to his liking.

And Saint Peter brave, king of fishermen,
Will after it give me his blessing then.

May Ariel, Gabriel, John withal,
Saint Raphael favouring, good Saint Paul,

Saint Columba tender in each distress,
Graced mild-white Mary of maidenliness,

To the ocean fishing-bank with us go,
And still the wave-crests to a gentle flow.

Be the King of kings at our course's end,
A lengthened life and long happiness send.

From the Three on high be the King's own crown,
Be the cross of the Christ to shield us down,
    From the Three on high be the King's own crown,
    Be the cross of the Christ to shield us down.

39. *The Little Mother's Song*   *South Uist*

Thou King of the moon, thou King of the sun,
Thou King of the spheres, of the stars each one,
Thou King of the world, thou King of the sky,
How lovely thy face, fair Beam from on high!

Two folds of silk for to wrap thy limbs in,
Two folds of silk for thy precious smooth skin:
And yellow-gold jewels ready around,
For thy fingers a fistful doth abound.

IV. SACRAMENTS

By marking of the dove-skimmed wave,
By pouring of the fountain lave,
By meaning waterdrops that save,
In Father, Son, and Holy Spirit named;

By Bread that Christ himself did break,
By holy Wine that Christ did take,
Eaten and drunk for his dear sake,
That we be not, O God, condemned nor blamed;

We sleep a noble company,
A King, a Prince our royal we,
A Spirit throned, the Trinity,
Each night a holy household strong and famed;

Forgiveness ours on dying bed,
Absolved, anointed, be we fed
With everlasting Wine and Bread,
And stand before our Father unashamed.

40. *The Water of the Spirit*

O may the Spirit satisfy,
His water poured on thee to lie,
Water of grace may he distil,
Salvation water for thy fill.

41. *Baptism at Birth*

In the name of the Father, Amen.
And in the name of the Son, Amen.
In the name of the Spirit, Amen.

Three to give thee lavation, Amen.
Three for purification, Amen.
Three for holy salvation, Amen.

Father and Son and Spirit, Amen.
Father and Son and Spirit, Amen.
Father and Son and Spirit, Amen.

42. *The Baptism of the Aid-Mother*

Berneray of Barra

In God's name, in Jesus' name, in the Spirit's name,
The Three in One of power and perfectness the same.

The little drop of water for the Father fall
On thy little forehead, belov'd one of us all.
The little drop of water for the Son to be
On thy little forehead, belov'd one, holily.
The little drop of water for the Spirit done
On thy little forehead, belov'd one, let it run.

The little drop of water to guard thee, to aid,
To surround, to shield thee, to keep thee safely laid.
To hold thee from the fairies of the fickle trail,
To shield thee from the hosts of evil that assail.
To sain thee from the gnome hither thither going,
And to deliver from the spectre shadowing.

The little drop of water of the Holy Three
To shield thee from the sorrow that may be to thee.
The little drop of water of the Holy Three
That their grace and pleasantness all be filling thee.
The little drop of water of the Holy Three
To fill thee with their virtue overflowingly.
O little drop of water of the Holy Three
To fill thee with their virtue overflowingly.

43. *A Small Drop of Water*　　　*Berneray of Barra*

A small drop of water slowly
To thy forehead, belov'd one,
Meet for Father, Spirit, Son,
Trinity of virtue holy.

A small drop of water slowly
To encompass, belov'd one,
Meet for Father, Spirit, Son,
Trinity of virtue holy.

A small drop of water slowly
For each grace's filling done,
Meet for Father, Spirit, Son,
Trinity of virtue holy.

44. *First Baptism*　　　*Barra*

The Father's little drop to fall,
My love, upon thy forehead small.

The Son his little drop to fall,
My love, upon thy forehead small.

The Spirit's little drop to fall,
My love, upon thy forehead small.

The drop to aid thee from the fays,
The drop to shield thee from the host;
To aid thee from the gnome thy days,
The drop to shield thee from the ghost;

To safeguard for the Holy Three,
To shield thee, to encompass thee;
To save thee for the Holy Three,
With all the graces filling thee;
Little drop of the Holy Three
With all the graces cleansing thee.

Water for thy form all glowing,
Water for thy voice so knowing,
Water for sweet sounds of crowing;

Water fortune fair bestowing,
Water for thy goodness showing,
Water for thy health and growing;

Water for thy throat a-going,
Water for thy courage throwing,
Water for thy graces flowing;
    Waters nine for graces flowing.

45. *The Prayer of Baptism*

The little wave for thy form complete,
The little wave for thy voice so meet,
The little wave for thy speech so sweet.

The little wave for thy means requite,
The little wave for thy generous plight,
The little wave for thine appetite.

The little wave for thy wealth at hand,
The little wave for thy life in land,
The little wave for thy health to stand.

Nine waves of grace to thee may there be,
Saving waves of the Healer to thee.

The fill of hand for thy form complete,
The fill of hand for thy voice so meet,
The fill of hand for thy speech so sweet.

The fill of hand for thy mouth so small,
The fill of hand for thy fingers all,
The fill of hand to make strong and tall.

43

The fill of hand for the Father one,
The fill of hand for God's only Son,
The fill of hand for the Spirit done.

Nine fills of hand for thy grace to be,
In name of the Three-One Trinity.

46. *The Baptism Blessing* *Benbecula*

O great Being who fillest the soaring height,
    Wash thou with thy tide at the time to bless,
Remember the child of my body so slight,
    In name of the Father of peacefulness;
    When the priest of the King is setting now
    The meaning water poured forth on his brow,
    O grant that the great Three Persons may bless,
The high-soaring Three Persons of fillingness.

O send down thy grace sprinkling on him to flow,
    Give thou the growth and the virtue to hand,
Give thou strength unto him and guiding to go,
    Give thou possessions and flocks of the land,
    The sense and the reason guileless and true,
    The wisdom of angels all his days through,
    That in thy presence reproachless he stand,
In thy presence reproachless always to stand.

47. *The Trinity Pouring*

Yours be the blessing of God and the Lord,
The perfect Spirit his blessing afford,
The Trinity's blessing on you outpoured
With gentle and gen'rous shedding abroad,
So gently gen'rously for you unstored.

48. God's Aid

God to enfold,
God to surround,
God in speech-told,
God my thought-bound.

God when I sleep,
God when I wake,
God my watch-keep,
God my hope-sake.

God my life-whole,
God lips apart,
God in my soul,
God in my heart.

God Wine and Bread,
God in my death,
God my soul-thread,
God ever breath.

49. The Meal

Give us, O God, our morning bread,
The soul by body nourishéd;
Give us, O God, the perfect bread,
Sufficiently at evening fed.

Give us, O God, milk-honey yield,
The strength and cream of fragrant field;
God, give us rest, our eyelids sealed,
Thy Rock of covenant our shield.

Give us this night the living fare,
This night the saving drink be there;
This night, for heaven to prepare,
Give us the cup of Mary fair.

Be with us ever night and day,
In light and darkness, be our stay,
With us, abed or up, alway,
In talk, in walk and when we pray.

50. Bed Blessing   South Uist

As is due I am lying me down to-night
The Christ my friend, Son of ringleted Maid,
Father of glory my friend, of gracious light,
The Holy Spirit my friend, of mighty aid.

45

With my God I am lying me down to-night,
And lo! my God to-night will lie down with me,
But with sin I will not lie me down to-night,
Nor shall sin nor a trace of it lie with me.

With the Spirit I will lie me down to-night,
And the Spirit this night will lie down with me,
With my love's Three I will lie me down to-night,
And the Three of my love will lie down with me.

51. Happy Death

Thou God of salvation great, outpour
On my soul thy graces from above
As up the sun of the heights doth soar
And on my body outpours its love.

Needs must that I die and go to rest,
Nor know I where or when it will be;
But if of thy graces unpossest
So I am lost everlastingly.

Death of anointing, repentance due,
Death of joy, death of peacefulness giv'n;
Death of grace, death of forgiveness true,
Death that endows life with Christ and heav'n.

52. Death with Anointing

Death with anointing, penitence-death,
Happiness-death that forgiveness saith,
Death that nor dread nor disgust conveys,
Death that nor terrifies nor dismays.

Dying the death of the saints on high,
By me, my Soul-Physician, be nigh,
The death of peace and tranquillity,
Good the day grant thou to bury me.

The Holy Spirit has angels sev'n,
And two angel-guardians more from heav'n,
Be they my shield, be this eve the night
Till the brightness comes and summerlight!

46

53. Blessed Dying

Death with anointing, death with light,
Death blessed, death with gladness bright,
    Death with penitential night.

Death without pain, death without fear,
Death without death, and horror sheer,
    Death without the grieving tear.

The Holy Spirit in his might
His seven flaming angels bright,
Two guardian angels eve and night
    Shield till come the dawn and light;

Shield me each evening and this night
    Till come the dawn and the light.

54. The Gates of the Kingdom   *Benbecula*

Give us, O God, the needs the body feels,
    Give us, God, the need-things of the soul;
Give us, O God, the balm which body heals,
    Give us, God, the soul-balm which makes whole.

Bliss give us, O God, of repentance-ease,
    Bliss give us, God, of forgiveness sought,
Away from us wash thou corruption's lees,
    From us wipe the blush of unclean thought.

O great God, thou who art upon the throne,
    Give to us the heart repentance true,
Forgiveness give us of the sin we own,—
    The sin inborn and the sin we do.

Give us, O God, a yearning that is strong,
    And the crown of glory of the King;
Give us the safe home, God, for which we long
    In thy kingdom's lovely gates to sing.

May Michael, archangel warrior white,
    Keep down hostile demons of the fall;
May Jesus Christ MacDavid guide our flight
    And give lodging in his peace-bright hall.

F   47

V. CHILDHOOD

When *legs beneath kilts grow sturdy and strong,*
    The grass soft-afoot dew-brimming,
While skurrying dogs run barking along,
    Stones on the water go skimming.

When bird-songs and hens fill the barnyard air,
    And from byre there comes the lowing,
When the mist on the hills is rising fair,
    All the little feet are going.

The game of "tig" and the bare pony-ride,
    The boat on the water gleaming,
The peat-fire of evening and tale beside
    Fill daytime till bedtime dreaming.

O God bless the girl and God bless the boy,
    No ragwort-whip may they merit,
And as they grow be they filled with thy joy,
    Thy kingdom may they inherit.

55. The Cat

Walking by night,
Walking by night,
Walking by night,
  Purred the grey cat;
Walking by night,
Stars out of sight,
Never a light,
  Purred the grey cat.

56. The Dog

  "Dee do",
The white dog's bark,
  "Dee do",
The white dog's bark,
  "Dee do",
The white dog's bark,
  "Dee do,
And how we go,
Lie on the rug,
All through the dark,
Happy and snug",
The white dog's bark !

57. The Goldfinch

"Golden goldfinch loveliest,
I will spend a Sunday then,
Sweeping out thy chamber-nest",
Said his silly golden hen.

58. Pins and Needles   *Benbecula*

The pins and needles in my toes,
The greyhound take them as he goes !
O greyhound, through the townland tramp,
Find some milk for the foot I stamp !

59. The Fox's Mouth *Benbecula*

This sneaky mouth of the fox, my love,
That sneaky mouth of the fox instead,
The beaky mouth of the moulting dove—
And you'll be better before you're wed!

60. The Mouse

O little mouse! O mouse so slight!
O little mouse, so kind and wee!
O little mouse of running flight!
O little mouse, make love to me!

O give to me, o give to me
A little tooth so golden-bright,
O give to me, o give to me
A little tooth so silver-white.

And I will give back unto thee
In recompense my precious fee,
A little tooth so lovely-white,
Boy's little tooth bone-bound to bite,
Girl's little tooth bone-bound aright,
Loud laughing sound of little mite.

61. The Ragwort-Switch

O ragwort, O ragwort, that whip of pain!
And you ragwort whipper-she so unkind!
If the dead from the grave could rise again,
I would bring your ragwort whipping to mind.

62. The Oath of the Red Dog

By the bramble, by the thorn,
By the water falling borne,
By the sky above thy head,
By the earth beneath thy tread,
By the sun in firmament,
By the moon to westward sent,
By the stars uplifted high,
On thy kids I set no eye.

63. Catch as Catch Can

Escape from the small thing,
Escape from the big thing,
Escape from the Death King,
Escape from the Grave King,
Escape I will from thee,
And if I can, stay free.

64. Killmoluag   Lismore

Uill hill, uill o!
In what kill shall he go?

Lismore Moluag-Kill-o,
Maggot-worms crawl and grow!

Uill hill, uill o!
In what kill shall he go?

Lismore Moluag-Kill-o,
Scorching sun stifling slow!

Uill hill, uill o!
In what kill shall he go?

Lismore Moluag-Kill-o,
He'll not rise when below!

VI. PILGRIMAGE

The great God's is the thunder voice,
None great but he of thunder noise,
                Heard far or near,
                Rumbling or clear
O'er mountain-top or ocean's face,
Reminder of the heavenly place.

So God our pilgrimage impels
To cross sea-waste or scale life-fells;
                A further shore,
                One hill-brow more
Draws on the feet, or arm-plied oars,
As the soul onward, upward soars.

Beyond the hills a wider plain,
Beyond the waves the Isle domain
                With richness blest
                And place for guest,
Where God doth sit upon his throne,
The soul by Christ nor left alone.

65. By Land and Sea

Saint Bride, Saint Mary, Saint Michael, three
Shield thee on the land and on the sea,
Each step and each path that beckons thee.

66. The Soaring of the Soul

The hero of courage thou wast indeed
  On the journey of prophecy going,
No lame-foot beneath thee to be thy steed,
  But great Michael's, his angel-mane flowing.
No bit in his mouth, but with wing outspread,
Thou didst leap o'er Nature's knowing ahead.

67. The Path of Right

With God be my walking this day,
With Christ be my walking this day,
With Spirit my walking this day,
The Threefold all-kindly my way:
Ho, ho, ho! the Threefold all-kindly I pray.

My shielding this day be from bane,
My shielding this night be from pain,
Ho, ho! soul and body, the twain,
By Father, Son, Spirit, amain;
By Father's, by Son's, and by Holy Ghost's sain.

The Father be he shielding me,
And be God the Son shielding me,
The Spirit be he shielding me,
As Three and as One let them be:
Ho, ho, ho! as Three and as One Trinity.

68. The Pilgrim's Aiding   South Uist

May God be with thee in every pass,
Jesus be with thee on every knoll,
Spirit be with thee by water's roll,
  On headland, on ridge, and on grass;

Each sea and land, each moor and each mead,
Each eve's lying-down, each rising's morn,
In the wave-trough, or on foam-crest borne,
Each step which thy journey doth lead.

69. *The Pilgrim's Hope* Morar

I bathe my face in water fresh,
As the sun his nine rays doth spread,
As Mary washed her Son's fair flesh
In the generous milk white-shed.

May mercy be my lips' attire,
May kindness to my face be lent,
May chasteness be on my desire,
And wisdom be in mine intent.

Love Mary laid her one Son on
May all the world give unto me;
Love Jesus-giv'n to Baptist John
Grant I give to each one I see.

Son of God, be at the outset,
Son of God, be surety, friend;
Son of God, make straight my way yet,
Son of God at my seeking's end.

70. *The Three*

In the Father's name,
And in the Son's name,
In the Spirit's name,
Three the same, One in name;

Father be my friend,
And Son be my friend,
Spirit be my friend,
Three to send and befriend.

God my holiness,
Christ my holiness,
Spirit holiness,
Three to bless, holiness.

58

Help of hope the Three,
Help of love the Three,
Help of sight the Three,
And my knee stumbling free,
From my knee stumbling free.

71. *Thoughts*

'Tis God's will I would do,
My own will I would rein;
Would give to God his due,
From my own due refrain;
God's path I would pursue,
My own path would disdain;

For Christ's death would I care,
My own death duly weighed;
Christ's pain my silent prayer,
My God-love warmer made;
'Tis Christ's cross I would bear,
My own cross off me laid;

Repentance I would make,
Repentance early choose;
Rein for my tongue would take,
Rein for my thoughts would use;

God's judgment would I mind,
My own judgment close-scanned;
Christ's freedom seizing bind,
My own freedom in hand;
Christ's love close-scanned would find,
My own love understand.

72. *Before Me*

Before me be thou a smooth way,
Above me be thou a star-guide,
Behind me o be thou keen-eyed,
For this day, this night, and for aye.

I weary and heavy am driv'n,
Lead me on to the angels' place;
'Twere time now I went for a space
To Christ's court and the peace of heav'n;

If only thou, God of life, give
Smooth peace for me, at my back near,
Be as star, as helmsman to steer,
From smooth rest till rising I live.

73. *The Soul's Healer*

Healer thou of my soul,
At eventide keep whole,
Keep me at morning ray,
Keep me at full noonday,
As on my rough course I fare.

Safeguard me and assist
That this night I subsist,
I am tired and astray,
And so stumbling my way,
Shield thou from sin and from snare.

74. *Protection Prayer*   *Barra*

O God, do thou hearken unto my prayer,
My earnest petition come to thee where
I know that thou hearest with loving care
As though with mine eyes I beheld thee there.

Upon my heart I am setting a bit,
A bit on my thoughts undisciplined sit,
A bit on my lips I securely fit,
And for safety's sake it is double-knit.

Aught that is amiss for my soul's estate
In my death's pulsing o may it abate,
Do thou, O God, from me sweep off its weight,
Be my shield in thy love's blood dedicate.

Into my heart let there come not a thought,
And unto mine ear no sound be brought,
Come to mine eye no temptation besought,
Within my nose may no fragrance be caught,

No fancy allow to come to my mind,
No ruffle allow my spirit to blind,
That this night my poor body hurt or bind,
Nor may ill my soul at my dying find;

But thou God of life thyself, sanctified,
Be at my breast, at my back, at my side,
To me thou a star, to me thou a guide,
From my life's inflowing to ebbing tide.

75. The Pilgrim's Relief

Each one, O God, do thou relieve
In all his suffering on land or sea,
In grief, or wound, or in tears, receive,
To thy peaceful halls his leader be
    As day doth fade.

I am weary and weak and chill,
Weary of travelling on land and sea,
Of crossing moor and the foam-white hill,
Grant peace anigh of thine ease to me
    As day doth fade.

O my God's Father, lovéd one,
Let the care of my crying suffice;
With thee I would wish atonement done,
Through the witness and the ransom price
    Which thy Son paid;

With Jesus to find restfulness
In the blest habitation of peace,
In the paradise of gentleness,
In the fairy-bower of release
    Mercy-arrayed.

76. The Travel-Shiela of God

Almighty Lord, thou God of might,
    Shield me this night and sustain,
Almighty Lord, thou God of might,
    This night and each eve again.

Sain me and save me from mischief whole,
    And from sin save me and sain,
Sain me my body and my soul,
    Each dark and each light again.

Bless me the land my hope doth prize,
    Bless me the thing faith shall see,
Bless me the thing my love descries,
    God of life, bless what I be.

Bless the journey whereon I go,
    And bless the ground under me,
Bless the matter I seek to know,
    Glory-King, bless what I be.

77. The Pilgrim's Nightkeeping

I wrap my soul and my body within
    Under thy guarding this night, O Bride,
    Calm Nurse-mother to Christ without sin,
Calm Nurse-mother to the Christ's wounded side.

I wrap my soul and my body so sure
    'Neath thy guarding this night, Mary dear,
    Tender Mother of Christ of the poor,
Tender Mother of Christ of sorrow's tear.

I wrap my soul and my body from fears
    Under thy guarding, O Christ, this night,
    Thou piercéd Son of the wounds, the tears,
May thy cross this night be shielding aright.

I wrap my soul and my body so sure
    Under thy guarding, O God, this night,
    Aid-Father to feeble pilgrims poor,
Protector of earth and heav'n in might,
    Earth and heav'n's Protector in might.

78. Heavenly Protection

Each saint, man, woman, within heaven's gate,
O God of living things, of goodness state,
Be taking charge of you in every strait,
On every side about you wait,
Watch every turning of your fate.

VII. MULL POEMS

Unto the Isle Iona pilgrims fare
O'er the sound-water from the Morvern shore,
Under Ardtornish and its walls foursquare,
The oakwood-margins past and by Glen More.

Near Ardura's heap and the Lussa stream
An eagle still, aspread-winged, bides his time,
As from the trees to open lochside gleam
The slopes are skirted up the passhead-climb.

Then from the brow by tumbling burn and heath
Down the drear wildness of the wind-marched glen,
The braes to Ben More reaching, while beneath
The pilgrim road slips past the bog and fen.

And so to Scridain's Loch and tangle brown,
The open undulating stretching Ross,
From blue heights soft, Ardmeanach looking down
Coracle-waters o'er, to Pennycross.

The standing stones, the Iron-Sworded Race
Confine the track that leads to granite red,
The silent distant guardians of the place,
The guide-escorters of the quick and dead.

While now and then beyond the olive-green
Appears the jewelled archipelago;
An island-squadron anchored floats serene
Or ocean-waters ebb or tides inflow.

Last, with a foot in boat, a foot on land,
The calm ass-riding over, stands the shrine—
The holy island fringed with silver sand,
The ground and holy house with God ashine.

79. *The Flower of the Flight* *Mull*

I will pluck the flower smooth and small,
The blessèd plant of Christ who died,
The plant of wise Columba tall,
The plant of Mary, plant of Bride,
      Plant of Mary lowly,
      Plant of Jesus holy.

I will pluck the flower smooth as silk,
The plant of joy, of peace divine,
The plant of fatness, plant of milk,
The plant of the essences nine,
      Plant of Mary lowly,
      Plant of Jesus holy.

I will pluck the flower smooth and spun,
To Three in One abiding long,
To the Father and to the Son
And to the Holy Spirit strong,
      Plant of Mary lowly,
      Plant of Jesus holy.

80. *He Who so Calmly Rode* *Mull*

He who so calmly, so calmly rode
    The little ass so fair of gait,
Who healed each hurt and each wound of blood
    That is each generation's fate :

Joy he gave to the outcast and sad,
    To restless and tired he gave rest,
Bond and unruly their freedom had,
    Old and young in the land were blest.

He oped the eyes of the blind to see,
    He waked the lame man's step to tread,
The tongue that was dumb he loosened free,
    He gave life to him that was dead.

He stemmed the fierce-rushing blood issued,
    He took the sharp awn from the eye,
He drank the draught that was bitter brewed,
    Trusting the heav'nly Father high.

To Peter and Paul the strength of rocks,
And strength to the Mother of tears,
He gave strength to Bridget of the flocks,
Limbs, sinews and bones he inheres.

Soothing and smoothing
With Columba's little flower,
Soothing and smoothing
With the King of nature's power.

Soothing and smoothing
With Columba's little flower,
Soothing and smoothing
With the Christ the kindly's power.

Soothing and smoothing
With Columba's little flower,
Soothing and smoothing
With the Holy Spirit's power.

Soothing and smoothing
With Columba's little flower,
Soothing and smoothing
With the Three-in-One's own power.

Soothing and smoothing
In the woven kisses sweet
From lips of soothing
As the kind Three tender greet.

Soothing and smoothing
In the due of kisses sweet
From lips of soothing
As the mild Three tender meet.

Soothing and smoothing
In protecting kisses sweet
From lips of soothing
Of the saints' quire-music meet.

Rubbing and bathing
In the woven honey kiss,
Rubbing and bathing,
King of nature's lips in this.

Power over Wasting   *Mull*

 I have over thee the power of the silver moon,
  I have over thee the power of the fierce sun,
 I have over thee the power of the rain's wet shoon,
  I have over thee the power of the dew spun;

 I have over thee the power of the ocean's sheen,
  I have over thee power of the firm land,
 I have over thee the power of the stars serene,
  I have over thee the power of planets spanned;

 I have over thee the power of the earthly sphere,
  I have over thee the power of the skies' space,
 I have over thee the power of the saints sans peer,
  I have over thee the power of the heavenly place,
 I have the power of heaven and God's power o'er thee near,
 Over thee the power of heaven, the power of God here.

 A part of thee away on the grey stones to shift,
  A part of thee hence on the steep mountains' side,
 A part of thee away on the waterfalls swift,
  A part of thee hence on the gleaming clouds bide;

 A part of thee away on the whales of the sea,
  A part of thee hence on the beasts out of doors,
 A part of thee hence on the rough sedge bogs to flee,
  A part of thee hence on the cotton-grass moors;

 A part of thee away on the great surging sea,
  She herself has the best means to endure thee,
 The mighty, surging, seething, foaming, breaking sea,
  She herself has the best means to endure thee.

82. *Charms for the Evil Eye*   *Mull*

  I make for thee and I fashion them all—
  The charms on the evil eye to bide
 From the bosom of Peter and of Paul
  And of my belovéd quiet Bride.

Against the eye of the man that is small,
  'Gainst the eye of the man that is great,
'Gainst the eye of the man of wayfaring call,
  The long highway ahead for his gait;

Against eye of bird that flies to the sky,
  'Gainst eye of bird that flies to the sea,
Against eye of the goose that passes by,
  Eye of the hosts that together flee;

Against eye of man rough-spoken and red,
'Gainst eye of pert woman, noisy, ill-bred,
'Gainst eye of red serpent's venomous head.

A drop, O kindly Columba, provide,
  A drop, holy Patrick mighty-blest,
A drop, O maid of the Boyne, quiet Bride,
  A drop, O great Mary ringlet-tressed.

Whole be the one who receives it in aid,
  Whole be thou in thy giving aright,
Whole be the one from the time it is made,
  Whole be thyself in thy health to-night.

Of the cattle of hoof the knowing guide
  By the fair Lake of Killarney's wave
Is the maid my belovéd quiet Bride,
  With her protection to heal and save.

Be it for the happiness and the wealth
  Of the one who abiding is there,
Of man or of wife, son, daughter, in health,
  Horse or cow, wife or little ones fair.

83. *The Widow's White Cow*   *Mull*

        "Put thou in, O Columcill,
            And heal the white cow so;
        Put thou in, O Columcill,
            And heal her bladder-flow !

        "Put thou in, O Columcill,
            And heal the fond cow here;
        Put thou in, O Columcill,
            And heal my cow so dear !"

"But how so, woman of hair,
    Am I to heal thy cow,
In the boat my one foot there,
    On shore the other now?"

To the knoll came Columcill,
    He on the cow set hand;
In the boat his one foot still,
    His other on the land.

"I myself thy swelling break,
    To kill thy tick I came,
Off thy prickliness I take,
    In King of ages' name!"

84. *Churning*   *Mull*

Shake, Columba kindly, dear,
    On the cream lustre spate;
See, neglected orphans here
The milky fountain's blessing wait.

Stillim! steòilim!
Strichim! streòichim!
Sending down the bits of him
And up the whole must swim!

Shake, O Bridget nursemaid fair,
    On the cream butter spate;
See, impatient Peter there
The white and yellow spread doth wait.

Stillim! steòilim!
Strichim! streòichim!
Sending down the bits of him
And up the whole must swim!

Shake, O Mary Mother mild,
    On the cream butter spate;
Paul and John and Jesus Child
The gracious butter there await.

71

Stillim! steòilim!
Strichim! streòichim!
Sending down the bits of him
And up the whole must swim!

85. *The Gracious Root* *Mull*

I will pull my gracious root from the earth
As Saint Bride did pull it with her one hand,
To give milk to the breast and fleshly gland,
To enrich the udder and kidney's worth,
For the butter and curd, fat, cheese and cream,
From fortune's bosom to pour as a stream,
As care-dropped honey doth fall on the land.

Anointed white One of the God of grace,
Keep thou for me the share that is mine own,
O keep thou for me the share of grace shown,
Keep thou from me, the share of foes displace,
Keep thou from me the tribes of men untrue,
Keep thou from me death's hardness and death's rue,
Keep thou from me harm's hardness and harm's pain,
Keep thou from me the stock-pairing-again,
O keep thou from me the calf born ungrown.

Theirs be the plant of the heath-grass afield,
The plant of sap-richness be mine to grace,
For while I keep the gracious root in place
There is blessing in all the harvest yield,
There is substance and increase in the stall,
In the herd-mating honour doth befall,
Anointed white One of the God of grace.

In mercy of God of the living things,
In the kind mercy of the health that glows,
Keep thou for me the share my wishing knows,
Keep for me the share to which my heart clings,
O keep thou from me the men of false gain,
Keep thou from me the hardness of the bane,
O keep thou from me the howling of foes.

Saint Bride came homeward and under her arm
Were the butter and the curd and the cheese,
And under the nine good locks she laid these—
All the nine stores securely locked from harm,

The store of the God of life to enfold,
The store of the Christ Son of love untold,
The store of the Holy Spirit to hold,
The Three-in-One of the grace that agrees.

86. *The Pearlwort* *Mull*

I'll pick the pearlwort from the land
    Beneath a Sunday's white sun,
Beneath the Virgin's gentle hand.
    Mine aiding she is the one,
In the might of the Trinity
Who granted it to grow for me.

I'll keep the pearlwort of the land,
    On my lips shall be no lie,
No bite or sting upon mine hand,
    No trick shall be in mine eye,
Mine heart from torment shall be free,
No heaviness in death for me.

VIII. MORNING

When morning in russet and saffron clad
Is mantling the hills in a dew-soft plaid
To the song of the moorland two-wings glad
        Let my heart upraise;

When light creeps in through the chinks of the door
When the mist ascends from the mountain floor,
When the ocean shimmers like burnished ore,
        Let me give the praise.

O God of the morning, Christ of the hills,
O Spirit who all the firmament fills,
O Trinity blest who all goodness wills,
        Keep us all our days.

87. Rising Prayer

Thou King of the moon and of the sun,
Of the stars thou lov'd and fragrant King,
Thou thyself knowest our needs each one,
O merciful God of everything.

Each day that our moving steps we take,
Each hour of awakening, when we know
The dark distress and sorrow we make
To the King of hosts who loved us so;

Be with us through the time of each day,
Be with us through the time of each night,
Be with us ever each night and day,
Be with us ever each day and night.

88. Night and Day

In the vista far I see, I see
Over the red bog-myrtle growing,
The son from the mother parting free,
And the mother from son a-going.

89. Morning Thanksgiving

That I have ris'n to-day, O God, the thanks be unto thee,
    To the rising of this life itself again;
O God of every gift, to thine own glory may it be,
    To the glory of my soul likewise a gain.

O great God, unto my soul give thine aid and make it full
    With the great aiding of thine own mercy whole;
Even as I am covering all my body with the wool,
    With the shadow of thy wing cover my soul.

God, be helping mine avoiding every sin that life fills,
    And my forsaking the cause of sinful ways;
And as flees the mist of morning on the crest of the hills,
    May there clear off from my soul each evil haze.

90. *The Morning Dedication* *North Uist*

      Let thanks, O God, be unto thee,
From yesterday who broughtest me
The morning of to-day to see,
Joy everlasting to earn whole
With good intention for my soul.
For every gift of peace to me,
Thoughts, words, deeds, and desires from thee
Each one bestowed, I dedicate.
And I beseech, I supplicate
That thou may'st keep me from offence,
To-night my aiding and defence,
For the sake of thy wounding red,
With thine offering of grace outspread.
      Let thanks, O God, be unto thee.

91. *Petition at Rising* *South Uist*

O holy Father of truth adored,
O kindly Father of mercy poured,
Deliver me from the spells that harm,
Deliver me from each evil charm.

Upon this day, and each single day,
O do thou sain me thyself alway;
Upon this night, and each single night,
O do thou sain me thyself till light.

O Father eternal, God of all,
O grant thy forgiveness at my call
In my wild thought and in foolish deed,
In my rough talk and speech without heed.

O Father eternal, God of all,
O grant thy forgiveness at my call
In hateful doing and false desire,
In worthless liking and courses dire.

O Chief, God of all, ward off the bane
Of the women who from speech refrain.

God and Father of all, ward the bane
Of the women who to wanton deign.

O Father eternal, God of all,
Ward the bane of women fairy-small.

O Father eternal, God of all,
Ward the bane of women's false enthrall.

O Father eternal, God of all,
Thy loving crown on my head install.

Allow no stain to blemish my soul,
Allow no spot to my body whole,
Allow no taint my breath to defile,
Father of tender and lovely smile.

As in the days before thou didst stand
When my life began, close at my hand,
Be thou nearby me again to stay
At my life's end as it ebbs away :

For now and for henceforth unto me
In my life, in my death, do thou be,
O Son and Abba Father of love,
And Holy Spirit of grace above !

92. *Dressing Prayer*   *Moydart*

Bless to me, O God, my body and my soul;
Bless to me, O God, belief, condition whole;
Bless to me, O God, my heart, my speaking too,
And bless to me, O God, the things my hands do;

Bless strength and busyness of the morn imposed,
Bless the frame and habit modestly disposed,
Bless the force of thinking and wisdom disclosed,
And, O God of virtues, thine own way be blest
Till at the close of day I lie down to rest;
      O God of virtues, thine own way,
      Until I rest at close of day.

93. *Morning Protection*

Be the eye of God between me and each eye,
Between me and each purpose God's purpose lie,
Be the hand of God between me and each hand,
Between me and each shield the shield of God stand,
God's desire between me and each desire be,
Be God's bridle between each bridle and me,
    And no man's mouth able to curse me I see.

Between me and each pain the pain of Christ show,
Between me and each love the love of Christ grow,
Between me and each dearness Christ's dearness stay,
Christ's kindness between me and each kindness aye,
Between me and each wish the wish of Christ found,
Between me and each will the will of Christ bound,
    And no venom can wound me, make me unsound.

Be the might of Christ between me and each might,
Be the right of Christ between me and each right,
Flow of the Spirit between me and each flow,
Between me and each lave the Spirit's lave go,
Between me and each bathe the Spirit's bathe clean,
    And to touch me no evil thing can be seen.

94. *Prayer this Day*

My prayer to thee, O God, pray I this day,
Voice I this day in thy mouth's voicing way,
As hold the men of heaven this day I hold,
Spend I this day as spends thine own household,
Under thy laws, O God, this day I go,
As saints in heaven pass pass I this day so.

Thou loving Christ who hangedst on the tree,
Each day, each night, thy compact mindeth me;
Lie down or rise unto thy cross I cede,
In life and death thou health and peace indeed.

Each day thy mercies' source let me recall,
Gentle, gen'rous bestowing on me all;
Each day in love to thee more full be I
For love to me that thou didst amplify.

From thee it came, each thing I have received,
From love it comes, each thing my hope conceived,
Thy bounty gives each thing that gives me zest,
Of thy disposing each thing I request.

God holy, loving Father, of the word
Everlasting, this living prayer be heard :
Understanding lighten, my will enfire,
Begin my doing and my love inspire,
My weakness strengthen, enfold my desire.

Cleanse heart, faith confirm, sanctify my soul,
Circle my body, and my mind keep whole;
As from my mouth my prayer upriseth clear,
May I feel in my heart that thou art here.

And, O God of life, do thou grant to me
That thou at my breast, at my back shalt be,
That thou give my needs as befits the gold,
The above-world crown to us promise-told.

And, Father beloved, grant thou that to me,
From whom each thing that is outfloweth free,
No tie too strict, no tie too dear between
Myself and this beneath-world here be seen.

O my God, in thee all my hope I set,
Father of the heav'ns, my living hope yet,
My great hope with thyself that I may be
In the far world that cometh finally.

Father, Son, Spirit, Holy Trinity,
Three in One Person and the One in Three,
Infinite and perfect, world without end,
Changeless through endless life, let praise ascend.

95. *Somerled's Supplication*   *Benbecula*

O Being of life ! O Being of peace !
O Being of time, and time without cease !
O Being, infinite eternity !
O Being, infinite eternity !

In good means of life be thou keeping me,
In all good intending, o keeping be,
Be keeping me always in good estate.
Far better than I know to supplicate,
  O better than I know to supplicate!

Be shepherding me for all this day long,
Relieve my distress, relieve me from wrong,
Enfold me this night with thine arms' embrace.
And pour upon me thy bountiful grace,
  O pour upon me thy bountiful grace!

My speaking and words do thou guard for me,
And strengthen for me my love, charity,
Illumine for me the stream I must o'er,
And succour thou me when I pass death's door,
  O succour thou me when I pass death's door!

IX. THE CROSS

When in their haste to Calvary they came
The Jews forgot the nails for Jesu's shame;
The whitesmith made them with a peatfire flame.

The aspen tree that grew within the wood,
Tall on the nearby knoll it clearly stood;
On it was stretched the Son of God so good.

And as the body crucified did bleed,
The vinegar uplifted on the reed,
The passion-flower did bloom and spring from seed.

For me he hanged, for me he wore the crown,
Beneath the darkened sky black lay the town;
For me he drooped, was pierced, was taken down.

His body women-tended gentle Bride
The head thorn red-scarred and lance-pierced the side
Washed for the garden-sepulchre to bide.

For the three days within the tomb he lay
Till rose the sun and danced with joyful ray
O'er mountains and the hills and far away,
On Crucifying Sunday, Easter Day.

O Cross of Christ, thou art my mighty shield,
Beneath thy shade my sins and wounds are healed,
The door to life is from the tomb unsealed.

96. The Aspen

A malison be on thee, aspen tree!
The mountains' King was crucified on thee,
Thou took'st the driven nails that caused his dying,
Exceeding sore that driving crucifying,
  Exceeding sore the Saviour's crucifying.

A malison be on thee, aspen hard!
The King of virtue died upon thy board,
Truth's Sacrifice, the spotless Lamb, death-going,
His dear life-blood in crimson streams down flowing,
  The Saviour's blood in crimson streams down flowing.

A malison be on thee, aspen cursed!
On thee the King of kings to death was nursed,
And malison be on the eye thee seeing,
If, aspen cursed, it curse not all thy being,
  If for the Christ it curse not all thy being!

97. Christ and the Horse
Berneray of Lewis

The Christ to the cross he did ride,
But the horse his leg he did sprain,
Christ went to the ground by his side,
And the leg it was whole again.

As that was made whole long ago
So for this the wholeness be done,
His will if it be to do so,
Through the heart of the Living One,
And the Three of the Three-in-One,
  The God of life, the Living One,
  The God Threefold, the Three-in-One.

98. Christ the Priest
South Uist

Christ is the Priest above us to reign,
Him did the Being of life ordain
For all alive salvation to gain;
Christ is the Priest of rising again,
  Christ is the Priest above.

85

To-night the anguish hanging is hailed,
The anguish cross to which Christ was nailed,
Christ is the Priest who this eve prevailed,
  Christ is the Priest of love.

Noble the Gift! and noble the Plight!
Noble the Man of this evening's night!
Christ is the Priest above us aright,
  Christ the Priest of the Bread.

Saint Bride the mild on her knee she went,
The King of life in her lap forspent,
Christ the Priest who to hang did consent,
  Christ the Priest of Blood shed.

I hear the hills, I hear the waves draw,
I hear all the floating angels soar,
Christ is the Priest above evermore,
  Christ is the Priest once dead.

Fine handsome Cairbre coming I hear,
Gently a friend, the charioteer,
Christ is the Priest above us so dear,
  Christ the Priest overhead.

Upon this knoll an assemblage great,
Man to man with no envious hate,
Christ is the Priest above us in state,
  Christ the Priest of the Wine.

The gillie of God the Son I be,
Rise thyself, open the door to me,
Christ is the Priest above we see,
  Christ is the Priest divine.

99. He who was Crucified

Lochalsh, Kintail and Harris

Thou who wert hanged upon the tree,
By people condemned, crucified there,
 Now that grown old and grey I be,
Pity, O God, my confession-prayer.

I wonder not my sins are great,
I am a clattering cymbal poor,
I was profane in youth's estate,
Forlorn in my ageing at the door.

Those to whom God hath no desire
Are people who lie, people who swear;
Fountain-tears hot-springing as fire
Rather would he, and genuine prayer.

100. *Blessing of a New House*

Christ's cross on your new dwelling place,
Christ's cross on your new hearth,
Christ's cross your new abode engrace,
Your new fire's blazing path.

Christ's cross upon your high-piled grain,
Christ's cross on fruitful wife,
Christ's cross upon sons' manly strain,
On daughters' wombs of life.

Christ's cross upon the serving maid,
Christ's cross on coming seed,
Christ's cross on your hill-shieling laid,
Your fattening herds that feed.

Christ's cross on living means and right,
Christ's cross on men and kin,
Christ's cross on you each dark and light,
Each day and night herein,
Life's day and night herein.

101. *The Prayer of Distress*   *Tiree*

May the cross of the crucifixion tree
Where the wounded back of the Christ we see
Deliverance grant from distress to me,
From death, from spell-binding to keep me free.

The cross of the Christ with no flaw at all,
Full outstretched to me to answer my call;
O God, bless unto me my mainmast tall
Ere I go forth and whate'er may befall.

What harm soever for me in it be,
O let me not take it away with me,
For the sake of Christ who from guile is free,
For the sake of the King, of virtues he.

In the name of the God of life above,
In the holy name of the Christ of love,
In the name of the Holy Spirit-Dove,
The Three-One together my strength enough.

102. *The Cross of Christ* *Barra*

Christ's cross 'twixt me and the folk of the hill
    That stealthily out or in do go,
The cross of Christ betwixt me and each ill,
    Each evil will, each misliking woe.

Be the angels of heaven shielding me,
    The heavenly angels for this night.
Be the angels of heaven shielding me
    Soul and body together aright.

The circle of Christ my compass around,
    From every spectre, from every bane,
And from every shame that comes to confound
    In darkness, and in power to give pain.

The circle of Christ my compass in might,
    My shielding from every harmful thing,
My keeping from each destruction this night
    Approaching me on destroying wing.

103. *The Mote*

Bonar Bridge and Kincardine (Ross)

In name of Father, Son, and Spirit at this hour,
Three-in-One Holy, all alike in might above,
Three-in-One of wondrous works, all alike in power,
Three-in-One, all alike in righteousness and love.

This is that which the Saviour Jesus Christ did write
When he was upstretched on the crucifying tree;
May the Mary gentle be by my hand in might,
And may the quiet Bridget near by my head be.

O thou Christ upon the tree,
All my hope I place in thee,
And the King of life to me,
That the thing within the eye,
Be it left or right, do fly
At my supplicating cry.

In name of the Father One,
And in the name of the Son,
In name of the Spirit too
                This I do.

Upon the King from on high,
Upon my Christ who is by,
On the Holy Spirit nigh,
Upon the Three I rely:
                This do I.

104. *The Reed*

O blessingless, thou reed,
O virtueless, thou reed,
O reed uplifted near
With numbing draught of fear;
Each lurching wind of moan
Over the knoll and mead
Makes deathly shiver-groan
Through every fear-curst reed,
        Through the fear-curst reed!

105. *Going to Rest*

Through Christ's crucifying tree,
Injury come not to me;
Through the Jesus-blood-avail,
Reiving act upon me fail.

No ill-doing come to me
Through bar, door-leaf, or turned key;
Nor oppression may I see,
King of glory leading me.

Light of lights take darkness' part
From thy place into my heart;
Spirit's wisdom music start
From my Saviour in my heart.

Spirit's peace this night be mine,
The Son's peace this night be mine,
Father's peace this night be mine,
Peace of peace this night be mine,
Life's each eve and morning-shine.

106. *Bedside Prayer*   *South Uist*

O Jesu, the one who art sinless quite,
Thou humble King of the meek and the poor,
Who wast brought low and crucified so sore
By sentence of the evil men of spite.
Do thou defend and shield me for this night
From traitor-ways and Judas-dark-steal flight.

My soul on thine own arm, O Christ, to lie,
Thou art the King of the City of Heaven,
Thou it was, Jesu, who my soul didst buy,
For by thee was my life-sacrifice given.

Do thou protect me because of my woe,
For the sake of thy passion, wounds, thy blood,
Take me in safety to-night as I go
Climbing up near to the City of God.

Of virtues loved thou passion-flower,
Made holy in a holy hour
By holy Lamb's blood that was shed,
Mild Mary's Son, 'twas his blood red,
By Bride of kine Son nourishéd,
Great Mary's Son, the people's aid,
Crucified Son of Mother Maid.

There is no land, there is no ground,
There is no lake, there is no deep,
There is no pool, no water round,
There is no wild, there is no steep,
That is not smooth and safe the hour
I wear the virtue passion-flower,
   That is not smooth and safe the hour
   I wear the little passion-flower.

X. THE WORLD

The world of the host and the world of the guest,
           The world of which great things are told;
The world of experience, world of the jest,
           The world that shall never grow old;

The world of the rogue and the world of the weak,
           The world of good fortune and ill;
The world long-ago that is now hard to seek,
           The world that is wonderful still;

The world of rejoicing, of repartee strong,
           The world where the great and small dwell,
The world of far lands, of sweet music and song,
           The heartbreaking world of farewell;

The world of the hills and the world of the young,
           The world of the good and the gone;
The world of God's arm so protectingly flung,
           The world that still goes on and on.

108. *The Mother's Compassing*

The joy of God be in thy face,
    Joy to each one beholding,
The ring of God thy neck embrace,
    God's angels shield enfolding,
    God's angels shield enfolding.

The joy of night and day be thine,
    Sun-joy and moon-joy showing,
Joy of men and women to shine,
    Or land or sea thy going,
    Or land or sea thy going.

Be every clime thy happiness,
    Each clime with brightness soothing,
Each clime be glad with loveliness,
    MacMary thy peace smoothing,
    MacMary-Maid thy smoothing.

The God of life's ring be it thine,
    The Christ of love's ring fending,
The Holy Spirit's ring divine,
    Thine aid and thy befriending,
      Donald, belov'd one best,
      Belov'd one of my breast;
    Thine aid and thy befriending,
      Mary, belov'd who art,
      Belov'd one of my heart.

109. *The Wicked*   *North Uist*

The wicked who would do me ill,
His throat let choking 'gluc-gloc' fill,
Up and down nasty whirling gobs,
With blood and lumps and sullen blobs.

Be harder than the stone to break,
Be blacker than the coal its head,
Be swifter-flying than the drake,
Heavier be it than the lead.

More galling, galling, grating, griping and grimmer may it be
  Than the hard hickle-hockle holly-o,
Be it sourer than the sacred, shining, sharp, salt, saline sea,
      Seven seven times so.

      Thither side to side,
      Hither far and wide,
      Down and down sagging,
      Up and up flagging.

      Out and out drivel,
      In and in snivel,
      Often out turning,
      Seldom returning.

The holding of each hand a straw,
His foot of each joist like a lag,
His leg like the jamb of each door,
A blood-spurt his driving and drag.

From heart, form, bones, let the blood pour,
From liver, breast, lungs, let it rise,
Scraping of veins, throat, kidneys sore,
For those who betray and despise.

In the God of virtues' great name,
Who breathed off from me every ill,
Who in might did shield me the same
From my breakers' snare and their will
      In loathing to kill.

110. *Winter Evening*

      The winter's eve so long and slow
      A stir there is to work for each,
      To tell the bairns what they must know
      The grey old-man doth patient teach,
      The daughter at her carding set,
      The mother at her spinning-wheel,
      The fisherman repairs his net
      With needle threaded from his reel.

The one for work is Jock o' the hay;
He's the one to lift, the one to lay,
The nimble one who whistles away,
He's up and about throughout the day,
The one of manners in all his way,
O Jock o' the hay, he works away.

O the wildcat from the cairn he'll bring,
The cormorant from the cliff he'll wing,
Stalking the deer on the hill he'll steal,
And from the skerry he'll bring the seal.

For combing and carding he's the one,
For smoothing and oiling ere 'tis spun;
He's the one to intercede and pray,
Bow head and knee to his God each day;
And Jock o' the hay, he works away.

112. *Saint Bride*

O Bride thou charming, Bride thou kind,
    The breath of thy mouth is well;
When myself with strangers I find
    Thyself hear the tale I tell.

113. *Uist of Old*   *South Uist*

Whenas the great sea spreading laid
    Was but a grey mossy wood,
I was a joyous little maid,
    And my wholesome breakfast good
Was Eager Rock dulse of the shore,
    Wild garlic of Cloud-cap Steep,
Water clear from Loch Darkhead's store,
    With fish from Ionnaire-mor deep,
Those my choice for sustaining me
So long as I would living be.

Nine lovely flax-rigs I would sow
In little Coradale trim,
And nuts my skirtful I would grow
Between Thor's two headlands grim.

114. *The Reay Bard*   *Reay*

I am a Gordon when in Tiriodh,
When in Assynt a Macleod I be,
When in Cataibh a Sutherland I,
When I go home I am a Mackay.

115. *Timber*

Choose the willow of the burnside mound,
Choose the hazel of the rocky bound,
Choose the alder with the marshes round,
Choose the birch by falling waters' sound.

Choose the ash-wood of the shady ground,
Choose the yew-wood of the springing bound,
Choose the elm-wood on the braeside found,
Choose the seasoned oak by sunshine browned.

116. *The Winds*

Wind from the west the fish and bread provides;
Wind from the north, bitter cold and flaying;
Wind from the east, the snow on mountain-sides;
Wind from the south, fruit on trees a-Maying.

117. *The Rock of Rocks*   *Barra*

On the Rock of rocks so tall
Peace of Peter and of Paul,
Of James and lovéd John withal,
And of the Lady Virginal,
    The Lady Virginal,

Peace of Father, seneschal,
Peace of paschal Christ exthrall,
Peace of gracious Spirit, fall
On us and on our children all,
Us and our children all.

XI. PROTECTION

Bless, O Chief of generous chiefs,
Myself and all anear me,
Bless me in all my joys and griefs,
In all my actions, thoughts, beliefs;
From all that would afear me
Make thou me safe for all my days,
Make thou me safe for always.
O thou who all mankind enfeoffs,
Bless, O Chief of generous chiefs.

(This poem is an abbreviated version of number 132).

118. *The Clasping of God*

May the Father everlasting
Himself take you, round you casting
His own gen'rous arm engrasping,
His own gen'rous hand enclasping.

119. *Prayer to Jesus*

'Tis from my mouth that my prayer I say,
'Tis from my heart that my prayer I pray,
'Tis before thee that my prayer I lay,
To thyself, O healing Hand, I call,
O thou Son of God who saves us all.

O thou dear Son of Mary benign,
With creed and pater to Father thine,
And after, prayer of Mary divine,
And thine own prayer taught us of old,
Son of the God of grace, I have told;

To magnify the greatness of heav'n,
And to magnify God's greatness giv'n,
To magnify thine own greatness prov'n,
And thy glory, O thou God the Son,
Thou Son of God of the Passion done;

To give praise to thee, Jesus content,
Alla of sea and of continent,
Alla of sun, moon and firmament,
Alla of all the beautiful stars,
The bright heavenly chariot cars.

Fountain of life for men's righteousness,
And faithful Brother of helpfulness,
Make thou my prayer availing to be
Unto my soul and unto body.

Lord God of the angels overhead,
Thy linen robe do thou overspread;
From every famine be shielding me,
From each shape of spectre set me free.

103

O strengthen me in every good thing,
In every strait thine encompassing,
Safeguard me in every ill and pain,
From every venom do thou restrain.

Be between me and each grisly scene,
Be between me and everything mean,
Be between me and the gruesome things
That dark come towards me on fearful wings.

Glorious Master of star and cloud,
Glorious Master of the sky browed,
Glorious Master of heav'nly place,
O blest by thee is each tribe and race.

O mayest thou for me intercede
With the great Lord of life indeed,
With the kind Father of glory's throne,
With the great Chief whom the nations own.

O Master bright-fragrant and endeared,
O Master bright-kindly, lov'd and feared,
Earnest and humble my prayer I make,
Lowly and tearful my prayer I take,
Kneeling before thee my prayer I wake,
In my death-passion do not forsake;

Rest everlasting grant I may find
In the great Trinity's resting kind,
Within the godly's Paradise place,
Within thy love's Vine-garden of grace.

Put thy salve to my sight to convert,
O put thy balm to my wounds that hurt,
Thy linen robe to my skin engirt,
Thyself, O thou healing Hand, I call,
O thou Son of God who saves us all.

O God of the lowly and the weak,
O God of the holy and the meek,
God of the righteous, the homesteads' shield;
Thou callest us thy praises to yield
With the mercy-mouth and glory-voice
Of the belovéd Son of thy choice.

Rest everlasting o may I find
In the home of thy Trinity kind,
Within the godly's Paradise bright,
Within thy love's Sun-garden of light.

120. *Appealing to God* *Barra*

Unto God appeal I make,
For Mary, Christ's dear Mother's sake,
The twelve Apostles and Saint Paul,
    To mine aid and shielding all.

I beseech the Lord the Son
'Gainst evil, evildoing done,
And Mary aye a Virgin Maid,
    To my succour and mine aid.

God mine aid, God my relief,
God mine aid 'mid the ocean reef,
God my safeguard in leper-place,
    God safeguard in narrow race.

God's Son shielding me from ill,
God's Son from harm be shielding still,
God's Son shielding from mishap-plight,
    God's Son shielding me this night.

God's Son shielding me with might,
Each one dealing with me aright,
God so deal with his soul each hour,
    God's Son shielding me with power.

May God free me from each sin,
Free me, God, from each ambush-gin,
Free me, God, from each dark ravine,
    Crooked road and bog unseen.

Every pass God open clear,
Christ open me each narrow sheer,
Each holy man and woman there
    In heav'n, path for me prepare.

From death's state, O God, upraise,
From torment-state to state of grace,
From world below and earthliness
To high heaven's holiness.

Fragrant Father high above,
Taking charge of my soul in love,
Thy loving arm my body's keep
Through each slumber here and sleep.

121. The Encompassing of the Three

The compassing of God be upon thee,
God of the living encompassing.

The compassing of Christ be upon thee,
The Christ of loving encompassing.

The compassing of Spirit be on thee,
Holy Ghost laving encompassing.

The compassing of the Three be on thee,
Encompassing Three preserving thee,
Encompassing Three preserving thee.

122. The King of Life Compass

The King of life compass, compass thee,
The loving Christ encompassing be,
The Holy Spirit, compasser he,
Unto the life-crown eternally,
Unto the life-crown eternally.

123. The Compassing of God

The compassing of God and of his right hand
Round my form and frame protecting may it stand;
High King's compassing and grace of Trinity
Round me abiding ever eternally,
Round me abiding ever eternally.

The Three's compassing my shield in my life-means,
The Three's compassing my shield through this day's scenes,
The Three's compassing my shield this night throughout,
From hate, from harm, from act, from evil about,
  From hate, from harm, from act, from evil about.

124. *Jesus the Encompasser* *Barra*

Jesu! Only-begotten mine,
God the Father's Lamb sacrificed,
Thou didst give thy body's blood-wine
From the grave-death to buy me right.
My shield, my encircler, my Christ, my Christ!
For each day, each night, for each dark, each light;
  My shield, my encircler, my Christ, my Christ!
For each day, each night, for each dark, each light.

Jesu! uphold me and be nigh,
My triumph, treasure, thou art now,
When I lie down, when stand, be by,
Whenever I watch, when I sleep.
My aid, my encircler, MacMary thou!
My strength everlasting, MacDavid, keep;
  My aid, my encircler, MacMary thou!
My strength everlasting, MacDavid, keep.

125. *Encompassment*

Encircling holy Apostles round,
Encircling of gentle martyrs crowned,
Encircling of the nine angels bound,
  My cherishing and my aid.

Encircling of Bride without a sound,
Encircling of Mary mild renowned,
Encircling warrior Michael found,
  My shielding and aiding prayed.

Encircling of God of life's abound,
Encircling of Christ so loving wound,
Encircling of Holy Ghost surround,
  My cherishing, aiding made.

107

126. *The Protecting Arm*

The arm of Mary Mother be thine,
The arm of Saint Bridget of the kine,
Saint Michael's arm, the victory sign,
  From every grief
  To ward and save.

Apostle Saint John's arm to befriend,
Apostle Saint Paul's arm thee to send,
Apostle Saint Peter's arm rock-fend,
  From all mischief
  To guard and brave.

The arm of the God of life to hold,
The arm of the loving Christ enfold,
And the Holy Spirit's arm to mould,
  Thy shielding chief,
  Surround, enclave.

127. *Shield-Prayer*   *Lorne*

Thou Michael to fight,
Thou Michael of wound-might,
O shield me from the spite
Of the hostile this night,
  The hostile this night.

Thou Bride of the kine,
Bride of plaid-swaddling fine,
O shield me from scorn-bine
That the knoll-fairies twine,
  The knoll-fairies twine.

Thou Mary so staid,
Mary Mother proud Maid,
O shield me, succour, aid,
With thy linen arrayed,
  Thy linen arrayed.

Thou Christ of the tree,
On the cross Christ for me,
From the snare tear me free
Where the vicious agree,
  The vicious agree.

Thou Father of stray,
The bare one's Father aye,
To house-shelter away
Draw me, Saviour, I pray,
The poors' Saviour-stay.

128. *Charm for Protection* *Barra*

Bridget's charm round her Fosterson,
And Mary's charm placed round her Son,
Michael's charm round his buckler giv'n,
God's Son's charm round city of heav'n.

Charm against sword, 'gainst arrow fierce,
Charm against spears so sharp to pierce,
Charm 'gainst bruises and water's drown.
Charm 'gainst firebrand and bolt from sky,
Charm 'gainst adder that coiled doth lie,
Charm 'gainst battlefield risk and down.

Charm 'gainst earth-child or fairy-child,
Charm against the enemy wild,
Charm against peril's deadly ill.
Charm 'gainst ravaging red icebound,
Charm 'gainst rending by swift-foot hound,
Charm 'gainst huntsman's fatal kill.

Columba's cowl over thee be,
Michael the soldier's cowl round thee,
Christ's cowl, belov'd, safeguarding fold,
Cowl of the God of grace thy hold;

To guard thee from behind thy back,
To save thee in a front attack,
From crown of head and brow, the whole
Down thy body unto thy sole.

An isle art thou in midst of sea,
A hill on land shelteringly,
A well art thou in desert place,
And health art thou in ailing's case.

In great fear for their lives they go
Who see the person charmèd so.

Columba companies to aid,
About thee his own cowl is laid;
Soldier Michael's succour is round,
And his great buckler fends thee sound.

129. *Heavenly Love and Affection*

Heavenly love and affection to you,
The saintly love and affection imbue,
The angels' love and affection as dew,
The love and affection of the sun,
The love and affection of moonbeam spun,
Be to you in your lives each day and night,
To keep you from harm, oppression, and spite,
O from them that harm, that oppress, that spite.

130. *The Guarding of the God of Life*

The God of life with guarding hold you,
The loving Christ with guarding fold you,
The Holy Spirit, guarding, mould you,
Each night of life to aid, enfold you,
Each day and night of life uphold you.

131. *The Form of Christ*

Christ in beauty to'rds me near,
Christ in beauty to me here,
Christ in beauty stand before,
Christ in beauty after sure,
Christ in beauty overhead,
Christ in beauty underspread,
Christ in beauty with me found,
Christ in beauty to surround,
Monday, weekday, Sunday bound;
    Christ in beauty to surround,
    Sunday, Monday, weekday sound.

XII. FAIRIES

When the angel of evil for the sake
 Of proud rebellion took to his wings
The gust of his flying drew in his wake
 A host of spirits and foolish things.

When God saw the headlong swooping descent
 He bade close the gates of heav'n and hell,
And as the great hinges revolving went
 A band was excluded as it fell.

O little people that dwell in the knoll,
 O little people, part good, part bad,
O little people of song-flitting soul,
 Mischief and aid from you can be had!

O little people of beautiful bowers,
 Whose ways are hid but whose life is gay,
Who dwell 'mid the rocks, the waves and the flowers,
 You spirit hither, thither away.

O God of all life, thou Father of grace,
 Have pity on all creatures that live;
The mischief ward, bless the aid of their race,
 To all of us thy salvation give.

132. The Chief of Generous Chiefs Benbecula

Thou Chief of gen'rous heroes bless
Myself and all things that are near,
Bless me in all my doingness,
Keep thou me ever safe and dear,
     Keep thou me safe and dear.

From every brownie and ban-shee,
From each ill-wish and sorrow's pass,
From nymph and wraith of stream and sea,
From fairy-mouse and mouse of grass,
     Fairy-mouse and mouse of grass.

From every troll among the bens,
From every siren pressing hard,
From every ghoul within the glens,
O till my day's end do thou guard,
     Until my day's end guard.

133. Mountain Lullaby South Uist

On milk of deer they reared me here,
    The milk of deer my fountain,
On milk of deer 'neath stormy sheer,
    On crest of hill and mountain.

134. The Spirit Hounds Benbecula

Mountain-ranger, Slender-fay,
Come away, o come away!
Lucky-treasure, Fairy-black,
Come to heel here, hairy back!
Seek-beyond, and Blue-greyhound,
Come to me in single bound!

135. The Bennan Brownie Arran

Ho, hi, ho! out the kine,
The cattle pretty of hoof and horn,
The cattle pretty a shining morn,
Ho, hi, ho! out the kine.

Macugan's cows, cows of Mackinnon,
Big Macfarquhar's cows of the Bennan,
Ho, hi, ho! out the kine.

Corpse and cairn for an English midden,
For they have slain my lover hidden,
Ho, hi, ho! out the kine.

To my shift they stripped me in their scorn,
My lover dear they have clubbed and torn,
Ho, hi, ho! out the kine.

An Arran night and an Islay night,
And green Kintyre of the birches bright,
Ho, hi, ho! out the kine.

136. The Benmore Calves
South Uist and Benbecula

Little she-calves, spotted hide,
Little she-calves, spotted hide,
Little she-calves, spotted hide,
Storm in rutting time to ride!

Little carle of Corrie vale,
Little carle of Corrie vale,
Little carle of Corrie vale,
Crageo and Coradale!
Little she-calves, spotted side.

Little carle of coat-no-tail,
Little carle of coat-no-tail,
Little carle of coat-no-tail,
Cragavig and Circidale!
Little she-calves, spotted pied.

Little carle of Pass's foot,
Little carle of Pass's foot,
Little carle of Pass's foot,
   Strength and health I wish to put
   For thy hand and for thy foot!
   Little she-calves, spotted bide.

137. *Fairy Wisdom*   *Benbecula*

The maiden-queen of wisdom dwelt
In Beauty's Bower of the single tree,
   Where she could see what humans felt,
And where no fool could her beauty see.

Loveliness shone around her like light,
Her steps were the songs of music bright.

The day that sense she lotted round
Not to be on the knoll was my fate,
   But had mine own share then been found
I would not to-night be in this strait.

138. *The Blue Flax*   *Tiree*

The fairy-queen's flax, the blue-eyed flower
   Be to shield me and keep me still
From hosts of the air and faery power,
   From evil deed and from ill-will.

139. *It is Mine Own Eye*   *Barra*

Mine own eye of seeing it is,
The eye of God's Being it is,
The eye of God's Son is for this,
To return it back, to repel,
To oppose, to fight with it well.

The person who made thee the eye,
O grim on himself may it lie,
And grim lie it on his desires,
And grim on his cattle and byres:

On his children, and on his wife,
His dear ones, the means of his life,
On his herds, and on his crop seed,
And upon his kine's comely breed;

His mares both the brown and the grey,
On his garrons ploughing away,
His flocks both the white and the black,
His grain-stores, his crushed meal astack;

On women of fairy so wee,
Mound-reelers and dancers they be,
Who bide in and out of the heath,
Who fill all the holes underneath.

140. *The Defence of the Holy Ones*

I pray and with my supplication sue
To druid Coivi and Columba true,
I pray unto the Mother of my King,
To modest Bridget maid petitioning,
To Michael of the warfare making prayer,
The high-king of the angels of the air,
That they give succour and they shield me round
From all the little folk of fairy mound.

XIII. SAINTS

When comes the new-born child, Saint Bride
    Doth quietly preside;
Saint Bride, when comes the new-born spring,
    Nurse gently fostering,
Gives warmth to earth and tends the birth;
The living flocks and herds she leads
To pasturage and watered meads,
With milk and butter for our needs.

Saint Patrick great apostle free,
    To show the One-in-Three,
Though once a captive, doth return
    And sees the homestead burn;
The folk he seeks, the faith he speaks,
The reptiles swiftly creep away,
The druids watch him, ashen-grey;
Green yet there blows the shamrock-spray.

Saint Magnus royal sailor guide
    The northern wave doth ride;
Unto his brother he doth yield,
    Yet not on battlefield;
Lest blood be shed himself instead
The noble earl to seal the peace
And cause the quarrelling to cease
Doth offer up his living's lease.

Saint Brendan of the ocean wide
    Doth master every tide;
His ship doth search the distant shore
    Traversing evermore
The endless space of waters' face;
The gospel message he doth spell,
To continents its echoes swell
From lonely sea-girt cliff-face cell.

Saint Mary Virgin white and mild,
    Mother of every child,
Mother of tears and of God's Son,
    Mother of everyone,
Pierced is her heart with anguish dart;
The fruit bows to the Mother fair;
"Under the wood" she foils the snare;
Smiling she stands with flower-crowned hair.

Saint Michael, angel of the sea,
    Lord of the horses he,
Saint Michael, of the angels king,
    Of war, of shepherding;
On steed he flies across the skies;
The first-fruits of the harvest corn,
The first-fruits of the flock-lambs born
Are his, he meets the soul forlorn.

The saints and angels watch o'erhead,
    Their wings and prayers o'erspread;
The righteous ones in heaven wait,
    Saint Peter at the gate;
In might arrayed they shield and aid;
Be with us e'er, archangel powers,
Be with us, angels, life's long hours,
O blessed saints, your life be ours.

141. *Love and Protection*

The love and affection of angels flying,
The love and affection of saints undying,
Heaven's love and affection satisfying,
O your guarding and cherishing let them be,
Your so loving protection eternally.

142. *Saint Bride Blessing*

South Uist and Benbecula

Holy maid Bride's ancestry is told,
Christ's high Foster-Mother of flame-gold.

Bride is daughter to Dugall the Brown,
From Aodh, Art and Conn coming down,
From Criara, Cairbre and Cas descent,
From Cormac, Cartach and Conn it went.

Bride of the veils, of the peat-heap stock,
Bride of the sight, of the plaited lock,
Bride of the quiet, of the white feet,
Bride of the kine, of the white hands neat,

Bride tress of Mary, of the peat piled,
Christ's Fostermother, Bride woman mild,
Each morning time and each eventide
That I repeat the descent of Bride,

I shall not be wounded, pierced, nor slain,
I shall not be prisoned, torn in twain,
I shall not be despoiled, nor be ripped,
I shall not be downtrod, naked stripped,
Hurt, blinded, rent, I shall not be left
By Christ overlooking me, bereft.

Nor fire, nor sun shall be burning me,
Nor the sickly moon shall whitening be;
Nor flood, nor sea shall be drowning me,
Nor shall waterfall my downing be.

Nor shall lift me seed of fairy host,
Nor shall lift me seed of airy host,
Nor earthly destroyer uppermost.

Fear of nightmare shall not lie on me,
Nor the black-sleep on mine eyelids be,
On me shall not lie the sleeping-spell,
Nor galloping-plant making unwell.

Under the shielding I shall abide
Each day provided by maiden Bride;
Under the shielding I shall abide
Each night provided by maiden Bride.
'Neath the Foster-Nurse of Mary's aid
I stand flow and draw, each light and shade.

Bride my friend-woman, woman of song,
Bride is my helping-woman along,
Choicest of women, my woman-guide,
Each choicest, dearest, each guiding supplied.

143. *The Shamrock of Saint Patrick*

Shamrock of the leaves so fair,
O thou shamrock-plant entwined,
O thou shamrock of the prayer,
Shamrock that I love to find.

Shamrock of my sorrowing,
Virtues' plant of Patrick friend,
Shamrock of MacMary King,
People's plant of journey's-end.

O thou shamrock-plant of grace,
Plant of joy, of tomb-sward scene,
'Twere my wish in death's embrace
That thou on my grave grow green.

144. *Saint Magnus*   *Kildonan and Orkney*

O Magnus who my love didst win,
Thy guidance may we find,
Fragrant body of life within,
O keep us in thy mind.

Mindful of us, thou saint of power,
  Defence-surround of men,
O aid us in our wretched hour,
  Nor e'er forsake us then.

Our flocks lift to hill pasturage,
  The wolf and fox subdue,
Keep from us spectre, giant, rage,
  Oppressing fraud untrue.

Surround the cows and cattle whole,
  Surround the lambs and sheep;
Keep off from them the water-vole,
  The field-vole off them keep.

Sprinkle the sky-dew on the stock,
  Give growth to grass and corn,
Give sap to plants, rush, cress and dock,
  And daisy morning-born.

Magnus of fame, when'er we stand
  Aboard the heroes' craft,
On crest of wave, on sea, on land,
  Help, protect fore and aft.

145. *Black Donald's Ploughing* *Barra*

Black Donald went to plough his lands
  Upon Saint Brendan's day;
Behind his horses two he stands
  And drives his plough away;
The mist caught hold with night-black hands
  And blotted out the day.

"O Brendan, Brendan", Donald cried,
  "Lift off the mist from me";
The mist did gently upward ride
  And showed him pygmy wee,
Two long-eared asses were beside,
  And distaff-handed he.

Black Donald went to plough again,
    He drove his asses two;
The mist came down as black as rain
    And blotted them from view;
Black Donald he was vexed with pain
    And knew not what to do.

"O Brendan, Brendan", Donald said,
    "God willing, wishing men,
Lift off the mist from o'er my head";
    The mist it left the glen,
And showed a fairy man instead,
    Coneys and spindle then.

Black Donald went to plough once more,
    He drove his coneys on;
The mist came down black as before,
    And lo! they were all gone;
Black Donald he repented sore
    And prayer began to con.

"O Brendan, Brendan", he did pray,
    "O hearken to my prayer,
As God doth will and men do say,
    Lift off the mist in air";
The mist rose up and showed the day,
    And they were as they were.

Black Donald he went home again,
    Sore sorrowful at heart;
The neighbours they did mock his pain,
    And disbelieved his part;
But one she did his love obtain,
    And soothed him with her art.

"My loving dark-haired one art thou,
    Let all sharp tongues assail,
One there is to be true knows how,
    And one heart will not fail.

"My dark-haired, dark-haired one art thou,
    Though poor and poor we be,
No rich old man could please me now
    Like thee, my love, like thee".

122

146. *The Feast Day of Saint Mary*   Benbecula

On sweet-smelling Mary's feast day 'tis done,
Mother from whom the Fold-Shepherd was born;
I reap me a cut of the new-grown corn,
Gently I dry it laid out in the sun,
From the husk sharply I rub out the grain
　　　　With mine own palms twain.

On Friday I grind the meal in the quern,
In a sheep-skin I bake it to a turn,
On a rowan-wood fire I toast it fine,
And I share it round with all that are mine,
　　　　With all that are mine.

With the sun I go round my dwelling-place,
In the Mother-name of the Mary of grace,
Her who to preserve me pledged her a vow,
Who did preserve me, and will preserve now,
In cattle for fold, in peace for our days,
In the uprightness that in the heart stays,
In any task, in the love that we know,
In our essence wise, the fondness we show,
O Christ of grace, for thy Passion's sake,
　　　　Do not thou forsake!

Thou who till the day that death doth me take,
The Christ of the grace, wilt never forsake,
　　　　Till death doth me take,
　　　　O never forsake!

147. *A Hail to Saint Mary*   Barra

To Mary, hail! to Mary, hail!
　　Queen of grace, Mother forgiving;
To Mary, hail, the non-pareil,
　　Source of our joy, fount of living!

Children we of Adam and Eve,
　　Night and day to pray beginning,
As we wail, and weep, and grieve,
　　Unto thee for all our sinning.

123

Root of gladness, on us to fall,
　Thou Cup of generous graces,
The faith of John, Peter and Paul,
　From Ariel's cloud-winged places.

O Branch of gold, a hall provide,
　In the Peace-land to us yielding,
From peril-wave and boiling tide,
　Fruit of womb Jesus our shielding.

148. *Ave Maria*   *Barra*

Mary Mother, hail unto thee!
For thou art full of loving grace,
The Lord God ever is with thee,
O blessed Mary, Queen of grace;
Blest amongst women all thou art,
Blest is thy womb-fruit set apart;
O holy Mary, Mother mild,
Thou Mother of the Jesus Child,
For me a wretched sinner plead,
Both now and in death's hour of need,
　Both now and in death's hour of need!

149. *Praise of Saint Mary*   *Morar*

The prayer that I say it is this
That with the anointing was made
For the Mary Mother the Maid
　　　　　Of bliss;

With the Paternoster and Creed,
And the Saving of Mary there,
And the Son of God's Passion Prayer
　　　　　For need;

Thine own honour to increase more,
More the Son of God's glory-state,
More the God of grace who is great
　　　　　Ensure.

Do thou plead with thy happy Son
That an answer unto my prayer
For my soul and my body there
                    Be done.

O Queen of the angels so rare,
O Queen of the heavenly height,
O Queen of the city so bright
                    And fair :

Do thou in each virtue enwreathe,
From each vice be compassing me,
And my shielding o do thou be
                    And sheathe.

O thou quiet Mother of fame,
Thou Mother of stars, great in grace,
Full-blest hast thou been of each race
                    And name.

Thou singly praised, worthy of praise,
Fervent prayer for me at my call
With the world-Chief, the God of all,
                    Upraise.

Happy Mary mild and white seen,
Forsake me not I humbly pray
In the pang of my dying day
                    So keen.

Shield of each home, shield of men all,
That sorely on the mercy kind
Of thy belovéd Son to find
                    Do call :

Thou the Queen of sweetness of heart,
The Queen who art loyal and true,
Queen of peace and of nations too
                    Thou art.

Thou the fountain of mercy mild,
Thou art of consoling the root,
Life-stream of maid, mother of fruit
                    And child.

Thou the shrine of the Christ the Son,
Thou the hall where the Christ is known,
Thou art Christ's ark, of him alone
           The one.

Thou the Queen of the sea so bright,
Queen of all the heavens on high,
Queen of the angels of the sky
           In light.

The God of all's temple thou art,
The God of all's shrine thou art still,
The God of all's hall, of the ill
           At heart.

The river of grace thou dost flow,
The well-spring of health thou dost rise,
Maidens' garden, the paradise
           They know.

Of the morning thou art the star,
The star of the night-watching long,
The star of the ocean-tide strong
           Afar.

The star of the earth is thy brow,
Of the heavens thou the star-one,
Of the Father of glory's Son
           Star thou.

In her corn thou art the earth drest,
Thou art the rich treasure of sea,
In homes here is waiting for thee
           The guest.

The vessel of sating to find,
Thou the cup of wisdom to seal,
And thou art the well-spring to heal
           Mankind.

Thou the orchard of virtues twined,
And thou art the hall of the glad,
And thou art the Mother so sad
           And kind.

Thou the lullaby of the great,
The orchard of apples art thou,
The world in beauty thou art now
                    To sate.

Thou the moon of the skies to show,
The sun of the heavens by day,
Thou art the star, and thou the way
                    Men go.

Since thou art the full ocean wave,
By sea be my pilot at hand;
Since thou art the dry shore, by land
                    O save.

The gem of the jewel thou art,
Preserve me from water, from flame,
From sky-men and wee folk whence came
                    The dart.

There is none who sings my song here
Or employs it, but Mary still
Thrice to him ere dying's end will
                    Appear.

150. *The Spell of Purest White*   *Benbecula*

The spell of purest white was sent,
From Mary Virgin forth it went,
To Dorail's daughter, lovely Bride
Of golden-yellow tresses tied,
Hither upon the mainland wide,
Hither upon the coastland side,
Hither upon the lakeland sheen,
Hither upon the ocean green,
To thwart the eye, to thwart the snare,
Malice to thwart, and hatred's stare,
To repel debility bred,
And to repel the measles red,
To repel running from the nose,
And to repel the deadly rose.

O Michael of the battlefield,
　　King of the angels arrayed,
Unto thy people be a shield
　　With thy shining might of blade,
Unto thy people be a shield
　　With thy shining might of blade.

Thy wing of feathers overspread
　　O'er sea and o'er land to go,
The east and the west overhead,
　　And shield from the evil foe,
The east and the west overhead,
　　And shield from the evil foe.

O brighten with the sun thy Day
　　From the heavens of the height;
Be with us in our circling way
　　And in the twists of the fight;
Be with us in our circling way
　　And in the twists of the fight.

Arch-chief of chiefs, thou angel-lord,
　　Arch-chief of the poor and low,
Be with us processing abroad
　　And in river's gleaming flow;
Be with us processing abroad
　　And in river's gleaming flow.

Arch-chief of chiefs, lord overhead,
　　Arch-chief of angels a-row,
Thy wing of feathers overspread
　　O'er sea and o'er land to go,
All their fullness is thine to shed,
　　Their fullness thine to bestow,
Thine own is the fullness to shed,
　　Fullness thine own to bestow.

152. Saint Michael of the Angels

O Michael of the angel-host afar
And of the righteous who in heaven are,
Give shielding to my soul with thy wing's shade;
In earth and heaven shield my soul and aid;

From foes upon the ground, foes underground,
From foes who hide protect and circle round
My soul beneath thy wing's defending aid,
My soul within thy wing's defending shade!

153. Steed of Saint Michael

Brian of Michael as white as the snow,
Snow of the peaks and the foam of the sea,
White as the cotton-grass meadow doth grow,
Near white as the angel of victory.

Brian as swift as the swift of the spring,
As swift as the March wind's turbulent breath,
Swift as the bolt deadly lightning doth bring,
Near swift as the fate-laden shaft of death.

Brianag white as the sun of the days,
Musical as the bards' harmony bliss,
As gentle as Bride of the herds that graze,
Near sweet as the lips of the mother's kiss.

154. Prayer against Consumption   The Black Isle

Healing I will give to thee,
Mary she will heal with me,
Mary, Michael, maiden Bride,
All the three with me abide.

All thy sickness and thy plight
To the earth-holes hence from sight,
On the grey stones hence away,
Of the firmest bed are they.

On the birds of air to rest,
On the wasps of swarming nest,
Be on the whales of the seas,
Of the swiftest body these.

Be upon the sky-clouds grey,
Showery of nature they,
Be upon the river's stream
Flooding to the wave's demesne.

155. *The Holy Spell*   *Baleshare of North Uist*

Unto mine eye I do place this spell,
As the King of life ordained it well,
The spell of Peter and Paul amain,
The spell of James and of John the twain,
The spell of Columba, kindness versed,
The spell of Patrick, of saints the first,
The spell of calm Bride, the cows in sight,
The spell of fair Mary of delight,
The spell of the kine and herds that chew,
The spell of the sheep and flocks in view,
The spell of greatness, the spell of means,
The spell of joy, and of peaceful scenes,
The spell of war, and bravery done,
The third best spell that is 'neath the sun,
The virtuous spell of the Virtues Three,
Father, Son, Spirit, e'erlastingly.

156. *The Saints and Angels*

The circle of the saints around you wound,
The circle of the angels o'er the ground,
O circle yours of all the saints be found
And of the angels nine for you around.

XIV. LOCHABER POEMS

Lochaber of the soaring bens,
Lochaber of the mighty glens,
  Of towering sweeps and cloud-capped steeps,
Lochaber of the prayers that rise
As mist unto the morning skies.

Olympian the navel-place,
Ben Nevis of the summit grace,
  The topmost crest of Highland blest,
The heavenly print of lasting snows,
A virgin whiteness of repose.

Lochaber where the waters fall,
Lochaber where the curlews call,
  Sound rising here so fresh and clear,
Fresh as the dews the offered prayer,
Lifted clear as the mountain air.

Lochaber of the axes keen,
Lochaber of the battle scene,
  Of galleyed fleet and marching feet,
A dedicated holy art
Reveals thy single faithful heart.

157. *Before Prayer*   *Lochaber*

The Father who created me
With eye benign beholdeth me;
The Son who dearly purchased me
With eye divine enfoldeth me;
The Spirit who so altered me
With eye refining holdeth me;
In friendliness and love the Three
Behold me when I bend the knee.

O God, through thine Anointed One,
The fullness of our needs be done—
Grant us towards God the love ordained,
Grant us towards man the love unfeigned;
Grant us the smile of God's good face,
Grant us God's wisdom and God's grace;
Grant us to fear and reverence still,
Grant in the world to do thy will
As done in heaven by saintly hands
And myriad of angelic bands;
Each day and night, each dawn and fall,
Grant us in kindness, Lord of all,
Thy nature's tincture at our call.

158. *Morning Prayer*   *Lochaber*

O Jesus Christ, all thanks be to thee,
Who hast brought me safely through last night,
To the morning joy of this day's light,
To win everlasting life for me,
Through the blood that thou didst shed for me.

O God, for ever praise be to thee,
For the blessings thou bestow'st on me—
For my food, my work, my health, my speech,
For all the good gifts bestowed on each,
O God, for ever praise be to thee.

I pray thee now to shield me from woe,
From sinning, this night to consecrate,
God of the poor, and I poor and low,
O Christ of the wounds, thy wisdom great
Along with thy grace on me bestow.

May the Holy One make claim on me,
And protect me on the land and sea,
Step by step leading me on my way
To the City of e'erlasting day,
Peace of the City that lasts for aye.

159. *Nativity Prayer* — *Lochaber*

O God, in each thing that I do,
In word and wish and thinking through,
In what I want, and when I sleep,
In dream, repose, and what I keep
Within my mind, in soul and heart,
May our dear Lady have a part
And that promised Branch of Glory
Famed in holy Gospel story;
May the blessed Virgin Mary,
And the fragrant Branch of Glory
Be in my heart and soul always
To have my worship and my praise,
  O in my heart and soul always.

160. *Prayer to Saint Mary the Mother* — *Lochaber*

O thou Mary Maid,
There was not known e'er
An one who was laid
'Neath thy gen'rous care,

Who thy mercy prayed,
Who thy shield prayed too,
Who prayed for thine aid
With heart that is true,

Found not solace made,
Who found not thy rest,
Who found not the aid
For which he made quest.

That gives unto me
The hope very great
That inn-room with thee
Be found for my state,
That my tears and prayer
Find a welcome there.

My heart is content
Thy footstool to near,
My heart is content
That thou grant and hear;

To come before thee,
Fair smiling thy face,
To come before thee,
Fair womanly grace;

To come before thee,
Thou Princess of man,
To come before thee,
Princess of world-span;

To come before thee,
O branch-wreath of flower,
To come before thee,
White wreath of sky-bower;

To come before thee,
The Grace-Lamb who bore,
To come before thee,
The Mother adore
Of Paschal Lamb sure;

To come before thee,
Seed-river of dream,
To come before thee,
O peace-bed of stream;

To come before thee,
O fountain to heal,
To come before thee,
Well-spring of grace-weal;

To come before thee,
Thou fine dwelling-place,
To come before thee,
Thou home of peace-grace;

To come before thee,
Thou jewel of cloud,
To come before thee,
Thou jewel star-browed;

To come before thee,
Dark Mother of woes,
To come before thee,
O Mother whence grows
God's glorious rose;

To come before thee,
Thou Maid of the poor,
To come before thee,
The Mother adore
Who Christ Jesus bore;

With woe and with keen,
With prayer and with cry,
With grief and tear seen,
With asking and sigh;

That thou have me spared
Scorning and disgrace,
That thou have me spared
Fawning and shame's face;

That thou have me spared
Woe and mourning sore,
That thou have me spared
Anguish evermore;

That my soul thou aid
On the great King's road,
That my soul thou aid
On the path peace-strowed;

That my soul thou aid
In the mercy-door,
That my soul thou aid
On the justice-floor.

Star of the sea thou,
Lead me o'er the sea;
Star of the land thou,
Ashore my guide be.

Star of the night thou,
In the dark my light;
Sun of daylight thou,
Afield my shield-might.

Angelic star thou,
On earth watching send;
Star-paradise thou,
To heaven befriend.

O shield me by day,
O shield me by night,
O shield night and day,
O Queen gracious, white,
Of heavenly light.

Grant me my love-prayer,
Grant shielding-request,
Grant me my pain-care
Through Son of thy breast
Of the blood shed best.

My God, not as naught,
My Christ, not as naught,
O kind Spirit sought,
Count me not as naught,
Nor leave me to stay
Deficient for aye.

161. *For the Household*   *Lochaber*

God, bless the world and all that in it dwell,
God, bless my partner, children dear as well,
God, bless the eye that stands set in my head,
And, God, the handling of my hand o bless;
What time I rise in morning's earliness,
What time I lie down late upon my bed,
   My rising bless in morning's earliness,
   And my late lying down upon my bed.

God, guard the household members and the hall,
God, consecrate the mother's children all,
God, all the flocks and young in safety keep;
Be after them and tend them from the fold,
What time the herds ascend the hill and wold,
What time I lie me down in gentle sleep,
   When slow the herds ascend the hill and wold,
   When tired I lie me down in peace to sleep.

162. *The Protection of the Cross*   *Lochaber*

The cross of the saints over my head
And of the angels overspread
Down from my face to where my feet tread.

O Michael mild, O Mary of fame,
O gentle Saint Bride, hair golden-bright,
My shielding be in my feeble frame,
My shielding three on the path of right,
   O shielding three on the path of right.

My shielding be in the soul-shrine low,
My shielding be when naked and weak,
My shielding be lest I stumbling go,
My shielding three for to-night I seek,
  O shielding three for to-night I seek.

The cross of the saints over my head
And of the angels overspread
Down from my face to where my feet tread.

163. *The Guardian Angel*　　　　　*Lochaber*

Thou angel of God in charge over me
From the fragrant Father of all mercy,
The fold of the saints and shepherding kind
This night round about me be sure-entwined;
The compassing kind of the Sacred Heart
Be made this night round my soul-shrine apart,
    Round my soul-shrine apart.

Drive forth each danger, temptation to sin,
On the waters of evil hull me in,
In the narrows and currents keep my boat
'Mid the rocks and the reefs always afloat;
All perils, distresses from me enforce,
On the ocean of right compass my course,
    O encompass my course.

Before a bright flame, above guiding star,
And below a smooth path for travelling far,
To-day, to-night, and for ever, behind,
Thou angel of God, be my shepherd kind;
Before me, I pray thee, make thy fresh light,
Beauty-white angel, on this very night,
    O white angel, this night.

Weary am I and a stranger as well,
And so lead me to where the angels dwell;
Be steering my boat on the waters' crest
To the haven of tranquil waves at rest;
For me it is time now to make home-tryst
In the peace of heaven and court of Christ,
    In the roadstead of Christ.

O Jesu, this nightfall,
Who dost fold-herd the poor,
Without sin thou at all
Who didst suffer full sore,
By the wicked's decree,
Crucified thou for me,

From ill be my safeguard,
And safeguard me from sin,
Save my body and ward,
Make me holy within,
O Jesu, this nightfall,
Nor leave me till light fall.

O endow me with might,
Virtue-Herdsman of light,
Do thou guide me aright,
Do thou guide me in might,
Thine, O Jesu, the might,
Keep me safe until light.

165. *The Soul-Shrine*   *Lochaber*

God, give thy blest angels charge to surround
Watching over this steading to-night,
A sacred, strong, steadfast band be they found
To keep this soul-shrine from mischief-spite.

Safeguard thou, O God, this household to-night,
Themselves, their means of life, their repute,
Free them from danger, from death, mischief-spite,
From jealousy's and from hatred's fruit.

O grant thou to us, O God of our peace,
Whate'er be our loss a thankful heart,
To obey thy laws here below nor cease,
To enjoy thee when yon we depart.

166. Resting Supplication *Lochaber*

O God, preserve the house, the fire, the kine,
All those who here to-night in sleep recline.
Preserve myself, my love-fold children's band,
From attack keep us and from harm withstand;
Keep us this night from foes and hatred shun,
For the dear sake of Mary Mother's Son,
Here and each where to-night they resting dwell,
This evening's night and every night as well,
    This evening's night and every night as well.

167. Death beyond Price *Lochaber*

Grant thou unto me, O God, as due
Each meal of need for my body's feed;
Grant thou unto me, O God, anew
Each light of need for my mental rede;
Grant thou unto me, O God so true,
Each healing balm that my soul doth need.

Grant thou unto me, O God, to show
A repentance unreserved, sincere;
Grant thou unto me, O God, to know
Repentance whole-hearted, without fear;
Grant thou unto me, O God, to owe
A repentance lasting, to thee dear.

Grant thou unto me, O God, to see
The precious death of the unction here;
Grant unto me, O God, that to me
May the Healer of my soul stand near;
Grant thou unto me, O God, there be
The death of bliss and of peace so dear.

Grant thou unto me, O God, to dare
To confess the death of Christ on tree;
Grant thou unto me, O God, in prayer
To meditate on Christ's agony;
Grant thou unto me, O God, to care
To make warm Christ's love, so warm to me.

O thou God of heaven good and great,
Draw thou my soul to thyself apart,
That repentance I may consecrate
With a just, a strong, a steadfast heart,
With a heart of bruised and broken state,
That stiff, adamantine will not start.

O thou great God of the angels high,
Bring me unto peace's dwelling-place;
O thou great God of the angels nigh,
Save me from the ill of fairy-race;
O great God of angels, hear my cry,
Bathe me in thy bathing-water's grace.

O great God of grace, that it may be,
Grant thou to me the virtue-Spirit's sway;
O Great God of grace, grant thou to me
The immortal Spirit, lasting aye;
O great God of grace, grant lovingly
The Lamb's loving Spirit for my way.

XV. THE HOME

Bless, O Lord, each wall of four,
Bless, O Lord, within the door,
Bless, O Lord, the hearth and floor,
    Bless the homestead ours.

Bless, O Lord, the resting bed,
Bless, O Lord, the meat and bread,
Bless, O Lord, those nourishéd,
    Bless the daylight hours.

Bless the home and keep from strife,
Bless the children, bless the wife,
Bless the loom and means of life,
    Bless, O Lord, with powers.

Calm the day or stormiest
Going in and out be blest,
Bless the stranger and the guest
    That a welcome dowers.

Bless, O Lord, the whole household,
Bless, O Lord, the cattlefold,
Bless the crops, the increase told,
    Bless the milk that showers;

Bless the pasture, bless the grain,
Bless the eye with holy sain,
Bless us also once again
    Through the darkness hours.

Bless the sowing, bless the seed,
Bless the harvest for our need,
All our days o bless and lead
    To the lasting bowers.

168. House Blessing

God bless the house from ground to stay,
From beam to wall and all the way,
From head to post, from ridge to clay,
From balk to roof-tree let it lay,
From found to top and every day
God bless both fore and aft, I pray,
Nor from the house God's blessing stray,
From top to toe the blessing go.

169. The Heath-Fire

As would Mary so within the hearth
I raise the fire. Bride and Mary's path
Encompass round the fire, round the floor,
Round the household all within the door.

Who are they upon the bare floor all?
Great Saint John, Saint Peter, and Saint Paul.
Who are they who stand at my bedside?
Her Fosterson and the beauteous Bride.
Who are those who watch upon my rest?
Fair-love Mary and her Lamb so blest.
Who is that who is anear to me?
Of the fire-sun King himself is he.
Who is that who is behind my head?
Beginningless, timeless he doth tread,
The Son of Life, my all-worshippéd.

170. Family Blessing

Bless, O our God, the fire here laid,
As thou didst bless the Virgin Maid;
O God, the hearth and peats be blest,
As thou didst bless thy day of rest.

Bless, O our God, the household folk.
According as Lord Jesus spoke;
Bless, O our God, the family,
As offered it should be to thee.

Bless, O our God, the house entire,
Bless, O our God, the warmth and fire,
Bless, O our God, the hearth alway;
Be thou thyself our strength and stay.

Bless us, O God Life-Being, well,
Blessing, O Christ of loving, tell,
Blessing, O Holy Spirit, spell
With each and every one to dwell,
    With each and every one to dwell.

171. *The Homestead*

O God, bless my homestead,
    Bless thou all in there.
O God, bless my kindred,
    Bless thou my life-share.

O God, bless my speaking,
    Bless thou what I say.
O God, bless my seeking,
    Bless thou all my way.

O God, sin decreasing,
    Increase thou belief.
O God, woe surceasing,
    Ward off from me grief.

God, from guilt be my shield,
    With joy be I filled.

O God, of my body
    Let naught harm my soul
When to great MacMary
    I enter in whole
In fellowship union
    Of his communion.

May the Great Being's blessing light
Upon the dwelling of this site;
May Jesus blessing send aright
Upon the dwelling of this site;
The Spirit's blessing in his might
Upon the dwelling of this site;
The Holy Three with blessing be
Upon the dwelling of this site;

May Bridget send her blessing bright
Upon the dwelling of this site;
May Michael blessing wing in flight
Upon the dwelling of this site;
Be Mary's blessing, gentle-white,
Upon the dwelling of this site;
Columba dear with blessing near
Upon the dwelling of this site :

On roof and frame, on stone and beam,
On wattle and the clay and seam;
On window, timber, summit, found,
On head and foot from thatch to ground;
On man and wife, on children's joy;
On young and old, on girl and boy :

Plenty of beds, of drink, of food,
And plentiful the ale and good;
Full riches, people, merriment,
A lifetime full here ever spent :

Warrior, poet, beam and clay;
And gear and thong and tie and stay;
Bairn, father, wife and children own;
Maiden and stripling, young and grown.

The King of life to be its aid,
In charge the King of glory stayed;
Christ the belov'd, MacMary Maid,
The Spirit-fountain gentle played;
King-angel soldier Michael, ward,
Watching o'er with power of sword;
White cotton-grassed, fair-gentle Bride,
The rich-gold-tresséd maid, beside;

Gentle-white Mary fireside by,
Columba kindly blessing nigh,
Each promise be fulfilled aright
Upon the household of this site,
  Upon the household of this site!

173. *The Peace of God and Men*

God's peace to me, peace of mankind,
And Saint Columba's peace, the kind,
Mild Mary's peace, a loving thing,
And peace of Christ the tender King,
  The peace of Christ the tender King,

Be on each window, on each door,
Each cranny-light upon the floor,
On house four corners may it fall,
And on my bed's four corners all,
  Upon my bed's four corners all;

Upon each thing mine eye doth see,
Upon each food that enters me,
Upon my body of the earth,
And on my soul of heavenly birth,
  Upon my body of the earth,
  Upon my soul of heavenly birth.

174. *The Well*

Mary Mother to surround
Holding hand and foot to ground
As forth I go to the well,
Safe to bring me home to dwell,
  Safe to bring me home to dwell.

Warrior Michael be mine aid,
Quiet Bride's preserving made,
Be sweet Brianag my light,
And go with me, Mary white,
  O go with me, Mary white.

I will raise the hearth-peats for the night,
As would Mary raise them in her sight,
Bride's and Mary's compassing aright,
The hearth-fire over, over the floor,
Over the household within the door.

Who outside on the grass is the one?
My trusty Michael white as the sun.
Who are they in the midst of the hall?
Saint John and Saint Peter and Saint Paul.
By my bed-post front who are they there?
The sun-white Mary with Son so fair.

The mouth of God ordained it to be,
The angel of God vowed it to me,
An angel white o'er the hearth below
Till white day come to the embers' glow,
  A white-flame angel o'er hearth below
  Till white day come to the embers' glow.

176. *Rest Benediction*   *Benbecula*

Bless to me, O God, the moon above my head.
Bless to me, O God, the earth on which I tread,
Bless to me, O God, my wife and children all,
Bless, O God, myself to whom their care doth fall;
  Bless to me my wife and children all,
Bless, O God, myself to whom their care doth fall.

Bless, O God, the thing on which mine eye doth rest,
Bless, O God, the thing to which my hope doth quest,
Bless, O God, my reason and what I desire,
Bless, thou God of life, o bless myself entire;
  Bless my reason and what I desire,
Bless, thou God of life, o bless myself entire.

Bless to me the partner of my love and bed,
Bless to me the handling of my hands outspread,
Bless to me, O God, my compass compassing,
Bless, o bless to me sleep-angel mine a-wing;
  Bless to me my compass compassing,
Bless, o bless to me sleep-angel mine a-wing.

XVI. LOVE

She stood in her snood and arasaid
    Beneath the trees of the wood,
The buckled plaid round her shoulder laid,
    She looked for him as she stood.

He came to her running o'er the heath,
    A present was in his hand,
And upon his dirk drawn from the sheath
    They plighted their troth to stand.

The mavis was singing in the tree,
    The lark was high in the air,
Happy was he and happy was she
    As they stood together there.

He held her close in his arms' embrace,
    Their eyes and their lips did meet,
He looked down into her lovely face,
    And her heart did faster beat.

The clouds flew over the mountain crest,
    The spray was flecking the sea,
She drew him close to her throbbing breast,
    Her prisoner for aye to be.

They went to kirk an it came the day,
    And the book the priest did take;
He in his kilt was so bright and gay
    As his promise he did make.

She stood at his side so white and fair,
    Her white fingers fair to give,
The priest handfasted them then and there,
    And he blessed them long to live.

O God give the joy and God the love
    To those who are lovers true,
Shed down benediction from above
    As in one are joined the two.

177. A Love Charm *Barra*

This charm for thee when deep in love
  Is water drawn through a straw,
The warmth of one to keep in love,
  With love unto thee to draw.

Betimes on Sunday do thou stir,
  To the flat rock of the beach
Take with thee pointed butter-bur
  And the priestcap foxglove reach.

A little of the embers' heat
  In thy kirtle's lifted fold,
The seaweed specially plucked and sweet
  In a wooden shovel hold.

Three old man's bones to serve thy turn,
  From the earth-bed newly torn,
Nine kingly wands of royal fern,
  By the axe-head newly shorn.

A fire of faggots do thou start,
  And burn into ashes fine;
Sprinkle them on thy lover's heart
  'Gainst the north-wind's venom whine.

For good luck go the fertile round,
  The circuit of turnings five,
And I will vow and warrant sound
  Thy lover shall cleave alive.

178. The Suitors *Skye*

The two gave love to the damsel bright,
But on Goll was her lovely blue eye,
He came to her in her dreams by night,
And deep in the woods he made her sigh.

"O thou Duaran, why didst thou stand!
But O Goll, my Goll, why didst thou fall!
Why, Duaran, ever in the land
Was heard a praise of thy race at all!"

The lovely damsel was found in woe,
And from her lover she would not go,
But lips unto lips and breast to breast
With white arm twining she did invest
As ivy round ageing tree caressed.

179. *The Mount of Mist*

O in the mount of mist,
We two together kist,
Callain cile,
Na vo hi o.

Would were my love and I,
On the mist-mountain high,
O my brown maid ho hu,
Hi ill u ho ill au.

180. *The Dart of Love*

The dart of love as piercing flies
As the seven-grooved spear to fling;
Brown maiden of the liquid eyes,
Warm as my plaid the love I bring.

The damsel there who sang so sweet,
She in a chair of gold demure,
A silken carpet 'neath her feet,
Myself I blessed her face so pure.

Sweet are the birds beside the sea,
Sweet are the swans upon the mere,
Sweeter my lover's voice to me
When a song she pours in mine ear.

O'er the meadows on a calm day
Sweeter than mavis unto me
My lover's voice, a ho, a hey,
Beautiful maid my love is she.

Sweeter to me her kissing lip
Than the honey and spruce-tree beer,
Though we twain the mead were to sip
From two glasses together here.

181. *The Red-Kilted Hunter*

Late it was that I saw yesterday
    A red-clothed man down in the glen;
My heart did welcome him on his way,
    I thought 'twas thyself it was then.

I thought it was thyself it was then,
    Venison-chaser of dun deer's speed,
Traveller o'er heather and moor and ben,
    Hunting a thousand stags of breed.

When hunting a thousand stags of breed,
    Close to thee be the mild Saint Bride,
Mild Mary by thy body indeed,
    Mild-white Michael thy head beside.

182. *Michaelmas Promises*

"My lover a little knife did give
To cut me the withe-sapling white,
To cut the soft and the hard aright,
Long may the hand of the giver live.

"A snood my lover he promised me,
Promised, and a brooch and comb for hair,
And I by the wood promised that there
At rising of sun our meeting should be.

"A mirror my lover he promised me
That I might see mine own beauty there,
Promised, and a coif and ring so fair,
And a string-tuned harp for melody.

"He promised those and a fold of cows,
An ambler firm of the steeds to ride,
A birlinn, pinnacled white beside,
That through ocean dangers safely ploughs.

153

"A thousand blessings and virtues be
To my love who left late yesterday,
He gave me the promise lasting aye,
His own Good Shepherd, God's Son be he".

183. *The Trout of the Well*

Thou speckled little trout so fair,
The lover of my love, o where?
Is he beyond the ocean's storm,
With heroes holding combat warm?

Thou speckled little trout so fair,
The lover of my mind, o where?
Out on the gloom-hills doth he stride,
Cairn-brownie maiden at his side?

Thou speckled little trout so fair,
The lover of my heart, o where?
The Isle of Youth, is that his bound,
The champions of old around?

Thou speckled little trout so fair,
The lover of my breast, o where?
In Ireland or in Alba steep?
Behind the sun is he asleep?

Thou speckled little trout so fair,
Is with my love MacMary there?
And may I let my sorrow go
In the unfailing River's flow?

Thou speckled little trout so fair,
My lover, o my lover where?

XVII. GRACES

Grace of form and grace of strength
    Be unto arm and hand,
Grace of speech throughout life's length,
    And grace throughout the land;

Grace to shepherd and to till,
    Grace in the ocean stream,
Grace at home and on the hill,
    Grace in the hours of dream;

Grace of finger, grace of thread,
    Grace by the glowing fire,
Grace of foot and grace of head,
    Grace of the mind's attire;

Grace of children, grace of means,
    Grace of the comely face,
Grace of this life's closing scenes,
    To thee the Lord's own grace.

184. *The Grace of God*

> May the great God give his grace
>   And may it lie on thee,
> And MacMary Virgin grace
>   And mayest thou it see,
> And the perfect Spirit grace
>   And may it with thee be,
>   Gently and gen'rously.

185. *Bridal Song*   *South Uist, Tiree and elsewhere*

> For bathing fingers showering wine,
> Flame lustral-lingers to refine,
> Nature's elements sevenfold—
> Of fire, of air, of earth, of snow,
> Of water, ice and winds that blow—
> The raspberry juice, and honey-sweet
> The milk where warmth and sweetness meet;
> And in thy fair fond face so fine
> I place the pure choice graces nine—
> Fortune and goodness in thy face,
> The grace of form, the grace of voice,
> Of wisdom, charity, the grace,
> The grace of maidenliness choice,
> The loveliness that fills the soul,
> The speaking fair, the graces whole.
>
> O dark and strange is yonder town,
> And dark and strange the people there,
> Thou art the young swan feathered brown,
> Thou goest in amongst them fair.
> Their hearts are under thy control,
> Their tongues are underneath thy sole,
> Nor will they utter hostile word,
> Offence and hurt shall not be heard.
>
> In noonday heat thou art a shade,
> And from the cold a shelter made,
> Eyes art thou for the blind to see,
> For pilgrim thou a staff to be,
> At sea thou art an island port,
> On land thou art a battled fort,
> A well thou art in desert ground,
> Thou to the sick his healing found.

Thine is the Fairy Woman's skill,
Thine the virtue of Bride serene,
Thine the faith of Mary the still,
Thine the tact of the Grecian queen,
Thine the beauty of Cuchulainn's wife,
Darthula-tender is thy life,
Thine the courage of Maeve the strong,
Thine the charm of the Mouth of Song.

Thou the joy of all joyous things,
Thou of the sunbeam art the light,
Thou the door of hospitable kings,
Thou the guide-star surpassing bright,
Thou the step of hill-breasting deer,
Thou the step of steed on the plain,
Thou the grace of swan on the mere,
Thou all loveliness I would fain.

The lovely likeness of God's Son
Is o'er thy pure face shed upon,
The likeness loveliest and best
That ever on the earth did rest.

The day's best hour be it for thee,
The week's best day with thee to be,
The year's best week unendingly,
Thine the Son's world's best year to see.

The saints have come, Peter and Paul,
James and John, to thy festival,
Muriel, Mary Lady here,
Uriel all-bestowing, dear,
Ariel, beauty-youth, is near,
Gabriel, Virgin Lady's seer;
Raphael, prince of might, is by,
Michael, chief of the hosts that fly;
And Jesus Christ the mild descends,
Truth's guiding Spirit here transcends,
While at the helm the King of kings
Love and affection to thee brings,
    Love and affection to thee brings.

186. *Invocation of the Graces*

The grace Saint Bride was placing,
    The maiden of all grace,
On the daughter of the king,
Gillian of lovely face.

Form of Christ before thee go,
    The form of God behind,
Stream of Spirit through thee flow,
Succour thine and aiding kind.

The bloom of God on thy face,
    The bloom of Christ glows there,
The Spirit's bloom is thy grace,
To bathe thee and make thee fair.

Over thee grace upwards spread,
    Grace downwards overpoured,
Grace of graces ungainsaid,
Grace of Father and of Lord.

Grace of form, of fortune fine,
    The grace of voice's sound,
Comrade-grace Christ Jesu's thine,
The Lord's image-grace around.

Men's and women's grace to thee,
    Wise grace of council's sense,
Thine the grace of lover be,
Grace of sons and daughters thence.

Grace of knolls and grace of dells,
    Grace of a shelter place,
Grace of hills and grace of fells,
Of horses and heroes grace.

Grace of bread and grace of wine,
    The grace of music be,
Be the grace of guiding thine,
And the pilgrim's grace to thee.

Grace to travel, grace to roam,
    Town-grace, the city's grace,
Grace of the returning home,
Grace of land and water's face.

Grace of beauty's lovely smile,
    Effulgent grace of light,
Grace of good, of heavenly Isle,
Grace of day and grace of night.

Grace of form, cheek's healthy glow,
    Of sitting, walking's go,
Grace of cattlefold and herd,
Grace of churning and of curd,
Butter-grace and milky flow.

Mary's grace of mallard's flight,
    The fountain-swan's grace white,
Grace of sheep and woolly coats,
Grace of kids and grace of goats,
Lasting grace by day and night.

Of each night thou art the star,
    Gleam of each morn thou art,
Thou the news each guest brings far,
Enquiry of distant part.

Though thou traverse a rough ground,
    Thy foot shall not be red :
Jesus is thy guarding round,
Jesus by thy hand and head.

The King's crown is on thy head,
    Son's diadem on brow,
Spirit's might thy heart inbred :
Safely to and fro go thou.

Upward shall thy journey be,
    And down thou shalt come back,
Be thy journey o'er the sea,
Be hither again thy track.

Peril shall not thee befall
    On knoll or bank or brae,
Hollow, meadowland at all,
In mount or glen by the way.

Michael's shield o'er thee in might
    Cover thee, guard thee whole,
The king of the angels bright,
From thy summit to thy sole.

Nor shall man or womankind,
	Son, daughter prying make,
Nor wish, hate, eye, jealous mind,
Love, nor envy, durance take

That shall sunder thee in two,
	That shall on thee lay weight,
That shall lay thee low, subdue,
Wound or incapacitate.

No host, false one, fairy, world
	Sling or catapult make,
Arrow, spear or javelin hurled,
Hook or sword they shall not take,

That shall have effect on thee,
	Shall wound thee and confound,
That shall thine affliction be,
That shall overpower thee round.

No smith, tinker, mason, wright
	Make tool, machine, gear, arm,
Instrument, tackle for fight,
Or frame, or invention's harm,

Of stone, copper, iron, brass,
	Wood, silver, bronze, or gold
That shall check thee, rend alas!
That shall bridle and enfold,

Thither, hither, earth, or land,
	Down, up, or to or fro,
Over, under, sea, or strand,
In sky aloft, deep below.

Love-grace of the skies be thine,
	The star love-grace above,
Love-grace of the moon to shine,
Sun-grace thine of flaming love,
Grace of love and grace of crown
Sent to thee from heaven down.

Thou the kernel of my heart,
	Face of my sun downshed,
Thou my music's harp and part,
Thou crown of my sense and head;

Love of God of life thou art,
    Christ's tender love above,
Spirit Holy's love in heart,
Thou each living creature's love,
    Thou each living creature's love.

187. God's Grace Distilling

The grace of God on you distil,
The grace of Christ bedewing fill,
The grace of Spirit flowing still
Each day and night upon you pour
Of this life's share for you in store;
    O day and night upon you pour
    Of this life's share for you in store.

188. The Young Matron   Skye and South Uist

Thy coif is on, a thousand times hail!
Be thou whole through all thy course nor fail,
And may strength and days be thine in peace,
Thy paradise with thy means increase.

Thy double race starting, youthful wife,
Starting thy course, seek the God of life,
Fear not but he will right rule with care
Thine every secret needing and prayer.

Thou now hast this wedding crown onlaid,
Full oft it has given grace to maid,
Be filled with virtue, but gracious be,
Pureness in word and in hand to thee.

Be thou hospitable, yet be wise,
Courageous be, but calm otherwise,
Open be thou, but reserve display,
Be thou exact, but generous stay.

In thy giving no miserly proof,
Do not flatter, yet hold not aloof,
Ill speak not of man, though ill be he,
If spoken of, unresentful be.

For thy good name be thou full of care,
Be dignified, yet kind everywhere,
On thine helm the hand of God besought,
In act, in beginning, and in thought.

Beneath thy cross, o do not complain,
When thy cup is full good ware maintain,
Ne'er countenance evil or ill tales,
To thy coif a hundred thousand hails!

189. *The Wedding Dance*

> Each damsel is so brightly
> A-bowing of her head,
> And she would dance as lightly,
> As if parched corn to tread.

> "'Twas Donald, o 'twas Donald,
> 'Twas he the wedding made!
> 'Twas Donald, o my Donald,
> The famous wedding played!"

190. *A Maiden's Face*

> The beauty of God is in thy face,
> The Son of God is protecting thee
> From the wicked ones of world-disgrace,
> The King of the stars thy vanguard he.

> Saint Mary's beauty of love so deep,
> A modest, mild tongue of manners there,
> Fair hairs within thy two eyebrows peep,
> The fairness of Fionn MacCool's fair hair.

> Since 'tis Mary and Jesus her Son
> Who set this pleasantness in thy face,
> May mild honey's taste thy lips be on
> And on each word thou speakest in grace,

To simple, to noble, high and low,
To men, tender women, from this day
Till thine ending day relying so
On the Belov'd and the Pow'rs of aye,
On the life-God and his Son-shield-stay.

191. *Grace of Love*

Thine be the grace of love when in flower,
Thine be the grace of humble floor,
Thine be the grace of a castled tower,
Thine be the grace of palace door,
Thine be the pride of homeland place
And its grace.

The God of life to encompass thee,
Loving Christ encompass lovingly,
The Holy Ghost encompasser be
Cherishing, aid, enfolding to send
To defend.

The Three be about thy head to stand,
And the Three be about thy breast,
The Three about thy body at hand
For each day, for each night of rest,
The Trinity compassing strong
Thy life long.

192. *The Blessing of God's Grace*

God's grace with you, Christ's grace with you,
The grace of Spirit with you too,
And with your children may they be,
For moment, time, eternity.

XVIII. WISHES

As range the hills unendingly,
So be God's changelessness to thee;
As swell the seas contendingly,
So be God multiplied to thee;

As bursts the sunlight readily,
So be God's blessedness to thee;
As burns the moonlight steadily,
So be God's friendliness to thee;

As wings the mallard soundingly,
So be God's swiftsureness to thee;
As leaps the salmon poundingly,
So be God's urgency to thee;

As paws the horse from stable free,
So be God's liberty to thee;
As graze the herds on moorland lea,
So be God's sustenance to thee;

As grows the pine straight-risingly,
So be God's righteousness to thee;
As blooms the rose surprisingly,
So be God's fragrancy to thee;

As Father made so cunningly,
So be God's skilfulness to thee;
As Son did hang upon the tree,
So be God's sacrifice to thee;

As Spirit worked dumbfoundingly,
So be God's pow'rfulness to thee;
As God doth love aboundingly,
So be God's lovingness to thee.

193. My own Blessing

My own blessing with you go,
God his blessing to you show,
Spirit's blessing to you flow,
On your children to bestow,
On you, on your children so.

194. Each Day be Glad   South Uist

Each day be glad to thee,
No day be sad to thee,
Life rich and satisfying.
Plenty be on thy bound,
A son be at thy sound,
A daughter at thy nighing.

Serpent's strong aid be thine,
The fire's strong aid refine,
The strong aid of the graces.
Joy's love-death be to thee,
Love-death of Mary free,
Love-Saviour's arm-embraces.

195. The Three Rich and Generous

The eye of God with thee to dwell,
The foot of Christ to guide thee well,
The Spirit's pouring shower to swell
Thy rich and gen'rous fountain-well.

196. Good Wish

Eye that is good be good to thee,
Good of liking unto thee be,
    The good of my heart's desire.

Sons that are good to thee be born,
Daughters good to thee fair as dawn,
    The good of my sense's fire.

167

Thine the good of the good wide sea,
Thine the good of land fruitfully,
　　Good of Prince of heav'nly quire.

197. *God's Blessing be Thine*

God's blessing be thine,
And well may it spring,
The blessing divine
In thine every thing.

198. *A Joyous Life*

A joyous life I pray for thee,
Honour, estate and good repute,
No sigh from thy breast heaving be,
　　From thine eye no tear of suit.

No hindrance on thy path to tread,
No shadow on thy face's shine,
Till in that mansion be thy bed,
　　In the arms of Christ benign.

199. *The Creator's Love*

God the Father uncreate
　　Above,
Your Creator Potentate
　　In love,
Be with you in lovingness
　　And bless.

200. *The Creator's Gifts*

Wisdom of serpent cunningly,
Wisdom of raven black to thee,
Wisdom of eagle valiantly.

Voice of the swan thy clarity,
Voice of sweetness and honey-bee,
Voice of the Star-Son shiningly.

Thine be the plenty of the sea,
Thine be the land plentifully,
The plenty of Father heav'nly.

201. God's Goodness for Life

O be God his goodness to you sending,
And good, seven times good, be your spending
Of your lifetime here unto its ending.

202. Each Day Gladness

Each day be for thee with a gladness-fill,
And no day ill,
A life of joy, of satisfaction still.

Each meeting unto thee be a success,
And thine no less
The Lady Virgin Mary's grace to bless,
And thine the King of graces' fillingness.

203. Day and Night Blessing

May God's blessing be yours,
And good be it sent;
May Christ's blessing be yours,
And good be it meant;
Spirit's blessing be yours,
For life's good intent,
Day arising indoors,
Night lying down spent.

XIX. CHIEFS

Chief of the mountain and Chief of the plain,
Chief of the river and Chief of the main,
Chief of the sunlight, the rainbow, the rain,
      O my Chief, hear my prayer.

Chief of the fishes and Chief of the herds,
Chief of the creatures and Chief of the birds,
Chief of the singing, the echoes, the words,
      O my Chief, grant thy care.

Chief of the island and Chief of the land,
Chief of the highland and Chief of the strand,
Chief of the skyland and Chief of the sand,
      O my Chief everywhere,

Chief of the planet and Chief of the height,
Chief of the moon, mottled Star-Chief of might,
Chief of the morning and glittering light,
      O my Chief jewelled fair,

Chief of the night time and Chief of the day,
Chief of the heroes and Chief of the fray,
Chief of my life and when death calls away,
      O my Chief uncompare,

Chief of the mother and Chief of the child,
High Chief of the chiefs and the clansmen wild,
Chief of the wind-whisper, gentleness mild,
      O my Chief, hear my prayer.

204. Chief of Chiefs Kintail and Harris

Chief of chiefs beyond my ken,
O Chief of chiefs, Amen.

God be with me lying down,
And God be with me rising,
In the sunlight flying down
God with me, supervising,
No joy nor any light without him,
Nor any light without him.

Christ be with me sleeping hours,
And Christ be with me waking,
Through all watches aiding powers,
Christ with me undertaking,
No day nor any night without him,
Nor any night without him.

God be with me to protect,
The Spirit there to strengthen,
Lord be with me to direct
As span of life doth lengthen,
No time, no year, no hope, no fear,
No age, no space, no work, no place,
No depth nor any height without him,
Nor any height without him.

Ever, evermore, Amen,
O Chief of chiefs, Amen.

205. Prayer of Power

Power of the eye be thine to see,
Power of element thine to be,
Power of my heart's desire-land.

Power of the surf be thine to skim,
Power of the swell be thine to swim,
Power of my reason's fire-land.

Power of King Cuchulainn thine to sway,
Power of King of the world to prey,
Power of Sea-King of Ireland.

173

206. *Macdonald's Bride* *Skye*

"Thou daughter of the king of halls bright-lit,
On the night that thy wedding is to be,
If in Duntulm a living man I sit
With my gifts I will go bounding to thee.

"Badgers a hundred, dwellers of the banks,
And a hundred brown otters waterside,
For thee stags a hundred, wild spindle-shanks
The pastures green of the high hills astride.

"For thee a hundred steeds stately and swift,
And a hundred reindeer of summer-pride,
Red hinds hummelled a hundred for thy gift,
In the Wolfmonth unstalled of wintertide".

207. *Sleep has Forsaken Me* *Eigg*

Since Shrovetide sleep has forsaken me,
    Oft turning on my side
My hope is thy speeding ship to see
    On black-blue ocean tide.

Surpassing swift thy grey-timbered boat
    From Lochlann's steep hillsides,
Smooth each plank of her like the swan's coat
    That the loch water rides.

Three warriors great of Alba are,
    My sore grief one away,
No home, no people, afield afar,
    The Isle of Man his sway.

Would, O King, that thy load-sorrow were
    Spread in thy land for thee,
That upon each man there were his share,
    But three full shares on me!

The youths' love thou at the morning's birth
    In van of battle fray,
But women's love in the evening's mirth
    What time the harp doth play.

This I would ask, to thy hand a blade
    In a strait pass arise,
A meeting with them who hate thee made,
    And blood blinding their eyes.

There would come raven, carrion-crow
    At the first mouth of dawn,
And would drink from the pools' filling flow
    A blood-red brimming drawn.

208. *The Lady-Lord*   *Benbecula*

The sweet-singing lady-lord, who is she,
By the climb-down and the wave-lapping sea?

She is no guillemot, no duck is she,
She is no swan, nor stands she solit'ry.

The sweet-singing lady-lord, who is she,
By the climb-down and the wave-lapping sea?

She is no lark, no blackbird whistlingly,
No sweet laverock upon the bough is she.

The sweet-singing lady-lord, who is she,
By the climb-down and the wave-lapping sea?

No petrel of storm, fulmar of the sea,
No hill-ptarmigan murmuring is she.

The sweet-singing lady-lord, who is she,
By the climb-down and the wave-lapping sea?

No salmon-grilse of the water-leap she,
No wave-seal, no May maiden of the sea.

The sweet-singing lady-lord, who is she,
By the climb-down and the wave-lapping sea?

No dame of the distaff fireside is she,
No damsel of lyre, shepherdess of lea.

The sweet-singing lady-lord, who is she,
By the climb-down and the wave-lapping sea?

The sweet-singing lady-lord, God-like she,
God-like in gentle loveliness to see.

Daughter to king and her grandsire a king,
His sire, his sire's sire, and his sire a king,
Wife of a king and mother to a king,
Fostering, lullabying kingly thing,
He under her plaid, her little wee lad.

For Lochlann bound from Erin travelled she,
Wherever she goes the Three-in-One be,
Blessed Trinity to accompany,
Wherever she goes over land and sea.

209. *Queen of Grace* *Benbecula*

Fair is her foot and smooth is her hand,
And graceful her form upon the strand,
Winsome her voice and gentle her speech,
Stately her mien on the ocean beach,
Warm doth she look and mild is her face,
While swelleth her lovely breast of grace
Like black-headed seagull up and down
On the gently heaving water's crown.

Holy the lady of gold-mist locks,
With tend'rest babe at foot of the rocks,
No food for either 'neath arching sky,
No shelter to shield from foeman nigh.

The shield of God's Son doth cover her,
God's Son's inspiration over her,
The word of God's Son is feeding her,
His star is a guide-light leading her.

Night's darkness is as brightness of day,
The day to her gaze is joy alway,
Mary of grace doth everywhere dwell,
The sev'n beatitudes aid her well,
    The sev'n beatitudes aid her well.

Baby fair thou, fair thou, fair thou !
Baby fair thou, turn to me now !

My darling and my dear,
        Wouldst thou climb the hill,
A lad behind thee near
        To hold the hound still?

Baby fair thou, fair thou, fair thou !
Baby fair thou, turn to me now !

My loved one and my dear,
        Wouldst thou climb the height?
A sure hand on the sheer
        Yonder Blaaven bright.

Baby fair thou, fair thou, fair thou !
Baby fair thou, turn to me now !

My love-pride and my joy,
        Spindrift of the sea,
Kilt pleated on my boy,
        Red on fawn to see.

Baby fair thou, fair thou, fair thou !
Baby fair thou, turn to me now !

My love-sense and my joy
        Is Alpin's dark son;
With shield and bow's employ,
        The peak hunting done.

Baby fair thou, fair thou, fair thou !
Baby fair thou, turn to me now !

MacLeod ere Alba-bound
        Those heroes would cry
Our great chief was renowned
        In far Germany.

Baby fair thou, fair thou, fair thou !
Baby fair thou, turn to me now !

MacLeod ere Lochlann-forth
　　Those stalwarts could fight;
None would decry their worth
　　Though so few to-night.

Baby fair thou, fair thou, fair thou!
Baby fair thou, turn to me now!

211. *The Milk for the Nobles*

　　　　Give the milk, brown cow!
　　　　Give the milk, brown cow!
　　　　Give the milk, brown cow!
Heavy and rich let it down!

　　　　Give the milk, brown cow!
　　　　Give the milk, brown cow!
　　　　Give the milk, brown cow!
Nobles are coming to town!

　　　　Give the milk, brown cow!
　　　　Give the milk, brown cow!
　　　　Give the milk, brown cow!
Clanranald! MacNeill! MacLeod!

　　　　Give the milk, brown cow!
　　　　Give the milk, brown cow!
　　　　Give the milk, brown cow!
And thirsty the hero-crowd!

212. *Give thy Milk*　　　　　　　　　*Barra*

Give thy milk, brown cow, a rich and heavy flow,
For why should I hide it that thou shouldst not know?
The calf of yon cow in the next stall in view,
And the calf of my love in the pastures new,
　　　O! ho! in the pastures new.

Give thy milk, brown cow, o give thy milk, brown cow,
Give thy milk, brown cow, rich heavy-flowing now.

White-footed calves shall be to my lovely one,
And a tether fine kindly round her leg done;
No tether of hair, of tow, of heather strand,
But a tether dear brought from the Saxon land,
        O! ho! from the Saxon land.

And my maiden queen of beauty she shall get
A tether smooth softly around her leg set;
No tether of lint, of tow, of corded strand,
But a silk tether up from the Saxon land,
        O! ho! from the Saxon land.

There'll be grass for my love and a shelter-stand,
Pasture of green beach, of heath, of machair land,
Meadow-grass, club-rush, and stubble for her fill,
And there'll be wine from the tumbling mountain-rill,
        O! ho! from the mountain-rill.

213. *My Brown Heifer*   *Barra*

Ho my little heifer, ho brown heifer mine!
Ho my little heifer, ho brown heifer mine!
Dear little heifer of my heart, beloved mine,
The bright precious one thou art of the white kine.

Ho my little heifer, ho brown heifer mine!
Ho my little heifer, ho brown heifer mine!
Dear little heifer of my heart, beloved mine,
No calf from me to seek nor calf-skin of thine.

Ho my little heifer, ho brown heifer mine!
Ho my little heifer, ho brown heifer mine!
Little brindled heifer, dear and beloved mine,
Be a safe crossing of the mountain-crests thine.

Ho my little heifer, ho brown heifer mine!
Ho my little heifer, ho brown heifer mine!
O sweet little heifer, dear and beloved mine,
With me be a crossing of the wave-crests thine.

214. *Sleep-Dedication Prayer*

O my God and O my Chief,
In morning light to thee I pray,
O my God and O my Chief,
Again this night to thee I pray.
I give unto thee belief,
I give my mind, my yea and nay,
I give unto thee my lief,
Body, and soul that lives for aye.

Mayest thou be unto me
Chieftain and master for my sway,
Mayest thou be unto me
Shepherd and guardian lest I stray,
Mayest thou be unto me
Herdsman and guide that I obey,
O Chief of chiefs, with me be,
God of the skies, Father for aye.

XX. THE CHRIST

To men and beasts in sore distress
The ancient vision comes to bless,
Jesus the Christ, himself no less,
    The little leading Child;

His is the calm of land and sea,
His the birth with the maidens three,
With Faith, with Hope, with Charity,
    His is the Mother mild.

As the mild-white Mother and he
Into Egypt together flee,
So with a gentle hand they free
    The life by scourge defiled.

The Christ each healing doth provide,
The Christ who triumphing doth ride
Unto the place where crucified,
    Where scorned, and where reviled.

215. *Saint Mary of Motherhood*

Over the nine seas Saint Mary crossed
To gather the figwort as it tossed;
Loveliness round her shone as the light,
Her steps the music of songs in flight.

Her ringlets in beauty's folds fell down,
A curly and winding golden-brown;
She had the beauty surpassing fair
Of the famous Grecian woman there.

The fair-white Mary went on her knee,
The fair-white Mary of graces she;
When the three maidens lovely and slight
With the Christ were born the selfsame night.

216. *The White Spell of Mary*   *Benbecula*

The white spell that tender Mary sent,
Over stream and sea and land it went,
Against lies, 'gainst envy's glancing charms,
Against hostility's son in arms,
Against wolfine teeth and wolfine strength,
Against three herons of crooked length,
Against three bones that are crooked bound,
Against three wounds that are crooked found,
And against the long lint of the ground.

Whosoe'er made unto thee the eye,
O upon himself it is to lie,
May it lie upon his dwelling tower,
May it lie upon his cattle dower,
May it lie upon his fattening yield,
May it lie upon his fruitful field,
May it lie upon his means of life.
Upon his children, upon his wife,
Upon his descendants may it lie,
Whosoe'er made unto thee the eye.

The evil eye 'tis I will avert,
The evil eye 'tis I will convert,
The evil eye I will march from sight,
With arteries three that blood invite,
And the death-tongue from the bounds in flight.

Three lovely small maidens of the dawn,
Faith, Hope, Charity coming the morn
Of the same night on which Christ was born,
If alive be these three here to-night,
Life near unto thee, poor beast, alight.

217. *The Two Beetles*

Nuns' Heiskir of North Uist

When the Christ was underneath the wood,
And his enemies pursuing stood,
The crooked deceiver said so sly
To the black beetle and butterfly—

"Was it the day before or to-day
You saw God's Son of my love this way?"
Said the black beetle, "We saw! we saw!
Our Redeemer pass the day before".

"A lie! a lie! it's a lie you say!"
Said the small horse beetle of the clay,
"It was a great year from yesterday,
That the Son of God went by this way".

218. *Jesus and the Rose-Breast*

Harris

"Behold, O Son, the breast,
Filled with a swelling sore;
Give thou the woman rest,
The tumour-germ withdraw."

"Behold her, Mary blest,
For thou the Son didst bear;
Unto the breast give rest,
Relieve the woman there."

"O Christ, behold her breast,
Thou art the King of might;
Give thou the woman rest,
Put the tumour to flight."

Spake Christ, "I will behold,
To me 'tis as to thee;
The breast with health I fold,
The tumour cause to flee.

"Whole be the woman from this hour,
And shrunken be the swelling's power."

219. *Blindness*

The salve that Saint Mary placed
   To the salmon's sight
   As he leaped with might
While the river torrent raced.

Against eye of wildness-sight,
   Contemning, or stare,
   Consenting, pride, there,
Against eye's oppressing blight.

Against eye of downcast blight,
   Burning, grieving there,
   Eye-wounding, or snare,
And against eye's flustered sight.

A drop, tender Mary, sure,
   A drop, O Bride still,
   A drop, Columcill,
A drop, O Michael of war.

A drop, King of nature, more,
   A drop, meek Christ, bide,
   A drop, Spirit-guide,
A drop, O Trinity, pour.

Thou who didst fashion the light,
   Pupil in the eye,
   Search the mystery,
Befriend thou, O God, the sight.

Turn the evil in the light,
   Turn the virus by,
   Turn, King of the eye,
Give strength, O God, to the sight.

The light to-day sanctify,
    Sanctify the eye,
    The sight sanctify,
God, befriend the light of eye!

220. *For the Eye* *North Uist*

Peter and Paul and John are they,
In speech most beautiful three alone,
    Who did arise the spell to lay
Beneath the shield of the heavenly throne;

At God the Father's right knee, a band,
And at God the Son's right knee, at hand,
At God the Spirit's right knee they stand;

    'Gainst the women of eyes that peer,
And against the men that fawning glance,
    'Gainst the slender ones, eyes a-blear,
Against fairies seven of phantom dance.

    Four it is who on thee laid ill,
And four it is who thy hurting laid,
    Man and woman, conspiring still,
Man and woman, and youth and maid.

    The Three I set to check them each,
The Three I am sending to subdue,
    Father and Son I both beseech,
And the gracious Holy Spirit too.

    Four and twenty diseases fell
In both mankind and beast they inhere,
    In man and woman both they dwell,
Inherent in youth and maiden here.

    God to search them, God overthrow,
God to scrape them, and God to expel,
    From blood, from flesh, from water's flow,
From all thy smooth bones of fragrant smell;

    From kidney hard, from veins close-set,
Belov'd, from pith, from thy marrow's strength,
    From this day forth and each day yet
Till the ending day of life at length.

As Christ did pluck the fruit one day
From off the bushes that he did find,
    May he pluck now from thee away
Each spell, paralysis, eyesight blind;

    As Christ the sleep did pluck and clear
From the little son of earth and dust,
    May he pluck off from thee, my dear,
Each frown, each envy, each spiteful thrust.

221. *The Yarrow of Counteracting*   *South Uist*

I pluck the lucky yarrow from the land
That Christ was wont to pluck with his one hand.

The High King of the angels came with love,
His spirit-breath around my head above.

Hither to me came Jesus Christ the Lord,
Substance, and milk, and produce to afford,
The cow-calves in the stall, the dairy stored.

Be it upon the eye or large or small,
Over Christ's every thing protection fall.

In name of the Being of life applied,
With fullness of thy grace be I supplied,
The crown of the King of the angels o'er
That the milk from the udder and gland may pour,
Cow-calves to grass and young on byre-shed floor.

On you be the length of a sev'n years' end,
May no loss of calf or of milk descend,
No loss of life-means, no loss of dear friend.

222. *Toothache Charm*

The charm that Saint Columba placed
Around his friend's right knee to ring,
'Gainst pain and pang and stinging raised,
Against disease of tooth and sting.

Said Peter unto James in pain,
"From the toothache I get no rest,
Though I lie down and rise again
And jump on my feet in my quest".

Said Christ as he did cut their knot,
And their problem he did decide,
"The toothache and the rune shall not
Henceforth in the one head abide".

223. *The Red-Stalk of Christ*   *Ensay of Harris*

The Christ with his apostles walked,
He broke the silence and he talked—
   "To this plant what name appointed?
This plant henceforth is named red-stalked,
For God the Son's left foot here walked
   And his right hand-print anointed".

224. *Christ the Healer*   *Arasaig*

Early in the morning went out the Christ the Lord,
He found the legs of horses splintered on the sward;
Marrow to its marrow and pith to pith he knit,
Membrane to its membrane and bone to bone was fit,
Sinew unto sinew and blood to blood so red,
Tallow unto tallow and flesh to flesh he bred,
Fat to fat and skin to skin, hair to hair he drew,
The warm unto the warm, the cool to cool flowed through;
As the King of virtue that healing made anew
This is in his nature if 'tis his will to do.
   Through the One of life's bosom-kindness be it done,
   Bosom-kindness of the Three of the Three-in-One.

XXI. POEMS OF
THE FURTHER ISLES

Where two or three together are
In pasture isle and shieling far
    The Lord Christ there
    Doth hear the prayer;
For in their midst he doth abide,
    Is by their side.

The ocean cliffs of Barra Head,
By Barra's Sound the meadows spread
    With primrose fair,
    Both offer prayer,
Hearts from the Harris isles offshore
    Uplifted soar.

Columba's wort, the ivy there,
Are living tokens of the prayer,
    The club-moss found,
    The "mothan" bound,
The shamrock strewed a carpet seen
    Of gravesward green.

As once upon a princely strand
A new world called to a new land;
    Across the sound
    The soul is bound,
In the strong Saviour's holding laid
    And not storm-stayed.

225. *Madonna and Child*   *Mingulay of Barra*

The Virgin approaching, o behold,
Doth Christ so young on her breast enfold,
The angels making obeisance low,
The King of glory praising it so.

The Virgin hath locks bedewed with gold,
The Jesu whiter than snow-white cold,
The seraphs of song singing them, lo!
The King of glory praising it so.

226. *Christ and the Rose Breast*   *Fuday of Barra*

"My Son and Saviour, lo,
Thy Mother's swollen breast;
Unto the breast give rest,
Subdue the swelling so;
    Unto the breast give rest,
    Subdue the swelling so."

"O Queen and Lady, lo,
The Son was born of thee,
Thine is the breast to free,
Subdue the swelling so;
    Thine is the breast to free,
    Subdue the swelling so."

"The thing, O Jesu, lo,
Thou King of life, o see;
Thine is the breast to free,
The paps subduing so;
    Thine is the breast to free,
    The paps subduing so."

"I see," said Christ, "nor cease,
And I do as is best,
Unto the breast its rest,
And to the paps their peace;
    Unto the breast its rest,
    And to the paps their peace."

227. *Rose Charm* Scarp of Harris

Rose windy, deadly, swelling round,
 Leave that spot and part,
There is the udder in the ground,
 From the breast depart.

Behold, O Christ, the woman low,
 Her breast swollen there,
O Mary, thyself see her so,
 The Son thou didst bear.

Rose windy, deadly, thirsty near,
 Leave the breast and side,
Be off, for breast the healing here,
 The swelling subside.

Rose-redness thieving to infest,
 Quickly flee, red thief,
To swelling that was in the breast,
 To the paps, relief,
 Quickly hence, red thief.

228. *The Tree-Entwining Ivy* *Sandray of Barra*

I will pluck the ivy that entwines the tree,
 As Mary plucked it with her single hand,
As the King of life has ordained it to be,
 To put milk in the udder and the gland,
With the cow-calves speckled white-bellied to see,
 As was said in the prophecy would fall,
For a year and a day on this site to be,
 Through the kind God of life and the pow'rs all.

229. *The Missing Herdsman* *Hellisay of Barra*

The night that the Herdsman was away
No tether-rope went the cow to hold,
Nor ceased the calf its lowing till day,
Bewailing the Herdsman of the fold,
 Bewailing the Herdsman of the fold.

Ho my heifer! ho for my heifer!
Ho my heifer, my heifer awake!
Heart of my heart, kind, dear for ever,
Take to thy calf for the High King's sake.

The night they did miss the Herdsman dear,
In the Temple he was found to be.
The King of the moon to come down here!
The King of the sun, from heaven is he!
   The King of the sun, from heaven is he!

230. *The Priestly Flower*   *Grimsay of North Uist*

The gracious flower I'll pick me from the field,
The herb most precious that the knoll doth yield,
Of all the seven priests the sanctity,
And mine the eloquence within them be.

The gracious flower I'll pick me from the field,
The herb most precious that the knoll doth yield,
Their wisdom and their counsel be they mine,
As long as I possess the flow'ring twine.

231. *For Protection*
South Uist and Pabbay of Barra

As thou o'er the flock the Shepherd art here
Tend thou us to the cot and fold afield,
Safe-sained 'neath thy royal plaid keep us near;
Thou Buckler of protection, ever shield.

Be thou a claymore triumphant and hard
Surely to shield from the dread place beneath,
From fiends and from strait dank gullies to guard,
And from the abyss of the red-smoke wreath.

O trust thou, my soul, in the High King's hold,
And to meet my soul be Saint Michael bold.

232. *Saint Columba's Yellow Flower*

Vatersay of Barra

Saint Columba's yellow flower,
Without search or seeking found,
Saint Columba's yellow flower,
'Neath my arm for ever bound!

For luck of men to abound,
For luck of means to be round,
For luck of wish to be crowned,
For luck of sheep for the ground,
For luck of goats climbing high,
For luck of birds in the sky,
For luck of fields spreading nigh,
For luck of shell-fish for bait,
For luck of fish after spate,
For luck of produce and flock,
For luck of people and stock,
For war-luck and victory,
On land, on ocean, on sea,
Through the Three who dwell on high,
Through the Three who dwell anigh,
Through the Three eternally,
Saint Columba's yellow flower,
Now I pick thee for thy power,
   Now I pick thee for thy power.

233. *A Curse*

Eriskay of South Uist

A twain it was that issuing came,
From the City of Heaven forced to go,
A man and a woman, in their shame
Through the world to cause mischief and woe.

On the blear-eyed women curses seize,
On the sharp-eyed men let curses lie,
Curses on the four darts of disease,
That in man and beast with poison fly.

234. *The Fairies of the Proud Angel*
Mingulay of Barra

God between me and every fairy one,
Every ill wish and each druidry done,
To-day is Thursday on sea and on land,
I trust in the King they be not at hand.

For not of the seed of Adam are they,
Nor from Abraham father came away,
But of the Proud Angel they are the seed,
Extruded from heaven with all his breed.

235. *Wearing the Club-Moss*   *Taransay of Harris*

The club-moss is upon me as I go,
No harm, mishap arising shall I know;
No yew-bow shot to wound, no sprite to slay,
No water-nymph to tear me, nor a fay.

236. *The Shamrock of Joys*   *Fuday of Barra*

Thou shamrock of the virtues good,
　'Neath the bank a-growing there
Whereon the gracious Mary stood,
　The Mother of God so fair.

The seven joys are these to know,
　With no evil trace at all
On thee, bright shining one aglow
　Where the sunbeams warming fall—

The joy of keeping safe and health,
　The joy of a friendship true,
The joy of kine and cattle wealth,
　The joy of the sheep and ewe,
The joy of sons to be the heirs,
　And of mild-white daughters fair,
The joy of peacefulness from cares,
　The joy of the great God rare!

The four leaves of the upright spray,
　　The root of the hundred shoots,
Shamrock-promise of Mary's Day,
　　All times thy blessings and fruits.

237. *For Grace* 　　　　　　　　　　*Berneray of Barra*

I am bending low my knee
In the eye of those who see,
Father who my life supplied,
Saviour Son who for me died,
Spirit who hath purified,
In desire and love to thee.

Be the blessing heaven-sent
Richly poured on penitent;
City-Prince of firmament,
O forbear thy punishment.

Grant us, Glory-Saviour dear,
God's affection, love and fear,
God's will to do always here
As above in heaven clear
Saints and angels do not cease;
Day and night give us thy peace,
　　Give each day and night thy peace.

XXII. SAINT COLUMBA

Tall Saint Columba, prophet kind,
       The green-white isle doth find,
Both man and beast to understand,
       Soldier of healing hand;
East, south, and north the Word goes forth;
And when beside the sea to teach
His wind-borne voice, upraised to preach,
Across the green-blue sound doth reach.

His little yellow wort-flower still
       Doth grace the grassy hill;
The swan upon his coasts is heard,
       An Erin-parted bird;
The flounder lies with mouthed surprise;
The air vibrates with angels' wings,
Knoll-wisdom is the song it sings,
Safe-conduct is the news it brings.

238. *The Herb of Saint Columba*

I will pick my wort for beneath my arm,
    The noble herb of the women fair,
The herb of the drink of comforting balm
    That was in Fionn's court so richly rare.

'Tis the herb for male and for female kind,
  · The herb for cattle and calf to rear,
Columba's herb, of the kindly wise mind,
    Lovely herb of women mild and dear.

Its reward is better beneath my arm
    Than a jostling group of calving kine;
Better the reward of its virtues' charm
    Than a herd of cattle white ashine.

239. *The White Swan*

Columba went by
Mild dawn in the sky;
A white swan did lie,
    "Guile, guile",
Down on the strand nigh,
    "Guile, guile",
Of death was her cry,
    "Guile, guile".

A white swan maimed, maimed,
A white swan lamed, lamed,
White swan, two sights claimed,
    "Guile, guile",
White swan, two signs famed,
    "Guile, guile",
Both life and death named,
    "Guile, guile,
    Guile, guile".

"Thy coming whence fled,
Swan mourning the dead?"
Lov'd Columba said.
    "Guile, guile,
From Erin sea-sped,
    Guile, guile,

By the Fiann wounded,
    Guile, guile,
My sharp death-pain bled,
    Guile, guile,
    Guile, guile".

"White swan Erin-breed,
Friend I to thy need;
Christ's eye to wound-bleed".
    "Guile, guile".
"Eye-mercy, kind heed—"
    "Guile, guile".
"Eye loving decreed—"
    "Guile, guile".
"Full healing indeed".
    "Guile, guile,
    Guile, guile".

"O Erin-swan free—"
    "Guile, guile".
"No harm shall touch thee".
    "Guile, guile".
"And whole thy wounds be".
    "Guile, guile".

"O lady of sea,
    Guile, guile,
O death-song lady,
    Guile, guile,
Lady melody,
    Guile, guile—

"To Christ glorying,
    Guile, guile,
The Virgin's Offspring,
    Guile, guile,
To the great High-King,
    Guile, guile,
To him do thou sing,
    Guile, guile!
To him do thou sing,
    Guile, guile!
    Guile, guile!"

240. Saint Columba and the Flounder

Columba passing on his way
Came to the Sand-Eel Strand one day
And trod upon a flounder fair,
Hurting her tail a-trampling there.

The lovely little flounder cries,
And makes a sad loud voice arise—
"Thou Colum big, of clumsy gait,
With thy great crooked feet crosswise
The hurt thou doest me is great
When on my tail thy big foot lies".

Columba, angry he replies—
"If I have crooked-footed tread,
Be thou wry-mouthed within thy head".
And leaving her that way she lies.

241. The Strangles

Tiree

"A horse with strangles in the jaw,"
    The Saint Columba spake.
"I will turn back the swelling sore,"
    The Christ reply did make.

"On Sunday morning will it be?"
    The Saint Columba spake.
"Or ere the rise of sun thou see,"
    The Christ reply did make.

"Three pillars lie within the well,"
    The Saint Columba spake.
"I will upraise them whence they fell,"
    The Christ reply did make.

"Will that give healing from his ill?"
    Saint John the Baptist spake.
"Verily, verily it will,"
    The Christ reply did make.

242. *The Flower of Saint Columcill*

O flower of Columcill the kind,
I look not, seek not thee to find!
Be I not lifted in my sleep,
From iron's pinning-thrust, o keep.

I'll pick the leafy brown that grows,
The herb that at the hillfoot blows;
To woman, man, my present fair,
My thousand blessings and to spare.

I'll pick the brown one in my hand,
The herb that the Lord Christ ordained;
'Tis it my milk aright will set,
'Tis it will make my herds beget.

243. *Saint Columba and the Widow's Cow*   *Barra*

My heifer beloved, be not alone,
 Let thy little calf stand before;
Lo, yonder bramble-bush bending down,
 And bowing with blackberries score!

O he ho-li-vo's a vo ri ag,
 Ri ag vo, o take to thy calf!

To thyself thy treasure coax and bind,
 Till a herd to the fold thou send;
Columba shall tend thee them behind,
 For thyself this singing he penned.

The gentle proverb is sure and first,
 The cow of calves blessings doth show;
But the moorland cow is cow accurst,
 With no thirst-quenching milky flow.

The calfless cow oft away doth run,
 She seldom at home within call,
And the calfless cow the kine do shun,
 The kine-midden she of them all.

Leap of the dyke is the calfless cow,
    She the neighbours' vexing around,
Curse of the herdsman the calfless cow,
    With her head to the rocky ground.

A useless head is the calfless cow,
    And a head of mischief is she;
No lovely shape has the calfless cow,
    And no increase from her to be.

Head lifted up is the calfless cow,
    But head of no joy and no song;
Worst of the byre is the calfless cow,
    And the worst of all the kine-throng.

Head turned to shoulder the calfless cow,
    And with foot to the rock is she,
At the fold's edge is the calfless cow,
    And no profit from her to be.

On the hill-summit the calfless cow,
    Or in the glen-bottom away,
A moorland drifter the calfless cow,
    No butter is hers and no whey.

In desert glens strays the calfless cow,
    Ugly, bristling and rough to see,
Climber of walls is the calfless cow,
    And the dirt of the byre is she.

The black heifer now in gentle mood,
    To her treasure lowing will make;
Home thou wilt come with a herding-brood,
    And the hundreds' thirst thou wilt slake.

O my black heifer! heifer so black!
    The same lot for me and for thee.
The little black calf mayst thou not lack;
    My loved only son 'neath the sea.

O he ho-li-vo's a vo ri ag,
    And ri ag vo's a vo ri ag,
O he ho-li-vo's a vo ri ag,
    Ri ag vo, o take to thy calf!

203

Colum, my blessing till doom on thee,
  Of the baptism grace best son;
Thy praise and love gave plenty to me
  With thy coaxing my heifer dun.

She moves not against me foot nor head,
  And she moves neither hoof nor side;
She fills the pail and the bairns are fed,
  And the calf has his fill beside.

No more of thy speech say unto me,
  My liking is small for thy word;
Out of thy mouth come no flattery,
  For small in God's sight it is heard.

There has been no mother's son on earth
  So good as the Son from on high;
He brought the plain's footed thing to birth,
  Sea-swimmer and winged one of sky.

244. *Saint Columba's Herding*

May Columba's herding with you stay,
  Forth and home to compass you bound,
To compass in strath and on ridge way,
  And the marches of each rough ground;

To keep from the pit and from the mire,
  From the precipice, from the height,
From the loch and from the downfall dire,
  Every evening and failing light;

From ravaging mean to keep you all,
  From the withering of mishap,
From the unrecovered stumbling fall,
  And be safe from each fairy trap.

Yours as you graze be Columba's peace,
  Yours as you graze the peace of Bride,
And yours as you graze be Mary's peace,
  Safe-kept return home, safe abide.

245. The Surfeit-Swelling

Thou surfeit hither come to bloat
    Yon little bull of belling,
Columba's foot within the boat,
    He minishing thy swelling;
Thy minished prickliness doth go,
    Thy parasites he killing,
The pale and brown worms killing so,
He kills the beast of double flow,
    He kills the surfeit filling.

246. Surfeit   *Coigach*

The rune that Saint Columba made
    For the woman's single cow,
For bag and for the hide 'tis laid,
    And 'tis for the blood-veins now.

The four and twenty veins engrain,
    In the cow they twining go,
The vein of heart, the liver-vein,
    And the vein of kidney flow.

With sword that sharp and cutting cleaves,
    And with each red stroke it makes,
From cow the surfeit-swelling leaves
    And the weightiness forsakes.

O be it on the stones now set,
    Be it on the whales of sea,
That the little cow she may get
    The healing that needs must be.

247. Butter Charm   *Barra*

Columba did the spell,
    The maid in the glen,
Her butter increased well,
    Her milk surpassed then.

Come, rich lightly, come!
Come, rich lightly, come!
Come, rich lightly, pieces tightly,
Come, rich lightly, come!

Who in moon and sun set beam,
Who set food in herd and ear,
Who set fish in sea and stream,
Butter set betimes up here!

Come, rich lightly, come!
Come, rich lightly, come!
Come, rich lightly, pieces tightly,
Come, rich lightly, come!

248. *Saint Columba's Day*   *South Uist*

Kind Saint Columba's Thursday is the day
For setting sheep on lambing way,
For setting cow to calve with blessing bred,
For setting web in warping thread:

The day for setting boat upon the tide,
For setting staff on flagstone side,
The day for bearing, and the day to die,
To hunt the heights, watch quarry fly:

Day to set harnessed garrons to the field,
Day to set herds to pasture-weald,
The day for setting answer as we pray,
My loved one's Thursday is the day,
My loved Columba's Thursday is the day.

249. *Saint Columba's Plant*   *South Uist*

I will pick the flower on which I light,
My saint and I in common heart,
To subdue the wily men of spite,
And mad and silly women's art.

I will pick my arm-wort plant aright,
    A prayer unto my King to be,
That the arm-wort plant give me its might,
    O'er every person that I see.

I will pick the leaf up unto me,
    As hath the great High King ordained,
In the name of the glad Holy Three,
    Of Mary, the Christ's Mother pained.

XXIII. PRAYER

Spirit who aboundest give me,
Father great, profoundest, give me,
Thou whose praise renowned is give me,
    Jesus Son, thy shield to guard.

At night I lay me down to rest,
Thy strength hovering o'er my breast,
With Father, and with Jesus blest,
    And the Spirit's mighty ward.

(This poem is based upon number 512.)

250. *The Saint John's Wort* *South Uist*

I will pick my little arm-wort forth,
A little prayer it is unto my King,
To still the men of blood in their wrath,
To still the wiles of women wantoning.

I will pick my little arm-wort forth,
A little prayer it is unto my King,
That to me the flower may give its worth,
A power o'er those I see, each one and thing.

I will pick my little arm-wort aid,
Unto the Three it is a little prayer,
'Neath the Trinity of grace's shade,
And of the Jesu's Mother, Mary fair.

251. *At my Praying Hour* *Lochaber*

God, listen to my prayer,
Bend down to me thine ear,
My askings and my prayer
Rise upwards to thee clear.
Come, thou King of glory,
My down-protection be,
King of life and mercy,
The Lamb protecting me,
Thou MacMary Virgin,
O listen to my prayer,
Son of lovely Virgin
Pure, beautiful and fair,
O MacMary Virgin,
Protect me with thy power,
Be at my praying hour.

252. *From the Darkness*

O gentle Christ, ever thanks to thee,
That thou from the dark hast raised me free
And from the coldness of last night's space
To the gentle light of this day's grace.

O God of all creatures, praise to thee,
As to each life thou hast poured on me,
My wish, my word, my sense, my man praise,
My thought, my deed, my fame, and my ways.

253. *The Holy Spirit*

O Holy Ghost
Of pow'r the most,
Come down upon us and subdue;
From glory's place
In heaven space,
Thy light of brilliance shed as dew.

Lov'd Father One
To each bare son,
From whom all gifts and goodness flow,
Our hearts enshrine
With mercy's shine,
In mercy shield from harm and woe.

God, without thee
Naught can there be
Within man that can a price gain;
King of kings, lo!
Without thee so
Ne'er a sinless man without stain.

All on thee stayed,
Thou the best aid
Against the soul of wildest speech;
Food thou art sweet
O'er other meat;
Sustain and guide at all times each.

The stiff-joint knee,
O Healer, free,
'Neath thy wing warm heart's hardness lie;
The soul astray
Out of thy way,
O swing back his helm lest he die.

Each foul thing seen
Early make clean,
Each that is hard grace-soften through,
Each wound or blow
That pains us so,
Healer of healers, whole renew!

Thy people must
In thee place trust,
God, grant diligence to do it;
Help them each hour
With sev'nfold pow'r,
Thy gift, gen'rous Holy Spirit!

254. *Oblation* *Benbecula*

Oblation to whom shall I offer
In the name of Michael above?
A tithe of my means I will proffer
To the Glory forsaken of love.

Of his peace and his mercy knowing
O so much in all that I see,
Son of God, be not from me going,
But lift up my heart unto thee.

Remember me when in the mountain,
'Neath thy wing be shielding me here;
O do not forsake me, my Fountain;
Rock of truth, tow'r over me near.

Grant me wedding garment enfolding,
Angels' converse in my need's case,
The holy apostles' safe holding,
Mild Mary's, thou Jesu of grace,
Mild Mary's, thou Jesu of grace.

255. *Nightfall* *South Uist*

Come I this day to the Father of light,
Come I this day to the Son, morning-bright,
Come I to the Holy Ghost great in might;
Come I this day with God, blessing to find,
Come I this day with Christ, promise to bind,
Come I with the Spirit of potion kind.

O God, and Spirit, and Jesu, the Three,
From the crown of my head, O Trinity,
To the soles of my feet mine offering be;
Come I with my name and my witnessing,
Come I with my contrite heart, confessing,
Come I unto thee, O Jesu my King—
O Jesu, do thou be my sheltering.

256. *Sleep Consecration* *Benbecula*

I lie down to-night
With Mary mild and with her Son,
And with angel Michael pure-white,
With Bride beneath her mantle spun.

With God I lie down,
God himself will lie down with me,
With Satan I will not lie down,
Nor shall Satan lie down with me.

O God of the poor,
Give me thine assistance this night,
Turn me not away from the door
Of thy treasure-house stored and bright.

For many a slight
And wound on thee by me is done,
So many I cannot this night
Count all of them one by one.

Thou King of blood true,
Be mindful of me in thy hall,
Exact not the recompense due,
Include me in thy muster-call,
In thy muster-call.

214

257. *Night Sanctification*

Father, bless me and my body keep,
    Father, bless me in my soul;
Father, bless me through this night of sleep
    In my body and my soul.

Father, bless me as I live my days,
    Father, bless me in my creed;
Father, bless me in my binding ways
    To my life and to my creed.

Father, sanctify to me my speech,
    Father, sanctify my heart;
Father, sanctify my portion each
    In my speech and in my heart.

258. *The Incense*   *Morvern*

In the day of thy strength and health,
    Devotion thou wilt not proffer,
Thou wilt not give thy cattle wealth,
    Nor the incense wilt thou offer;

O head of haughtiness unstemmed,
    O thou heart, thy greed unchecking,
O thou rough ragged mouth unhemmed,
    Nor ashamed art thou, nor recking.

But there will come thy winter's day,
    And the hardness of distressing,
And heavy then thy head shall weigh
    As the clod in earth caressing;

And when thy strength is failed and drained,
    And thine aspect has gone flying,
And thou a weakling thrall enchained,
    On thy two knees ere thy dying.

259. Death Prayer South Uist

O God, of thy wisdom do thou give,
O God, of thy mercy that I live,
Of thine abundance, O God, provide,
In face of each strait be thou my guide.

God, of thy holiness consecrate,
O God, of thine aiding aid my state,
Of thy surrounding, O God, invest,
And in my death's knot give of thy rest;
   O of thy surrounding to invest,
   And in my dying hour of thy rest!

260. The Holy Ghost Distilling

May the Holy Ghost distilling,
   Down from heaven forth to ground,
Grant me aid and goodness filling,
   That my prayer be firmly bound
The King of life's great throne around.

May the Holy Ghost with blessing
   Wing the prayer I send as dove
In the fitting state and gracing
   Of thy holy will above,
O Lord my God of life and love.

Be I in God's love, God's dearness,
   Be I in God's will, God's sight,
Be I in God's choice, God's nearness,
   Be I in God's charge, God's might,
And be I in God's keep aright.

As thine angels fair, untiring,
   As thy saints, household entire,
They in heav'n above desiring,
   So on earth may I desire,
With Holy Ghost aflame in fire.

XXIV. THE DAIRY

Sing a song of the fold, sing a song of the herd,
Sing a song of the bulls and the kine,
Sing a song of the butter, the whey and the curd,
Ho hi holigan, dairy-wort twine!

Sing a song of the byre, sing a song of the stall,
Sing a song of the gleaming black hide,
Sing a song of white-flowing, of the milking's fall,
Ho hi holigan, silk-tether tied!

Sing a song of the cream, of the cheese, of the churn,
Sing a song against murrain and loss,
Used by Christ against thieving, a whipping-thong stern,
Ho hi holigan, bramble-bush gloss!

Sing a song of the boyne, sing a song of the farm,
Sing a song of the crown of the thorn,
Sing a song of the meadows, a prayer from all harm,
Ho hi holigan, proud hold thy horn!

261. *My Speckled Cow* *South Uist*

Columba with progeny will endow,
Coivi of increase her grass will provide,
She will give me her milk, my speckled cow,
With her little lady calf at her side.
    Ho my heifer! my heifer! my heifer!
    Ho for my heifer, the kindly, the calm!
My loved heifer gentle, gentle ever,
Thou dear of thy mother, keep from all harm.

Yonder the bramble bush spraying and stout,
Yon the bush bramble-gloss twined in and out,
'Tis like to my heifer of fox-red hide,
With her young she-calf that stands by her side.
    Ho my heifer! do thou keep from all harm.

The white-combed Bridget, so quiet and neat,
Will give my heifer the swan's lustre down,
While the gentle Mary, honey-combed sweet,
Will give her the mottle of moorhen's gown.
    Ho my heifer! do thou keep from all harm.

262. *My Lovely Cow* *South Uist*

Come, Brendan, o come from the ocean wave,
Come, Ternan, thou peerless of men, to me,
Come down, O thou Michael of war and brave,
That my cow of joy may favourable be.
    Ho, my heifer, ho lovely heifer,
    Ho, lovely heifer, mine for ever,
My heifer beloved, the best shieling cow,
For the High King's sake, to thy calf take now.

Come, Columba kind, from the fold in love,
O come, great Bride of the kine, come to me,
O come, Mary fair from the cloud above,
That my cow of desire obedient be.
    Ho, my heifer, ho lovely heifer,
    Ho, lovely heifer, mine for ever.

The dove will come from his nest in the tree,
The torsk will come from the wave of the sea,
And the fox will come and his tricks will lose,
Greeting to give to my cow of virtues.
    Ho, my heifer, ho lovely heifer,
    Ho, lovely heifer, mine for ever.

263. *Ho Hi Holigan*   *Skye and North Uist*

The charm Mary of graces placed to guide,
Early and late going home and away,
With Patrick the herdsman, the milkmaid Bride,
Sheltering, saining, and shielding you aye.
    Ho hi holigan, ho for my heifer,
    Ho hi holigan, ho be it ever,
    Ho hi holigan, ho for my heifer,
    My calving kine each side of the river.

For my fairy heifer rush tether-line,
For my calving heifer silk tether fine,
A tether of straw for the homestead kine,
A tether new for the loved heifer mine.
    Ho hi holigan, ho for my heifer.

Dost thou see on the plain yonder the cow,
Her frisking calf at her head in the field?
As before did she, little love, do thou,
O calf of the hero-ones, milking yield.
    Ho hi holigan, ho for my heifer.

264. *My Three Heifers*

My treasure thou, and thou art of the sea kine,
    Red-eared, notch-eared, and thy proud horn grows,
    The strength of thy grandsire's haunch yet shows,
From Monday to Saturday thou shalt be mine.
    Ho hoiligan, ho my heifer-kine!
    Ho hoiligan, ho my heifer-kine!
On each side of the stream my kindly herd-kine.

My treasure thou, and thou art of the land kine,
 Cream milk, curd milk, white as drifted snows,
 Milk from the meads where the club-rush grows,
Give me no grey water of the sand-dune brine.
 Ho hoiligan, my kindly herd-kine!

My treasure thou, and thou art of the world's kine,
 Gull-white, foam-white, sweet as honey flows,
 Milk from the slopes where the heather grows,
Give me no grey milk like the sour rowan wine.
 Ho hoiligan, my kindly herd-kine!

Bride of the songs gives the increase to thy line,
 Bright sheen, sleek sheen, Mary mild bestows,
 Michael of lustre thy guide-star shows,
Jesus Christ grants the peace and joy they are thine.
 Ho hoiligan, my kindly herd-kine!

265. *Milking Song*   *Barra*

 Come, Mary, and milk for me my cow,
 Come Bridget, and encompass her now,
 Come, O Columba kindly enow,
 And twine thy two arms around my cow.
  Ho my heifer, my lovely heifer,
  Ho my heifer, ho lovely heifer,
  Ho my heifer, my lovely heifer,
  Heifer my heart, kind, loving ever,
    To thy calf o take
    For the High King's sake.

 Come, Mary, take notice of my cow,
 Come, great Bridget the beauteous, now,
 Come, milkmaid of Jesus Christ, allow
 To set thy two arms beneath my cow.
  Ho my heifer, my lovely heifer.

 O splendid black cow, the shieling's pride,
 First cow of the byre with calves beside,
 The straw-wound cords for the townland wide,
 With tether-silk my heifer will bide.
  Ho my heifer, my lovely heifer.

O my black cow, and so black is she,
Like is the ill for me and for thee,
Thou for thy splendid calf wailingly,
I for my loved son under the sea,
   My loved only son under the sea.

266. *Milking Prayer*

The teat of Mary, the teat of Bride,
Teat of Michael, teat of God divine.
Let no hatred, no envy abide,
Nor be eye on desire-heart of mine.

Be there no ill-will, and no affright,
And no loss to my own Minnie's yield.
Be there no spell, and be there no spite,
Let the King of the stars be her shield;
   The King of the stars be her shield.

Be blessing, O God, my little cow,
And be blessing, O God, my intent;
O God, my partnership blessing thou,
And my hands that to milking are sent.

Be blessing, O God, each teat of four,
Be blessing, O God, each finger's pull;
Be blessing thou each drop that doth pour
Until, O God, my pitcher be full!

O give the milk, my treasure of kine!
O give the milk, my treasure of kine!
Give the milk, my treasure, be it mine!

O give the milk and reward is thine,—
Quern-corn bannock, and the wort-ale fine,
Honey and cream, and the chalice wine,
O my treasure, my treasure of kine!

O give the milk and thine is reward,—
The machair grass, and dew of the sward,
The music of lyre, and malted bere,
My treasure of kine, my treasure dear!

O give the milk, my treasure of kine!
Give the milk, my treasure, be it mine!

Give the milk and the blessing for thee
Of the King of earth, the King of sea,
The King of heaven, of the angels' King,
King of the City, my treasureling!

267. Cattle Croon   *Kintail and Harris*

My little black one,
    Ho hi ri!
My little black one,
    A ho seo!
My little black one,
    Ho ri ri!
My little black one,
    A ho seo!

I'll not give thee to the loud-mouthed folk,
To the sulking folk I'll not give thee,
I'll not give thee to the rheum-eyed folk—
For 'tis with the Gael that thou shalt be!

I'd not give thee to the wheedling man,
Who has not yet found the shame to be,
I'd not give thee to the mocking man—
'Tis to the dairy man I'd give thee!

I'd not give thee to the herdsman low,
Lest the people should be slandering me—
'Tis with the countrymen thou shalt go
Up in the fold of the shieling lea!

To the fiddler man I'd not give thee,
Nor at all into a tailor's claws—
For 'tis with the gentry thou shalt be,
Being milked up on the hill-top moors!

268. The Hornless Cow

Give thou the milk, O cow without a horn,
It is for thy calf thy moaning forlorn,
Give thou the milk, O cow without a horn.

Thou art of the seed of white-shouldered kine
That my grandfather in his fold contained.
Thou art of the seed of well-beloved kine
That my own people in the glens maintained.
Thou art of the seed of proud-headed kine
That to the nobles of the Straths pertained.

But I cease to croon and to sing my song,
In the linen shroud my loved one is wound.
My calf to the cold grave-stone doth belong,
And he shall not stir when the spring doth sound.

O I cease to mourn and my dirge to sing,
Since my loved one is deeply in his sleep.
O I cease to mourn and my dirge to sing,
'Tis idle for me to moan and to weep.

269. *Milking*

Ho-an, ho-an, I'll croon abroad;
Flow white flaxen flow, little cow,
Plant of sweetness, plant of the Lord!
With Christ to aid I plucked it now,
By it aright my milk is stored.

For Columba of my love be the flow first,
Thy closer of each pit and smoother of each hill,
Thy guide home to-night unharmed from any ill;
O the poors' blessing my loving herdsman fill!
The flax-milk, little cow, for my dear friend's thirst!

Ho-an, ho-an, I'll croon abroad;
Flow white flaxen flow, little cow,
Plant of sweetness, plant of the Lord!
With Christ to aid I plucked it now,
By it aright my milk is stored.

For the pilgrim and waif be thy second flow;
Naught aright for a cow in an ill-kept stall;
The pilgrim and waif, woe who recks not their call;
Let flax-milk and daisy-milk, little cow, fall!
Milk for weary pilgrim and tender child show!

Ho-an, ho-an, I'll croon abroad;
Flow white flaxen flow, little cow,
Plant of sweetness, plant of the Lord!
With Christ to aid I plucked it now,
By it aright my milk is stored.

For goodman and little son be the flow third;
May he grow by day and may he grow by night,
With the sun of fire and with the moon of light!
Primrose-milk, kind shamrock-milk, milk flaxen white,
Pour good milk and thick milk for butter and curd,
For my man and lovely boy the fatness stirred!

Ho-an, ho-an, I'll croon abroad;
Flow white flaxen flow, little cow,
Plant of sweetness, plant of the Lord!
With Christ to aid I plucked it now,
By it aright my milk is stored.

270. *The Staff-Churn*   *Barra*

The stoup-churn is now lost and away,
Its skin-cover is not seen to-day,
And new customs have arrived for aye
Determined in the country to stay;
For I stand beside a staff-churn queer,
A stick as long as a sail-mast here,
Like a great rudder it is to steer
Driven down to the churn-bottom sheer.

271. *The Virgin's Charm*   *South Uist*

Mary Virgin sent the spell
To the nun as she did dwell
On the green floor of the dell,
Up beside the cold high fell—
    The green floor of the dell,
    Beside the cold high fell.

225

Spell she put unto the wet,
That more butter should be set,
That her milk the less should get,
That her store-tale full be yet—
    More butter for her set.
    Less milk for her to get,
    And filled her store-tale yet.

272. *The Churn*   *Benbecula*

Come the loose, come;
Come the tight, come;
Come the dues, come;
Come the bright, come;
Come the sap, come;
Come the height, come;
Come the gap, come;
Come the bite, come;
Come the cheer, come;
Come the light, come;
Come the dear, come;
Come the sight, come;
Come yellow capped, the one
To set the churn a-run.

Loose a-coming,
Tight a-coming,
Dues a-coming,
Bright a-coming,
Sap a-coming,
Height a-coming,
Gap a-coming,
Bite a-coming,
Cheer a-coming,
Light a-coming,
Dear a-coming,
Sight a-coming,
World-filling to the brimming,
Churn a-running yet;
Kind Columcill with trimming,
Bride herdmaid yellow set.

A splash is here,
A plash is here,
A plash is here,
A splash is here,
A slop is here,
A plop is here,
A plop is here,
A slop is here,
An ambling soft snail is here,
And cow-milk without fail is here,
Surpassing honey sweet and beer,
A scarecrow yellow-pale is here.

A thing and more than meed is here,
A fist of priestly greed is here,
A thing and more than death is here,
A skull quite out of breath is here,
A thing and more than wine is here,
The pailful of Christy's gear
With life all soft and fine is here,
With life all soft and fine is here.

Come on, churning, come;
Come on, churning, come;
Life a-making; breath awaking;
Come on, churning, come;
Come on, churning, come;
Cuckoo braking; jackdaw taking;
Come on, churning, come;
Come on, churning, come;
Lark the heavens a-shaking,
Nun black-cap, turning come.

Come on, churning, come;
Come on, churning, come;
Come the merle, thrush a-whirl,
From the bower music skirl;
Come on, churning, come;
Come on, churning, come;
Come, old cat, wild at that,
Ease thy throat with the fat;
Come on, churning, come;
Come on, churning, come.

Doggy quiet, here's your diet;
Come on, churning, come;
Come on, churning, come;

Come, you spare; come, you bare;
　　Come on, churning, come;
　　Come on, churning, come;
Come, O beggar needy,
　Sad little man to feed;
　　Come on, churning, come;
　　Come on, churning, come;
Come, each creature greedy,
　And satisfy your need.

　　Come on, churning, come;
　　Come on, churning, come;
It's God of all did give the fruit,
And not a hag-charm with a root.
　　Come on, churning, come;
　　Come on, churning, come;
Come, O Mary fair-white,
　And be the dowry mine;
　　Come on, churning, come;
　　Come on, churning, come;
Come, O Bridget calm-bright,
　And bless the milk of kine.

　　Come on, churning, come;
　　Come on, churning, come;
The Mary-made churning,
　In glen far a-turning,
Her milk away decreasing,
Her butter so increasing;
　　　Butter-milk wrist,
　Arm with butter kist;
　　Come on, churning, come;
　　Come on, churning, come.

273. *Spelling a Beast*

The spell is placed in thy right ear
For thy good, not thine ill, to bind;
Love of the land underhoof here,
Dislike of the land left behind.

My love to-night rests on the land,
And the mountain ridges are near;
Thy tether strong in my bare hand,
Thine iron lock, Whitefront, is here.

274. Milking Croon

My heifer will wait, my heifer will stay,
My heifer will wait for me,
My black horned-heifer will wait all day,
On the knoll-summit stands she.

Though the kine of others should be outside,
Though out the others should be,
Though outside the kine of others abide,
My dark heifer, no, not she.

275. The Figwort of Saint Ternan
Lewis and South Uist

Saint Ternan's figwort I pluck in my hand,
With the fruits of the sea and of the land,
The plant of the luck and gladness that grows,
The plant of rich milk that flows.

As the King of kings ordained it to show,
To enrich the breast and the mother's teat,
As the Being of life ordained it so,
Rich substance in udder and gland to meet,
With milk for the cream and butter to flow,
With whey to dairy and churning to go,
With cheese, with speckled she-calves in the stall,
Without any useless bull-calves at all,
With joy, with progeny, and with increase,
With love, kindness, luck, with peace;

Without any man of evil intent,
Without any woman of evil eye,
Without spite, or envy, or harassment,
Without any wide-hipped bear to be nigh,
Without any wilderness wolf-dog sent,
Without any beast of the borderland,
The tasty treat snatched away from the hand
That caused the richness to stand,
Saint Ternan's wort of the spray-gleaming strand,
The figwort wherein the substance doth stand,
With the fruit, the luck, the joy of the land.

XXV. CATTLE

The kine of the townland graze by day
    'Neath the milkmaid Bride's quiet eye;
She croons them home from the hills away
    When the shadows on lea-grass lie.

The kine of the townland on the strand
    The wave-ploughing Brendan will guide;
Red, black, white, dun and spotted they stand
    To come with the inflowing tide.

The kine of the townland give the milk
    O'erwatched by mild Mary fair-white,
Tether to foot as soft as the silk,
    Safe-kept at the stall for the night.

The kine of the townland slowly go
    With a lowing to shieling far;
Columba the kindly to and fro
    Leads and tends where the dangers are.

The kine of the townland far and wide
    O'er-roam the fresh pastures and new,
The mighty Patrick by their side
    Their path shielding the season through.

The kine of the townland proud of horn,
    Bride with them and Mary is here
To aid the calf that is being born
    At his mother's side to stand near.

The kine of the townland swim the straits
    When they take the long droving road;
Soldier Michael their coming awaits,
    Soldier Michael guards their abode.

The kine of the townland know the song
    That the Herdsman the Christ doth sing,
As day by day they shamble along
    To the call of the herding King.

The kine of the townland wintertide
*   Are kept warm by the heat of the fire;*
By the great God of life is supplied
*   The winter-long life of the byre.*

276. The Cattle Grazing   Benbecula

Smooth pastures, long, and wide to roam,
Beneath your hoofs rich meadowland,
Friend God the Son to bring you home
To fields where springs eternal stand,
        Fields where springs eternal stand.

May every pit to you be closed,
Each knoll for you diminished stand,
May you be warm whene'er exposed
The cold side of the mountain land,
        Cold side of the mountain land.

The care of Peter and of Paul,
The care of brothers James and John,
Fair Bride's and Mary's care withal,
To meet you and to tend you on,
The care of all the saintly band
To comfort, aid on either hand,
        Comfort, aid on either hand.

277. Blessing of the Herd   South Uist

The keeping of God and the Lord on you,
The keeping of Christ be dwelling with you,
The keeping of Cormac, Columba too,
The keeping of Cairbre for come and go,
The keeping of Ariel may you know,
        The gold-bright Ariel's keeping on you.

The keeping of Bride, aid-mother, on you,
The keeping of saffron Mary on you,
Of Jesus the Christ, Son of peace is he,
The King of the kings, of the land and sea,
Yours ever the Spirit, peace-giving, be,
        The Spirit peace-giving e'erlastingly.

233

These cattle I will set before me as they wend,
    As the King of all the world did ordain,
Saint Bridget to keep them, to watch them, and to tend,
    On the ben, on the glen, and on the plain,
Saint Bridget to keep them, to watch them, and to tend,
    On the ben, on the glen, and on the plain.

Arise, O thou Bridget the gentle-white so fair,
    Since thou madest to them the noble charm,
And so take thou thy lint, and thy comb, and thy hair,
    Safely to keep them from loss and from harm,
And so take thou thy lint, and thy comb, and thy hair,
    Safely to keep them from loss and from harm.

From the rocks, from the drifts, from the streams'
                      rushing flow,
    From crooked passes, from pits where beasts die,
From the slender ban-shee and the shafts of her bow,
    From envy's heart, and from the evil eye,
From the slender ban-shee and the shafts of her bow,
    From envy's heart, and from the evil eye.

Mother Mary, do thou all the offspring enfold,
    O fair-handed Bridget, my cattle shield,
Columba the kindly, saint of virtues untold,
    The kine-mothers compass, herds to me yield,
Columba the kindly, saint of virtues untold,
    The kine-mothers compass, herds to me yield.

279. *The Herding of God's Son*   *North Uist*

Travelling the highland, travelling the townland,
    Travelling the bogland long and wide,
God the Son's herding round your hoofs' downland,
    Safe and whole return home to bide,
God the Son's herding round your hoofs' downland,
    Safe and whole return home to bide.

Columba's and Cormac's holy folding
 Your refuge, home or forth you fare,
And milkmaid Bride's, her hands gently holding,
 Brown her tresses of golden hair,
And milkmaid Bride's, her hands gently holding,
 Brown her tresses of golden hair.

280. *Driving the Cows*

Closed be to you each pit so deep,
Smooth be to you each hilly place,
Warm be to you each windy sweep,
Close to the mountains' chilly face.

Yours Mother Mary's holy keep,
Yours the keep of Bride, beloved friend,
Yours victor Michael's holy keep,
Your strength and your fill let them tend.

Handsome Cormac be your defence,
And Brendan the shipman to fend,
Holy Maolduin be your defence
Through the rocks and bogs as you wend.

Yours Mother Mary's fellowship,
Bride's fellowship yours, of the kine,
Yours victor Michael's fellowship,
As you nibble, and chew, and dine.

281. *The Driving*

Yours the assistance of Oran the dun,
Yours the assistance of aid-mother Bride,
Yours Mary's assistance, the Virgin one,
 'Mid marshes and rocky ground awide,
 'Mid marshes and rocky ground awide.

Yours the keeping of Ciaran, dark his down,
Yours be the keeping of Brendan the fair,
Yours be the keeping of Dermot the brown,
 As you thread the meadows here and there,
 As you thread the meadows here and there.

Yours be the safeguarding of Fionn MacCool,
Safeguarding of Cormac, fair to the eye,
Yours the safeguarding of Conn and of Cool,
From the wolf and birds that preying fly,
From the wolf and birds that preying fly.

Yours the protecting of Columcill laid,
Yours the protecting of Maolrubha true,
The protecting yours of the milking Maid,
To search you out and enquire for you,
To search you out and enquire for you.

Yours be Maoloran's encircling you round,
Yours be Maoloighe's encircling to fend,
Yours be Maoldomhnaich's encircling your ground,
To give you assistance and to tend,
To give you assistance and to tend.

The Fenian king o'ershading your march,
Yours be the shade of the King of the sun,
Yours be the King of the stars' shading arch,
When into risk and distress you run,
When into risk and distress you run.

The King of kings' shielding yours with his arm,
Yours be the shielding of Lord Jesus Christ,
The shielding yours of the Spirit of balm,
From evil deed and quarrel devised,
From the wild dog and red fox devised.

282. *The Cattle Away*   *North Uist*

The cattle to-day are on their way,
Hill-i-ruin is o hug o,
Ho ro la ill o,
Hill-i-ruin is o hug o,
To eat the cemetary grass, away,
Hill-i-ruin is o hug o,
Their herdsman driving, tending them true,
Ho ro la ill o,
Hill-i-ruin is o hug o,
Herding, turning them, fending them true,
Hill-i-ruin is o hug o,

For milking them be the gentle Bride,
 Hill-i-ruin is o hug o,
Be the lovely Mary at their side,
 Hill-i-ruin is o hug o,
Their Herdsman Friend at their journey's end,
The Jesu Christ at their journey's end,
 Hill-i-ruin is o hug o.

283. *Herd Charm*   *Lewis and South Uist*

For the lasting life I charm the words
On your broad and full and lively herds,
And the cattle lying on the hill,
To rise up with life and healthy still.

Success and blessing as down they pace,
Up with their vigour and mating's chase,
No envy, malice, ill-will to fall,
No eye too large and no eye too small,
Nor the five eyes of neglect at all.

I will suck this, the envious vein
For the house-head, for the town-folk's bane,
Each evil deed, and attribute ill
Part of your nature, be theirs to fill.

If tongue has cursed you, yet a heart blessed;
If eye has hurt you, wish prospered best.

An upside-down and confusion chased,
The holly's prick and withering waste,
That their bullock-calves and all their ewes
For the nine and nine score years they lose.

284. *Cattle Dyke-Crossing*   *South Uist*

Ditch of Mary, ditch of Mary;
 Long heron shanks, heron shanks;
Ditch of Mary, ditch of Mary;
  Underneath you heron shanks,
  Safe ahead a bridge of planks.

237

Fair Mary set a wand in it,
And Bridget set a hand in it,
Columba set a foot and hold,
And Patrick set a flagstone cold.

Ditch of Mary, ditch of Mary;
  Long heron shanks, heron shanks;
Ditch of Mary, ditch of Mary;
  Underneath you heron shanks,
  Safe ahead a bridge of planks.

For myrrh in it set Muriel,
And honey in it Uriel,
And wine in it set Raphael,
And power in it set Micha-el.

Ditch of Mary, ditch of Mary;
  Long heron shanks, heron shanks;
Ditch of Mary, ditch of Mary;
  Underneath you heron shanks,
  Safe ahead a bridge of planks.

285. *The Two Bulls*

'Tis on the heather that I was born,
The Highland bull on the heather ridge high,
'Tis on the heather that I was born,
And upreared on the loved cow's milk was I.

'Tis upon the floor that I was born,
Upon the big house floor the Lowland bull,
'Tis upon the floor that I was born,
With the honey, beer, wine, and grasses full.

The Highland bull on the heather ridge bred
On the Lowland bull turning killed him dead.

286. The Cattle-Fold   *South Uist*

I drive the kine within to stay
By the stock-opening's narrow way,
The call bemoaning of the dead,
The call of bull with lifted head,
The call responsive of the mate,
The dun cow's call within the gate,
White-headed call, strong-headed call,
The milking call within the stall;
Between each stall the upright stone
For ever safely stand alone,
Like a full-weighted tether strong
Behind your rump to trail along,
Till come day white with morrow's light.

Father, Son, Holy Spirit, bide
To save, to aid, to be your guide,
Till mine or I be at your side.

287. *As I was Going to Rome*
                          Lewis and South Uist

Whenas I was going to Rome one day,
There met me Columba, Peter, and Paul,
The talk that they had and their mouths did say
Was of loud-lowing speckled she-calves all,
As it was said and most surely foretold
On this site for a year and day to hold,
Through the Lord's bosom-kindness to befall,
The God of the living and virtues all,
The Chief of the chiefs and the Powers alway,
The Powers everlasting above for aye.

XXVI. THE FARM

The croft, between the hills and sea,
    Stands closely to the ground;
The peat-fire reek incessantly
    Arises to the sound
Of barnyard noise and cocks that crow,
Of bleating sheep and beasts that low.

The double walls stand sturdily,
    Though wind and rain surround,
With thatch and ropes in symmetry
    The house is firmly crowned;
The byre and stacks in ordered row
The means of life affording show.

With crooked spade or coulter-vee
    Upturned the sparse-deep ground
'Mid bog and rock so pressingly,
    The run-rig strips abound,
And lazy-beds of labour slow
Cover the hillside slopes below.

Clipped are the lambs and running free
    O'er upland knoll and mound,
With sheep nose-down on pasture lea
    And cattle by rough bound,
While tangle-heaped from ocean-flow
The garrons from the shore-face go.

The God of life doth oversee
    And bless the circuit round;
He guides the crafts and artistry
    Within the townland found;
O God of life, watch and bestow
That increase unto crofters grow.

Thou Michael of victorious might,
Beneath thy shield I make my round,
O Michael of the charger white,
And of the brilliant lances bright,
Victor of dragon underground,
Thou at my back in hour of strife,
O circler of the heavens' height,
O warrior of the King of life;
   O Michael of victorious might,
   Be thou my pride, my only guide,
   O Michael of victorious might,
   Rest-glory of mine eye beside.

I make my round, the saint my friend,
From machair-plain to pasture's end,
To slope of heather I ascend
Where wind blows cold; he doth defend:
And though I cross the wide wide sea,
And hostile places frown at me,
No harm can e'er encompassed be
Beneath thy shield's protecting lee;
   O Michael of victorious might,
   Thou jewel of my life and heart,
   O Michael of victorious might,
   God's shepherd good and true thou art.

May the glorious Holy Three
Be evermore at peace with me,
With all my horses strong of hock,
With all my woolly sheep in flock,
With all my beasts, all crops in field,
With every ripening sheaf and yield,
On all the machair-plain, the moor,
In cock or stook or stack at door.
   Each thing on hill or in the glen,
   Each herd and implement of men,
   Belong the glorious Holy Three,
   And Michael great of victory.

Saint Mary the tender to keep the sheep,
Quiet Bride attender to keep the sheep,
Columba commender to keep the sheep,
Maolrubha defender to keep the sheep,
Saint Cormac contender to keep the sheep,
From the wolf and the fox of cunning deep.

Let Saint Oran appear the kine to keep,
Let Saint Aidan be near the kine to keep,
Let Saint Donnan be here the kine to keep,
Saint Moluag from fear the kine to keep,
Saint Maolruan the seer the kine to keep,
On the soft bogland and hard rocky steep.

The strong Spirit of aid the droves to keep,
The MacMary of Maid the droves to keep,
Glory-Being emprayed the droves to keep,
The great Three all arrayed the droves to keep,
From tearing of wounds and the death-loss sleep,
  From tearing of wounds and the death-loss sleep.

290. *Charm for Farm-Stock*   *South Uist*

The charm that by Saint Bride was laid
Around her cattle and her kine,
Around her goats and horses made,
Around her sheep and lambs to twine;

For every day, for every night,
And for the heat, and for the cold,
For the morning and evening light,
For the bright and the dark's enfold;

To keep them from the marshy place,
To keep them from the rocky ground,
To keep them from the pit's embrace,
To keep them from the bankside bound;

To keep them from the eye that finds,
To keep them from the omen forth,
To keep them from the spell that binds,
To keep them south, to keep them north;

To keep them from the venom bite,
To keep them east and west it goes,
To keep them from the envy's spite,
And from the wiles of wicked foes;

To keep them from the lurcher's tear,
And from each other's horns that toss,
From the birds of the hollow lair,
From the beasts of the mountain-moss;

To keep them from the wolf that howls,
From ravage-dog of savage bound,
To keep them from the fox that prowls,
And from the Swiftsure Fingal hound.

291. *Saint Bride's Charm*   *South Uist*

The charm put by Bride of the virtues all,
On her goats, her sheep, and her kine to fall,
On her horses, chargers, and beasts in drove,
As forth early and homeward late they rove.

To keep them from rocks and from ridges sheer,
From the hoofs and horns of each other near,
From the birds of the Red Rock swooping low,
From the Swiftsure Fingal hound as they go.

From Crag Duilion's grey peregrine hawk,
From Ben Ard's brindled eagle's aery stalk,
From the falcon swift of the Castled Tor,
From the Bard Rock's raven of stubborn soar.

From the wily fox, from the Mam's wolf-prowl,
From the pole-cat of noisome smell so foul,
From the grizzly wandering great-hipped bear,
From every hoofed four-foot forth from his lair,
From every hatched two-wing parting the air.

292. The Black Mare

O kicking is a black mare,
    Amid the rocky ground,
O kicking is a black mare,
    And she a-running round.
Fill your hand o then and there
With red rowan berries fair
    To keep her safe and sound,
O red rowan berries fair,
    And she a-running round.

293. Sheep Saining

The charm did Mary place
Upon her flock of sheep,
From birds, from dogs to keep,
From beasts, from human race,
From hounds, from thieves that seize,
From martens, pole-cat claws,
From eye, from envy's maws,
From pain, and from disease.
In hollow you collect,
God aid you and protect;
When down you lie on knoll,
Then be your rising whole.

294. Lamb-Marking   *Benbecula*

New and sharp and clean, with no stain be my blade,
My plaid beneath my knee with my red coat laid,
The first cut for luck to the right round my breast,
And the next one with the sun as it moves west.

Out on the plain let a spotless he-lamb go,
All a colour, no flaw, nor check the blood-flow,
If the drop remain red on the heather top,
My flock without spot while unmarried I stop.

The Three up above in the City of might,
My sheep and my kine be shepherding aright,
In the heat, storm, or cold tending them with care,
With the blessing of might driving them from there
To the shieling fold down from the hill-slopes bare.

Ariel's name, and he beautiful to see,
Gabriel's name, the Lamb's harbinger is he,
Raphael's name, he a princely one of might,
Surrounding, saving them by day and by night.

Muriel's name and the Virgin Mary's name,
The name of Saint Peter, of Saint Paul the same,
The name of Saint James and the name of Saint John,
Each angel and apostle on their track gone,
    To keep them alive and their young to thrive,
    To keep them alive and their young to thrive.

295. *Shearing Blessing*   *South Uist*

Off with thee shorn and come with a fleece,
And be dam to the she-lamb of May,
Bride the mild to give thee the increase,
Mary white to sustain thee for aye.
    Mary white sustain thee for aye.

Michael of war thy shield everywhere,
From wicked dog and fox of the hill,
From the wolf and from the cunning bear,
And from clawing birds of deadly bill,
    From clawing birds of crooked bill.

296. *The Cow, the Sheep and the Goat*

Wet on the grass, the delight of the cow,
    Warmth, the delight of the sheep,
Wind, the delight of the goat, on the brow
    Of the open rocky steep.

297. *Hatching Blessing*
South Uist and the Small Isles

Early Monday morning up will I stand,
My verse will I sing and my prayer,
Sunwise I will move, my cog in my hand,
To my hen's nest for success there.

Unto my breast my left hand is to go,
My right hand by my heart is found,
The Being's loving wisdom may I know,
Whose broods, and flocks, and young abound.

Quick will I shut my two seeing eyes each,
As in blind-man's buff slowly steal;
My left hand over that side will I reach,
To my hen's nest yonder I feel.

The first egg I shall bring unto me near,
Round my head withershins it goes
With my right hand into my cog set here,
And within shall one egg repose.

I will lift my left hand above again,
Swiftly I reach unerringly,
Down here will I lift to me eggs the twain,
There then in the cog shall be three.

I will reach my right hand again to bring,
This time I lift three in my hand,
My ruling will I seek me from the King,
Six at wish in the clutch shall stand.

I reach my left hand the second time light,
Four down will I lift with it then,
In the name of Christ the King of all might,
In the cog there now shall be ten.

The stronger to take is the right grasp yet,
Two I lift in its fingers then,
At the end my hatch entire will I set
Underneath the big speckled hen.

With soot on their two ends mark them I will,
 And I dumb as the dumb thus far,
In name of the Maker of sea and hill,
 Of saints and apostles that are.

In the Trinity's name, the holy Three,
 In name of Columba kind,
On Thursday the eggs will be set for me,
 On Friday a glad brood to find.

298. *The Catkin-Wool*   *Skye and South Uist*

Now I will pull me the catkin wool,
Through her palm as did Christ's Mother pull,
For virtue, for kine, for milking's flow,
For herds, for increase of stock to show,
No loss of lamb, nor of sheep be there,
No loss of goat, no loss of mare,
No loss of cow, nor of calf at all,
No loss of means, nor of friends befall;
The Being of life opens his heart,
The courses together play their part.

249

XXVII. THE CROPS

The wind has blown the tangle ashore,
Torn from the deeps of the ocean floor,
Brought by the tide and the breakers' roar,
      The heaps of the wrack
      For the furrows' lack.

The seed is sown in the earth each year,
The rye, the barley, the oats, the bere,
The cornstalk sprouting forth with the ear;
      In its serried rows
      The potato grows.

As crops become riper from the ground
The townland is circuited around,
That no intruder or stray be found;
      The fields are a-sway
      While the breezes play.

And so to cut for the parching's burn,
A sickle-stroke for the grinding quern,
A Lammas-lop for the quick-meal's turn,
      Or more slowly reap
      For the stackyard heap.

Thou who providest the corn and bread,
Who like the cornseed sprang from the dead,
With thyself our souls be ever fed,
      Thou the Bread, the Wine,
      The true feeding thine.

299. *The Land*

> Uncertain is the hunter's toil,
>   Rely not on the fishing,
> But set thy trusting in the soil,
>   It ne'er deceived man's wishing.

300. *God of the Sea*   *Iona and elsewhere*

> O God of the heaving sea,
> Give the wave fertility,
> Weed for enriching the ground,
> Our life-giving pouring sound.

301. *Come is the Seaweed*

> Come and come is the weed of the deep,
> Come and come is the breakers' red heap,
> Come is the yellow weed, come the mop,
> Come is the wrack-mass of wave-wash crop.
>
> Come is Michael of war, fruit to bless,
> Come is Bride quiet of gentleness,
> Come is mild Mother Mary to bide,
> Come is glorious Patrick to guide.

302. *Prayer for Seaweed*

> Fruit of the sea to the land,
> Fruit of the land to the sea;
> Who betimes acts not at hand,
> His share but meagre shall be.
>
> Seaweed cast up on the land,
> Being of giving, o give;
> Fruit for wealth cast up to hand,
> Christ, grant my share that I live!

I will go out the seed-corn to sow,
In the Being's name who made it grow;
I will turn forward to the wind's blow,
And on high a ready handful throw.
Grain that may fall on the rock-face bare
Will have no soil for a growing share;
As much as into the earth falls there,
The dew will swell it and bring to bear.

Friday, it is of blessings the day,
Drops will descend in welcome array
To every seed that in sleeping lay
Since the loveless cold arrived to stay;
Each seed its roots in the earth will grow,
As the King of nature wished it so,
With the fall of dew the braird will show,
Drawing its life when the soft winds blow.

I will come round, my pacing begun,
To the right I will move with the sun,
In Ariel's name, nine angels', done,
By Gabriel, kind Apostles, run.
Father and Son and Holy Ghost, Three,
Let growing and gentle substance be
To each live thing of the moss to me,
Until the day of the fruit I see.

Michaelmas Day, of blessings the day,
Around my sickle-stroke I will lay
The root of my corn the natural way;
Quick I will lift the first cut away;
Round my head with it three turns in flight,
The while I saying my rune aright,
My back to the northern pole from sight,
My face to the sun of blessings white.

Far off I shall throw the cut from me,
Twice mine eyes I shall close not to see,
If in one sheaf its falling should be
My stacks will last us productively;
No sheaf-hag with bad times for our land
To ask for the bannock of the hand,
What time the rough gales lowering stand
All dearth and hardship from us be banned.

304. *Silverweed*

Honey beneath the ground
The springtime silverweed;
Honey and spices found
A whisked-whey summer-feed;
Honey and ripe the fruit
The autumn carrot root;
Honey and crunching bite
Nuts for a winter's night
From Andrewmas to last
Till Christmastide be past.

305. *Reaping*   *South Uist*

O God, thyself my reaping bless,
Each ridge, and meadow, mossy-field,
Each sickle's hard curved shapeliness,
Each ear and binding of the yield,
   Each ear and binding of the yield.

Each maiden bless, each youth so slight,
Women and tender young ones all,
Mark them beneath thy shield of might,
And guard them in the saints' wide hall,
   And guard them in the saints' wide hall.

Each goat, each little lamb, each sheep,
Each cow, and horse, and barnstore-hold,
The flocks and herds, surrounding keep,
And tend them to a kindly fold,
   And tend them to a kindly fold.

For Michael's sake, the war-host's head,
White-breasted Mary, branch of grace,
Of Bride white-gentle, ringleted,
Columba of last resting place,
   Columba of last resting place.

Rise of the sun Tuesday of the feast,
Corn-ear back to the point of the east,
Sickle 'neath arm I forth to the crop,
The first deed the harvest-cut to lop.

Down I will lower my sickle-blade,
The fruitful ear in my grasp is laid,
Up mine eye I will lift from the ground,
Quickly on my heel I will turn round,

Right hand as the sun journeys to rest
From the east point reaching to the west,
With movement calm from the northern bound
To the dead centre of south point round.

I will bring praise to the King of grace
For the ground-crops growing in the place,
To us and the flocks food he will give
As he bestoweth that we may live.

On James and John, on Peter and Paul,
Light's fullness, Mary white-love I call;
On Michaelmas Eve and Christmas Day,
Bannock to taste for us all I pray.

307. *Parching*   *Mingulay of Barra*

Flame slender, curling, smoky-grey,
Rising from topmost pores of peat,
Flame leaping, spreading, giving heat,
Come nigh me not with sparks astray.

A burning steady, gentle, due,
Around my grass-roots drying slow,
Fire fragrant, kind, of comfort-glow,
No scorch, dust, sadness coming through.

Parch my fat seed, o warmness red,
Food to my little child to bring,
In name of Christ, Creator-King,
Who blest and gave us corn and bread,
    In name of Christ, Creator-King,
      Who blest and gave us corn and bread.

308. *The Quern* *Barra*

On the Shrove night
Meat for our bite,
That is our right,
That is our right.

Hen-cheek to chew,
Barley cakes two,
Enough is due,
Enough is due.

Mead shall we have,
Beer shall we have,
Feed shall we have,
Cheer shall we have.
We shall have wine,
Milk, honey fine,
Sweetness and cream,
Nectar of dream,
Such shall we have,
Much shall we have,
Much shall we have.

Tune shall we have,
Harp large and small,

Rune shall we have
With the horn's call;
Lute shall we have
For dancing feet,
Flute shall we have,
Clear is the beat,
Melody's string,
Lyre of a king,
Songs shall we sing,
Songs shall we sing.

The calm fair Bride
With us abide,
Mild Mother Maid
Mary beside,
Of shining blade
Michael to fight;
The King of kings
With us in might,
Christ Jesus dear,
The Spirit brings
Peace and grace near,
Grace with us here,
Grace with us here.

309. *The Blessings of Life*

Mary Mother's love be thine,
Thine be Bridget's love, of kine,
Love of victor Michael fine,
Their arm around
Each hour surround.

Thine great goodness of the sea,
Earth's great goodness to thee be,
Thine great goodness heavenly,
Thy life be strong
And fruitful long.

257

Father, give to thee mild grace,
Loving grace of Son embrace,
Spirit's loving grace emplace,
    So laving thee,
    Pow'r-saving thee.

XXVIII. GAIRLOCH POEMS

Waters of Gairloch that swell from the sea,
Waterside pinetrees that shade Loch Maree,
Waterbed salmon of Ewe leaping free,
          Your saint's ancient power
          At our praying hour.

Waters of strength and of cleansing inflow,
Minch-waters of fierceness where gale-winds blow,
Thy peace, God of waters, at ebb-tide show,
          Grant thou for each ill
          The faith and the skill.

Waters of healing on man and beast lie,
Water and grass-blade for cataract-eye,
Water for mote-pang, for worm that must die,
          The subduing blest
          To pining and breast.

Waters of Ewe where the tides run in free,
Waters of well from the Island Maree,
Waters of Gairloch swell in from the sea,
          A prayer at each flow,
          And God's blessing so.

310. *Prayer for the Day* *Gairloch*

Do thou, O God, bless unto me
    Each thing mine eye doth see;
Do thou, O God, bless unto me
    Each sound that comes to me;
Do thou, O God, bless unto me
    Each savour that I smell;
Do thou, O God, bless unto me
    Each taste in mouth doth dwell;
Each sound that goes unto my song,
    Each ray that guides my way,
Each thing that I pursue along,
    Each lure that tempts to stray,
The zeal that seeks my living soul,
The Three that seek my heart and whole,
    The zeal that seeks my living soul,
    The Three that seek my heart and whole.

311. *Christ and the Swollen Breast* *Gairloch*

Death to thy germ that it may cease,
    And death be thy swelling's dower,
Unto thy breast let there be peace,
    The peace of the King of power.

Let whiteness be unto thy skin,
    And let thy swelling subside,
Wholeness be to thy breast within,
    In thy pap fullness abide.

In the kind Father's holy eyes,
    The Son's holy eyes to thee,
In holy eyes of Spirit wise,
    Mercy's eyes holy the Three.

312. *The Pining-Away* *Gairloch*

A woman to close her heart too fain!
    And a generous husband dying;
The pining is piercing him with pain,
    And the Christ on the awn lying.

Death to the germ in the pining fell,
    To the bitter colic, dying;
May the hospitable man rise well,
    On the awn Christ himself lying.

313. *Cataract*   *Gairloch*

In my hand the water lies
In the Father's holy name,
In Son's holy name I rise,
In the Spirit's holy name,
Holy name of Three the Same
Everlasting, kind and wise.

Sure to me they will afford
That by prayer which I must gain,
Which is of their mind's accord,
That which now doth cause the pain,
The thing worthy to attain,
Kind just Trinity's award.

God the Father, God the Son,
God the Spirit, be it done,
Guidance, mercy, pity won.

314. *The Fleshworm*   *Gairloch*

Death-rune to creeping insect black,
Death-rune to insect's evil rack,
Death-rune to insect's wasting track
    Of every sort within.

Fierce worm within the body's seat,
Fierce fleshworm of the many feet
That caused the great tormenting heat
    Throughout the flesh and skin.

315. *Cattle Surfeit*   *Gairloch*

I have a charm for my sickly cow,
I have a charm for bag-swelling now,
For the black disease I have a charm,
A charm for the red disease's harm,
A charm for the surfeit-fill's alarm.

It is the charm that Columba made,
For the one cow of the woman laid.

O Beastie, shake thou it off from thee,
Push, Beastie, push, Beastie, push it free!
Beastie my dear, come running to me!

316. *Peace between Neighbours*   *Gairloch*

Peace between neighbours near,
Peace between kindred here,
Peace between lovers dear,
In love of the King of us all.

Peace man with man abide,
Peace man to wife allied,
Mother and bairns to guide,
And peace of the Christ above all.

Bless, O Christ, bless my face,
My face bless every face,
Christ, bless mine eye with grace,
Mine eye give a blessing to all.

XXIX. THE PEACE OF GOD

When war did cease upon the earth,
The stars looked out, the heavens rang,
The small Lord Jesus came to birth,
A lilt of peace his Mother sang.

A lilt of peace 'mid snow-clad sheen,
Goodness-peace, forgiveness of sin,
Confession-peace, penitent-clean,
Peace with God and the peace within.

Peace with God and goodwill to men,
The peace of triumph on the Tree,
The rising peace that followed then,
The peace of God for you and me.

The peace of God, lake-waters by,
The peace of God, mist o'er the sea,
The peace of God, ascending high,
The peace of God, unceasingly.

317. The Peace of God

Peace of God be unto you,
Peace of Christ be unto you,
Peace of Spirit be to you,
Peace be to your children too,
To your children and to you.

318. For Forgiveness   Harris

On this thy day, on this thy night,
  O God be with us, Amen.
On this thy day, on this thy night,
  To us and with us, Amen.

It is full clear within our sight
That since we came to this world's light
We have deserved thy wrath's despite;
  O God be with us, Amen.

O God of all, o thine own wrath,
Stretch, O God, thy forgiveness forth,
  To us forgiveness, Amen,
  Forgiveness with us, Amen,
  To us and with us, Amen.

Thine own forgiveness to us give,
Merciful God, by whom we live,
Merciful God of all, forgive,
  O God be with us, Amen,
  To us and with us, Amen.

Anything that to us is ill,
Or that may stand against us till
We come where is our longest day,
  Lighten it to us aright,
  O darken its ugly light,
  O banish it from our sight,
Forth from our heart chase it away,
For everlasting and for aye,
  Ever and ever, Amen,
For everlasting and for aye,
  Ever and ever, Amen,
  O God be with us, Amen.

Jesu MacMary, have mercy upon us;
Jesu MacMary, thy peace be upon us;
      Where we shall longest be,
      With us and for us be,
      Amen, eternally.

Jesu MacMary, at dawn-tide, the flowing,
Jesu MacMary, at ebb-tide, the going;
      When our first breath awakes,
      Life's day when darkness takes,
Merciful God of all, mercy bestowing,
      With us and for us be,
      Merciful Deity,
      Amen, eternally.

Condition and lot, to thee make them holy,
Condition and lot, to thee take them wholly,
      King of all kings that be,
      God of all things that be,
      Amen, eternally.

Our rights and our means, to thee make them holy,
Our rights and our means, to thee take them wholly,
      King of all kings that be,
      God of all things that be,
      Amen, eternally.

Our body and heart, to thee make them holy,
Our body and heart, to thee take them wholly,
      King of all kings that be,
      God of all things that be,
      Amen, eternally.

Each body and heart, the whole of each being,
Each day, each night also, thine overseeing,
      King of all kings that be,
      God of all things that be,
      Amen, eternally.

Holy Father of glory, kind Father of power,
All thanksgiving to thee, O thou Father of love,
For each harvest, each favour, each aid from above,
That on us thou bestowest in each needing's hour;
For we are thy children, whate'er fortune befall
In our portion and lot and the path where we stand,
O grant to us with it the rich gifts of thy hand,
And thy joy-giving blessing pronounce to us all.

God, with guilt we are filled and defilement within,
In our spirit and in body and in our heart,
In the thought, in the word, in the deed of our part,
In the sight of thine eyes we are stiff-necked in sin;
O the power of great love put thou forth for our sake,
Leap o'er the transgressions of our far wasteland height,
With the blood of atonement, o wash us as white
As the hill cotton-grass, as the lily of lake.

When steep is the highroad of our wayfaring's call,
To our flesh be it easy or uneasy here,
Be its music-sound to us or clear or unclear,
May thine own perfect guidance be over us all;
Be shield from the false one laying traps for our feet,
Shield from the arch-slayer arrow-goading behind,
And in each secret thought, warp and weft of our mind,
Be thyself at the helm, be thyself at the sheet.

Though there be dogs and robbers for reiving our fold,
Valiant Shepherd of glory, be shadowing near;
Whatever the matter, reason, heart's desire dear
Would fit us for torment and sore wounding's dire hold,
Or that would bear witness at the last to our face,
At yon side the great river of dark-shadow flow,
O do thou dark-blur it, from our sight make it go,
And for aye from our hearts do thou hound it in chase.

Praise now to the Father who created all life,
Praise now to the Son who did redeem man's estate,
Praise now to the Spirit, the strong Comforter great :
Be buckler and safeguard from the wounds of the strife,
Be o'er the beginning and the end of our race,
Grant us to see glory and to join in the song,
In the peace, in the rest, in the harmony long,
Where no tear shall be shed and where death has no place,
    Where no tear shall be shed and where death has no place.

321. Blessing and Peace

My own blessing to be with you I give,
And be God's blessing with you while you live,
The blessing of the saints with you to go,
The resting peace of life eternal so,
To resting peace of life eternal so.

322. Confession   Lochaber

Jesu, give unto me the forgiveness of sin,
Jesu, be mine erring not forgotten within,
Jesu, give me the grace of repentance's school,
Jesu, give me the grace of forgiveness in full,
Jesu, give me the grace of submissiveness due,
Jesu, give me the grace of sincerity true,
Jesu, give me the grace of humility's part,
My confession to make at this time from my heart,
At throne of confession condemnation to own
Lest condemnation I find at the judgement throne;
Jesu, give me the strength and the courage, alone
At throne of confession condemnation to own
Lest condemnation I find at the judgement throne.
More easy is a season of chastening to me
Than a descent unto death for eternity.
Jesu, give unto me all my guilt to confess
With the urgency of death's importunateness.

Jesu, take pity, o take pity on me,
Jesu, upon me have mercy, mercy whole,
Jesu, do thou take me, o take me to thee,
Jesu, give thou aid, o give aid to my soul.

Sin is of grief a cause, o a cause,
And a cause of sore anguish is death,
But repentance is of joy a cause
And the cleansing stream's life-giving breath.

O Shepherd, who leavest the ninety and nine,
Good Shepherd, who seekest the sheep that hath slipt,
The angels of heav'n will have joy that is mine
That in the confession-stirred pool I am dipt.

O my soul, lifted up and rejoicing be,
God willeth for thee an atonement above,
Seize his hand while it is stretched out unto thee
To announce to thee an atonement of love.

Withdraw not they hand, O my God, from me here,
O Chief of the chiefs, o withdraw not thy hand,
For Lord Jesus Christ's sake my Saviour so dear,
That I go not to death's everlasting land.

323. *Peace for this Life*

The peace of God be unto you,
The peace of Jesus unto you,
The peace of Spirit unto you,
Be peace unto your children too,
Peace unto you, your children too,
Each day and night let there be peace
Till of this world your portion cease.

324. *The Peace of Everlasting*

Peace of all felicity,
Peace of shining clarity,
Peace of joys consolatory.

Peace of souls in surety,
Peace of heav'n's futurity,
Peace of virgins' purity.

Peace of the enchanted bowers,
Peace of calm reposing hours,
Peace of everlasting, ours.

325. Peace to the End

The peace of God o dwell with you,
The peace of Christ to dwell with you,
The peace of Spirit dwell with you,
And peace dwell with your children too,
From the day we have here to-day
To the last day of your life's way,
Till come the day that ends your way.

XXX. HEALING

When Jesus dwelt in Galilee,
    He preached the Gospel word;
When Jesus went beside the sea,
    His gracious voice was heard.

When Jesus in the gloaming stood,
    The people to him came,
He gave to them his healing good
    And walking to the lame.

They brought to him the deaf and dumb,
    They brought to him the blind,
The paralysed to him did come,
    His healing hand was kind.

The outcast lepers were his care,
    And poor demented folk;
To evil spirits, which did tear
    The frame, he sternly spoke.

The raging fever he allayed,
    The crooked he made straight,
From bed he raised the lifeless maid,
    He cured the wanton's state.

When Jesus on the ass did ride
    And through the gate did fare,
With nailèd hands and wounded side
    He healed the world's despair.

And afterward upon the ben
    Unto the chosen ones
He gave his powers for healing men
    That we might be his sons.

The holy twelve did heal amain,
    Saint Peter and Saint John;
And kind Columba for our pain
    The power handed on.

O power of the blest Trinity,
    The power to loose and bind,
O'ershadow us, O Holy Three
    So infinitely kind.

326. Jesus-Praise

Harris

It were as easy, Lord, for thee
As to wither the sapling new
Anew to green the withered tree
Were it thy will the thing to do,
    O Jesu, Jesu, Jesu,
      Unto whom all praise is due.

There is no plant in all the land
But blooms replete with thy virtue,
Each form in all the sweeping strand
With joy replete thou dost endue,
    O Jesu, Jesu, Jesu,
      Unto whom all praise is due.

All life that is within the sea,
In river every dwelling thing,
All in the firmament that be
Thy goodness overflowing sing,
    O Jesu, Jesu, Jesu,
      Unto whom all praise is due.

Each single star fixed in the sky,
Each bird arising on the wing,
They that beneath the sun do lie
Thy goodness all proclaiming sing,
    O Jesu, Jesu, Jesu,
      Unto whom all praise is due.

327. Childlessness

Skye

The water from the little fall doth shine
As on the forelock of my hair it stays;
The sunbeams of the dawn outspreading nine,
In thy name, God of life, thy servant prays;
Away the red miscarriage from me raise;
The woman's hope of hurrying is mine.

328. *Charm for the Rose Disease*   *South Uist*

Behold the udder, O thou Son,
And the rose with its deadly swell;
That to our Lady do thou tell,
For 'tis she who did bear the Son.

O thou rose, do thou get thee hence,
Let me see the back of thy feet;
Let the udder be whole and sweet,
And drained let the swelling be thence.

Thou rose, swelling and ruddy drest,
Hard and scabby and foul infest,
Leave the udder and leave the breast;
Back the swelling and pap distrest.

329. *Fionn's Charm*   *South Uist*

The charm that by Fionn MacCool was made,
    Made for his own sister dear,
Against rose and pang and reddening laid,
    'Gainst germs of the moorland drear;

Against fairy elfin darts so fierce,
    Against elfin darts of charm,
Against the darts of the hosts that pierce,
    Against darts of winging harm;

Against the great creeping monster jaws,
    And against the gnawing cranes,
Against rose that to the udder draws,
    And against the breast's dread pains.

In trust of Father, and Son of woe,
    And perfect Spirit of might,
Hide not thy power on Sunday to show,
    Reject not who prays in plight.

In trust of the Father and the Son,
    In trust of compassion kind,
Reject not compassion's prayer begun,
    Thy Sabbath-healing to find.

276

The charm by the lovely Bride was laid
As God's Mother's thumb she bound with braid,
On flax, on wort, and on hemp the charm,
For worm, for venom, for teeth from harm.

For flax, for head, and for agony,
The charm for ocean and coast and sea,
For water and loch and marshy lea.

The torture worm has come born and bred
In the white teeth that stand in my head,
Hell by my teeth pressing hard beside,
The teeth of hell appear gaping wide.

O Christ, do thou now my healer be,
The teeth of hell are so close to me;
While I live on until I am dead
May my teeth live on within my head.

331. *For Sprain*

In the Father's name, in the name of Son,
In the Spirit's name, the Three of threes One.

The bone unto bone, the vein unto vein,
The balm unto balm, to the foot of pain.

The sap unto sap, the skin unto skin,
Tissue to tissue, to the foot within.

The blood unto blood, the flesh unto flesh,
Sinew to sinew, to the foot afresh.

Marrow to marrow, the pith unto pith,
The fat unto fat, to the foot forthwith.

Fibre to fibre, membrane to membrane,
Moisture to moisture, to the foot of pain.

The God of gods, Healer of healers best,
The Spirit of eternity who laves,
The Three of threes, the Trinity who saves,
Unto the foot of pain be granting rest.

332. *The Moving of Chest-Constriction*

The Black Isle

The first third of thee upon the grey clouds be,
They themselves have greatest nimbleness to flee,
In name of Father, Son, Holy Spirit, Three.

The next third of thee on the gulfing bogs go,
They themselves have greatest drawingness below,
In name of Father, Son, Holy Spirit, so.

The third third of thee on the fair meadows spread,
They themselves have greatest enduringness bred,
In name of Father, Son, Holy Spirit shed.

I make now this charm to compass thee around,
Donald son of Ewen, that thou mayst be sound,
In name of Father, my two hands on the ground,
In name of the Son, my two hands on the ground,
In name of Spirit, my two hands on the ground,
The Three who possess the heights that have no bound.

333. *Against the Wasting-Away*   *Bonar Bridge*

Jesus Christ unto Simon Peter said
That his own people he must fill with bread,
To his own people he must teach belief,
That his own people he must shield o'erhead,
To his own people he must give relief,
That his own people he must save from thief,
From traitor and from all deceiving led.

Mine appeal and my prayer to thee I bring,
For that thou art the King of each good thing,
For that thou art the King of heavenly sway,
That thou mayest lift each wasting away,

Each weariness and each lying down faint,
Each seizure of chest and every complaint,
Each soreness, unease, that malady brings,
Each sickness, disease, that from illness springs,
That unto this maiden stubbornly clings.

O set them upon the beasts of the height,
On the wilderness creatures let them be,
Set them upon those of peak-circling flight,
Set them upon the great whales of the sea.

O set them upon the streams of the glens,
On the monsters of ocean let them lie.
O set them upon the tops of the bens,
O set them upon the birds of the sky.

Keenly, o keenly, I pray unto thee,
I call closely, closely, imploringly,
That thou mayest lift each clot right away,
Each mischief, each binding, lift them I pray.

As rain from the rain parts drops that are shed,
As water from water parts in its bed,
As a wave from a wave parts and is free
Through all the wideness of waters of sea.

As haze disperses from haze of the shore,
As mist dispersing from mist is no more,
As clouds dispersing from clouds swiftly fly
In the deep of the great storm-song of sky.

As agony breaks from agony free,
As birds break from birds upstarting to flee,
This night may the God of life-giving break
Each ill and affection thy flesh doth take.

No loss it will cause them, nothing to fear,
For thee a fountainhead good springing here
O Margaret Calder, mine own sister dear.

334. Cough-Wasting

I tread thee down, thou wasting pest,
As on the sea the whale doth tread,
Wasting of back, wasting of chest,
Thou rotten throat-wasting so dread.

Of living things the mighty Chief
Destroy all thy body's disease,
From the crown of thy head relief,
To the sole of thy heel give ease;

From thy two thighs hither above,
From thy two thighs thither below,
With the power of the Christ of love
And the seasons' Creator so;

With the aid of the Holy Ghost
And with all the whole Powers to heal,
With the aid of the Holy Ghost
And with the whole Powers for thy weal.

335. Chest-Conflict

Noisy seizure of chest, I tread on thee
As upon the mountain moorland this night;
On thyself, King Geigean, thine arrow be!
Piercing and fearful the wound of thy flight.

The charm that Patrick the generous did lay
Upon the mother of Ireland's great king
To kill the beasts that did fasten and prey
On the veins of her heart, her vital string.

On the four and twenty ailments to fear
That in men and in beasts inhere and dwell,
That in man and in woman both inhere,
That inhere in son and in daughter as well.

On the running water of mountain stream,
On the running water that keeps apart,
On the rigid stones of the rocky seam,
And upon the weakness of fainting heart.

On smallpox and on the jaw that is locked,
On jaundice and sickness of tawny brand;
On bleary eye and the skin that is pocked,
On the running nose and the swollen hand;

On quivering ague and cough's hooping note,
On the dry fever, on the wasting rot;
On disease of chest, on disease of throat,
On the dropsy and on the measles spot.

336. *The Chest Disease*

Around thee God's hand,
O'er thee his eye stand,
The love of heaven's King
Thy pang emptying.

Hence, hence, hence, away!
Dumb, dumb, dumb, obey!
Venom in the ground,
Thy pain in stone downed!

Arrow bringing fright,
The salt healing blight,
The prayer that Christ prays,
Fairy arrow stays.

337. *The King's Evil*   *Kinlochewe*

May God, my dear, be thy healing One;
I set my hand upon thee this day
In name of Father, in name of Son,
In name of Spirit of power, I pray,
Three Persons who compass thee alway.

Full healing to thy red blood within,
More healing unto thy soft flesh be,
Another healing to thy white skin,
In virtue's name of the Holy Three,
   In virtue's name of the Holy Three.

338. *For Rupture* *Kintail*

O God of all grace, my body satisfy;
O Christ of the Passion, satisfy my soul;
O Spirit of wisdom, grant light on me to lie,
And restore to me repose, making me whole.

O Father of life, do thou strengthen mine hand;
O Christ the Son of love, do thou soothe the pain;
O Spirit Holy, reduce the swollen gland,
And in all lovingness make me whole again.

339. *Checking of Blood*

Strath Spey and Kilmorack

The blood-flow stay,
The blood-charm-lay,
The blood congeal,
The wound shall seal.

Salve of the Maid,
Christ's Mother, laid,
Shield us and aid,
Help us afraid.

In Father's name,
In the Son's name,
In Spirit's name,
Life-Three the same,
Spare us and aid.

XXXI. THE EYE

God gave the eye to man at birth,
　　And set it in his head,
That he might see the things of earth,
　　The loveliness there bred.

The eye looks out and sees the hills,
　　It sees the living things,
It sees the light that eachwhere fills,
　　It lends the body wings.

The eye unto the man doth show
　　The path of daily tread,
It warns of danger lairs below,
　　It lifteth up the head.

The eye of man holds his desire,
　　On things he lets it rest;
Cool it looks or speaks with fire,
　　The eye of seeing best.

The eye reveals the inner man,
　　The window of the soul,
The single eye of honest scan
　　That comprehends the whole.

The eye of good, the evil eye,
　　They each in man inhere,
The eye of envy's hatred sly,
　　The eye of laughter clear.

Throughout our days safeguard the eye,
　　God grant we be not blind,
Ward off the cataract, the stye,
　　The rheum, the mote unkind.

Grant us to live with vision clear
As the MacMary taught,
Grant us the heavenly vision here
For travelling as we ought.

O Father mighty, bless the eye,
That in our human head doth lie.

340. *The Eye of God*

O may the great God's eye upon you lie,
The God of glory's eye upon you lie,
MacMary Virgin's eye upon you lie,
The gentle Spirit's eye upon you lie,
To aid you and to shepherd be it nigh;
O the Three's kindly eye upon you lie,
To aid you and to shepherd be it nigh.

341. *The Sight*   *North Uist*

God over me, and God below,
God before, and God after me,
O God, on thy path may I go,
Thou, O God, in my walking be.

The sight Mary made for her Son,
The gift with her hand that Bride bore,
Didst thou, King of life, see it done?—
Said the King of life that he saw.

The sight Mary made for her Boy,
When those days amissing was he,
Knowing true, not false, be my joy,
That my seeking truly I see.

King of life, whom fair Mary bore,
Give me eyes to see all I seek,
With grace never failing, before,
Never snuffed nor shadowed and weak.

342. *Lifting the Eye*   *The Aird*

A little drop of water I lift,
In the holy name of Father One;
A little drop of water I lift,
In the holy name of God the Son;
A little drop of water I lift,
In the holy name of Spirit done.

O shake off thy harm, my love, from thee,
O shake off from thee thy jealousy,
O shake off thine illness, be thou free,
In name of the Father may it be,
In name of the Son eternally,
In name of the Holy Spirit, Three.

The evil eye who shall lift away?
Who but thou, O God of life, to-day!
By heart of Peter, by heart of Paul,
By the Three's heart, best glory of all.

A pater of Mary pray I one,
A pater of Mary second done,
A pater of Mary now the third,
A pater of Mary fourth be heard,
Fifth pater of Mary word by word,
Sixth pater of Mary now be given,
And pater of Mary number seven.

The paters of Mary's sevenfold might
Upon the stones and the trees alight,
Upon the wild duck of swampy lakes,
Upon the withered trees of the brakes;

On the pawing creatures of the plain,
The bear of the spaces be it lain,
Upon the whale-blowers of the sea,
Upon the beasts of the holes to flee;

On the brown stag of the mountainhead,
Upon the green grass beneath my tread,
Upon the birds that wing in the sky,
Upon the fish of the waves to lie;

For they themselves can endure the best,
Who in their form are the shapeliest.

On the evil eye I trample here,
As tramples the duck upon the sound,
As tramples the swan upon the mere,
As tramples the horse upon the ground,
As tramples the cow on grazing share,
As tramples the marching host on air,
   Tramples the elements' host on air.

Over the evil eye to dispose
Mine is the might of the wind that blows,
Mine is the might of the anger's ire,
Mine is the might of the burning fire,
Mine is the might of the thunder crash,
Mine is the might of the lightning flash,
Mine is the might of the gales that ride,
Mine is the might of the moon of tide,
Mine is the might of the blazing sun,
Mine is the starry might that is spun,
Mine is the might of the spreading sky,
Mine is the might of the heavens on high,
Mine is the might of the spheres that roll,
   Might of the heavens, of the spheres that roll,
   My might the evil eye to control.

A part be on the stones that are grey,
Part of it on the hills that are steep,
Part of it down the swift falls away,
Part of it on the fair meadow sweep,
A part of it on the great salt sea,
For she can the best take it from thee,
   The great salt sea to take it from thee.

In the Three of life's name, Trinity,
And in the name of the Holy Three,
And in the name of each Mystery,
And of all the Powers in company.

344. *An Eye*   *Benbecula*

An eye saw thee beholding,
A mouth naming thee mentioned,
A heart thought thee enfolding,
A mind desired, intentioned.

Three Persons sanctifying,
Three Persons thine aiding be,
Father and Son supplying
And perfect Spirit to thee.

Four thy hurt have been making,
Man, woman, and lad and maid;
Three against I am taking,
Father, Son, Holy Ghost prayed.

Who is there for repelling?
Who is there that will avert?
The Three Persons excelling,
Trinity Three will convert.

345. *Evil-Eye Counter*

O thou dear Blackie, I make unto thee
The spell of Mary, of the King of all kings,
The most perfect spell of all the world's things,
Which, God of all gods, thou hast given to me.

Against eye that is small, eye that is great,
'Gainst the eye of swift women of swelling greed,
'Gainst the eye of swift women's thieving breed,
'Gainst the eye of swift women of draggling gait.

'Gainst the own eye that belongs unto me,
Against the own eye that belongs unto thee,
Against the eye of the man who is grey,
The one who did come to the door yesterday.

Whoever hath brought thee to straits so sore,
With eye, with malice, and with envy, with hate,
O may her life be of unprolonged state
On the fresh sunny sheen by Loch Leargain's shore.

O grant that it lie upon their own eyes,
And grant that it lie on their own sorceries,
Grant that it lie on their envious blight,
And grant that it lie on their hatred and spite.

Grant that it lie on their calves that are she-s,
And grant that it lie on their calves that are he-s,
Grant that it lie on their fold of young pairs,
And grant that it lie on their own foaling mares.

Grant that it lie on their children when small,
And grant that it lie on their children when tall,
Grant that it lie on their bleating goats' leap,
And grant that it lie on their fleece-coated sheep.

O grant that it lie on their men of root,
And grant that it lie on their women of fruit,
Grant that it lie on their masculine sons,
And grant that it lie on their own daughters' wombs.

On their head, neck and backbone may it lie,
May it lie on their sinews, their leg and thigh,
May it lie upon each of this world's things
Which unto these people the most pleasure brings.

But be thy groaning, thy grieving's sore weight,
Thy yawning awide and thy heavy estate,
Thy weary sadness and the tears of thine eye,
Thy lamentation and thy dumb misery.

Be they upon the winged spoilers of sweep,
And be they upon the wild-beasts of the steep,
Be they on robbers of bough and of nest,
Upon the burnt heather of the rough hill-crest;

Be they on rangers that o'er the moors go,
Be they on the fish of the spate and the flow,
Be they on searchers of bough and of nest,
Since it is these themselves that can endure best.

Be one third to fall upon them to-day,
Be two thirds to-morrow to vanish away,
And each third to vanish until doomsday
On the day thereafter for ever and aye.

346. Checking the Evil Eye

I make for thee a thwarting spell
The evil eye to check, repel;

Against the nine paths winding wide,
Against the nine cries din-supplied,
Against nine cunning wiles and crafts,
Against nine fairy-women's shafts;

'Gainst the eye of old single man,
Against the old maid's eyeing scan,
Against old gaffer's eye of leer,
Against old woman's eye of peer.

If it be man with evil eye,
Like the pitch may it spit and fly,
But if it be a woman's eye,
May she want her breast's supply.

Her water be to her a flood,
And be there coldness in her blood,
In her cattle and sheep of wool,
In her people and portion full.

347. Mote Charm   Alness

O Bridget, be near to mine eye,
    O Mary, thine aid supply,
King of gladness, my knee be by,
    Loving Christ, my body nigh.

The mote in the eye of the head,
    O King of life, do thou place,
    O Christ of the loving grace,
O Spirit so Holy, instead
    Upon my palm do thou place.

May the King of life give the rest,
    The Christ of love give repose,
Give strength, Holy Spirit so blest,
    And the eye with peace enclose.

290

O Bridget veil-folded so calm,
    Mild Mary of poor man blest,
Soldier Michael of sword-glint arm,
    Be setting the hurt at rest.

348. *The Mote in the Eye*

The goad's pricking stab,
The rock's pinning grab,
The nine serpent's bane,
The roaring stag's pain.

The mote of the eye
For which my hopes lie,
For which I intend,
Which is my trust's end,
King of life above,
Lay, O Christ of love,
Holy Ghost, soft lay
On my tongue away.

349. *Mote Removal*   *Bonar Bridge*

Do thou place, O King of calm,
Place, O thou Christ of the tree,
Place, Spirit of guiding arm,
This mote on my hand to see.

The King at my hand beside,
At my foot the Christ be by,
At my knee the Spirit guide,
And rest be unto the eye.

Give ear, thou King of the eyes,
Thou Christ of the tree, give ear,
Spirit who guiding supplies,
Ease for the eye to-night here.

The King of life's name I pray,
The name of the Christ of love,
The Holy Ghost's name I say,
The Triune of rest above.

350. *Mote of Nine Motes*

Mote of nine motes and speck of nine specks,
Awn of nine awns and fleck of nine flecks,
Pain of nine pains and pang of nine pangs,
Leap of the stag over adder's fangs.

O the mote, the speck inside the eye
Whereunto now all my wishes lie,
O King of life, that the eye may see,
O come now to draw it out with me.

All the seven hounds of the Fingal race,
Let them attack the pain in the face;
King of the clouds, with love of the King
'Tis my desire to draw out the thing!

351. *I Sing of the Eye*   South Uist

I sing of the eye so keen and bright,
I sing of the guide-star's shining light,
I sing of the King of all the kings,
I sing of the God of living things,
    Song of King of all the kings,
    Song of God of living things.

I sing of Bride of the golden hair,
I sing of the Mary Maid mild-fair,
I sing of Virtue of all virtue,
I sing of the God of glory true,
    Song of Virtue of virtue,
    Song of God of glory true.

I sing of Peter and Paul a spell,
Of John of love and of Ariel,
I sing of God of all gods there were,
I sing of the God of grace so fair,
    Song of God of gods there were,
    Song of God of grace so fair.

The feast of Mary, and God's high feast,
The feast of the cleric and the priest,
The feast of the Christ, the King of might,
Who stablished the sun with strength for light,
    Feast of Christ, the King of might,
      Who strengthened the sun for light.

352. *The Eye of the Great God*

May the great God's eye, beholding,
God of glory's eye be seeing,
Eye of Virgin's Son be freeing,
Gentle Spirit's eye, enfolding,
Shepherd's aiding to thee showing
  In every time, in every clime,
  Each hour on thee outpouring be
In a gentle, gen'rous flowing.

XXII. FARRIERY

A beast a helpless thing doth stand
Exposed to all disease and pain;
But, King-ordained, the leech's hand
May make it sound and well again.

The cleansing waters by the shore,
The nine wells of the son of Lear,
Come pounding in with breakers' roar
To wash away the microbes clear.

The pure still waters of a well
Brought in name of the Holy Three;
Stream-waters for infection fell;
A knife's clean cut a beast to free.

The widow-woman's single cow,
The stall-cow with her calf beside,
The tethered one with lowered brow,
The ranging herd in all its pride;

O King of life, to each beast give
The healing and the increase best;
Grant thou the power that they may live;
The Highland cattle, be they blest.

353. *The Rough-Throated Heifers*   *Benbecula*

The gulping of gulping heifers' throats,
The gulping hairy ones resound,
The gulping of gulping heifers' notes
Forth from Rueval-top around.

354. *Healing Charm*   *South Uist*

I make for thee the charm of horses' breed,
The charm for cattle, charm for worm at need,
     And for the wiles of bout;

The charm for beast, the charm for wounding pain,
The charm for aching, and the charm for vein,
     And for the bone put out.

Death to thy pang, and to thy worm decay,
Fullness thy flow; if hurt be thine this day,
     To-morrow happy be.

In name of King of life, of Christ of love,
In name of Holy Spirit from above,
     The graceful Trinity.

355. *Udder-Rose*   *Skye*

Thou deathly, deadly, swollen rose,
Leave the cow's udder, the cow white-shanked,
Leave the cow's udder, the cow pied-flanked,
     Leave, leave that swelling, come not close,
     Begone where other swelling grows.

Thou cross-grained rose, obstinate grown,
In the cow's udder thy surly flush,
Leave the cow's udder, the swelling blush,
     Be off to the netherside stone.

To stone I set the rose anigh,
I set the stone on the earth to lie,
Milk I set for the udder's supply,
     I set drink for the kidney dry.

356. Red-Water Charm   *Harris*

I am down on the slopes below,
Abating wrath and anger now,
Charming against red water's flow,
To my lovely glossy black cow.

Milking, milkiness, milk in pail,
For the seething and frothing stream,
For curds and whey, milk without fail,
For butter, for cheese, and for cream.

For heifer calves and cattle seed,
For the rutting and fruitful bull,
For stock of choice and kine to breed,
With a blessing and increase full.

The nine wells of the great sea's son,
May they pour relief on thee now,
Stop thy blood, and let water run,
Cow of cows, thou glossy black cow.

Sea so mighty, waterfall red,
Stop the blood, flow water instead.

357. The Gravel Charm   *South Uist*

I have a charm for the gravel-blood disease,
     For the disease that refuseth to go,
And I have a charm for the red-flood disease,
     For the disease of painful bitter flow.

As runs a river with water cold and clear,
     As grinding by a mill is swiftly done,
O thou who didst ordain the land and sea here,
     Cease now the blood and let the water run.

In name of the Father, and of the Son,
In the Holy Spirit's name, be it done.

358. Chew the Cud South Uist

If the nine mountains' grass thou hast eaten whole,
And the nine hills' grass, and of every nine knoll,
If the nine torrents' water thou hast drunk full,
The nine streams' water, and of every nine pool,
Poor old hairy one of the paunch hard and bound,
Chew now thy cud, my love, chew it round and round;
   Poor old hairy one of the paunch hard and bound,
   Chew now thy cud, my love, chew it round and round.

359. Charm for the Surfeit

The healing that Christ made with his hand
On the poor woman's one cow to light,
A foot on sea and a foot on land,
A foot in the coracle to-night.

Across there are nine and twenty veins
Between the two broad flanks of the cow;
I will pierce the hide and ease the pains
And reduce the surfeit-swelling now.

Thy sickness and thy side-filling pain,
Be they upon the whales of the sea,
Woods and trees, the black beasts of the main,
And on the bears of the mountain be.

The God of life to heal thee I pray,
O Mooer, my quiet kindly friend,
From this day and on each other day
Unto the day when thy life shall end.

360. Bruise Charm Thurso

I have a charm for the limb that is bruised,
I have a charm for the blackening contused,
I have a charm for the matter-stream oozed
        And for running of sore.

I have a charm for disease that is known,
And I have a charm for disease unknown,
I have a charm for disease magic-sown,
      For relief that is sure.

Be there no venom nor moan of complaint,
Be there no blemish nor maggot acquaint,
Upon thy four quarters be there no taint,
      Thou poor beast, fond delight,

That shall not be taken away from thee
With the whine of the north wind blowing free,
With a cold flowing stream cleansingly
      And man's water to-night.

      Bite and drink, gulp and chew;
      If to live, live anew;
      If to live not, away;
      If to come, come to-day;
      If to come not, then stay;
      If to live, live anew,
      If to live not, so do.

361. *The Black Spaul*

Mine is a charm for spaul turning black,
    And a charm for bruise is my prayer,
Mine is a charm for festering's rack,
    And for rotting of skin and hair.

Mine is a charm for disease of side,
    And a haunch-disease charm I know,
Mine is a charm for disease spell-plied,
    And for hissing of water's flow.

If good arising for that so be,
    Better arise for this sev'nfold,
For each complaint that might come to thee,
    And, my love, for each evil told.

    So munch and drink, and gulp and chew,
    If thou wilt live, live on anew;
    If not to live, begone from view!

Teasel to tease for relief,
Comb to comb, and card to card,
Cat to scratch and tear thee hard,
In thy need and in thy grief;

And a yellow hag and sere,
Clawed and purring for thy hide,
Flecking streaks upon thy side,
Moving thy hide-binding here.

In comfort and peacefully,
Full of marrow, sap and meat,
Full of tallow, fat and heat,
Full of pith and full of power,
Flesh and blood and vigour's flower
May I thee beholding see!

Be of God thy healing now,
Of the Being nigh at hand,
Sea's Creator and of land,
Man's Creator and of kine,
The Creator thine and mine,
O thou hide-bound shrivelled cow!

363. *The Living Charm of Saint Bride*

The charm of life from quiet Bride it went
To Patrick, noble one of beauty, sent
For hurt, for worm, for throat of guiping ring,
For rose, for swelling, for the kidneys' spring,
For wound, for fester, mange, and ulcer's pains,
For snake, for poison, for distempered veins;
But be it for thy virtue and thy good
Upon thy cattle and thy young o'erstood;
If up thou hast it 'twixt the ear-tips twain,
If 'twixt twin bases of thy soles again,
Then may it downward ebb away from thee
As ebbs away the ocean's mighty sea,

Into the great whale's belly gaping wide,
Into the very beasts themselves inside,
Until one from another these divide;
As Jesus for the people once did feel,
As then of nature, 'tis in him to heal
Each one of these distresses that are real.

XXXIII. THE CALENDAR

The guiser bands with a tremendous din
Climb round the house to bring the New Year in,
    With stick and hide they beat outside,
They circle around with their fuming skin
And blessing give to all the house within.

The winter-blast winds, the winds of the spring,
The Wolf to freeze, and the Whistle to sing,
    The Garron-steed gallops indeed,
The rage-Hag scurries, the Broom sweeps awing
While Bride with her finger draws the sting.

The knoll-fire is kindled on Beltane Day,
Neid-fire on townland hearths the year to stay;
    All cattle-stock and every flock
Lustrated stand and start to move away
To summer shieling in procession gay.

Bannock and horse are for Michaelmastide,
The circuiting made and the bare-backed ride,
    Ponies apace in strand-long race,
The carrots for gifts the lasses provide,
And the evening ball is the dancers' pride.

The Lord's Day is kept as a day of rest,
The weekdays all observed as each is best,
    And God will keep, awake, asleep,
With safety he will each and all invest,
And through the years the household shall be blest.

364. The New Year
Skye, North Uist and elsewhere

God bless to me the new day that is here,
Nor ever yet before designed for me;
It is to bless thy countenance so dear
This time, O God, thou givest me to see.

O bless thou unto me my seeing eye,
And mine eye bless each one that it doth see;
My neighbour I will bless who liveth nigh,
My neighbour give his blessing unto me.

O God, give me a heart of cleanliness,
Nor be I from thy watching eye offstood;
And unto me my wife and children bless,
Bless unto me my stock and livelihood.

365. The Hogmanay Bag
North Uist

Bag's Hogmanay, bag's New Year's Day,
Beat the hide, beat its side.
Bag's Hogmanay, bag's New Year's Day,
Beat the skin, beat it thin.
Bag's Hogmanay, bag's New Year's Day,
Down with it! up with it! beat away.
Bag's Hogmanay, bag's New Year's Day,
Down with it! up with it! beat in play.
Bag's Hogmanay, bag's New Year's Day.

366. Hogmanay Carol
Barra and Benbecula

Now since we have come this country way
To renew to you the Hogmanay,
Time will not let us tell it to you,
For it was a thing our fathers knew.

The wall of the house I now ascend,
To the door again I now descend,
I will sing my song becoming well,
Politely, slowly, mindfully tell.

305

In my pocket the Hogmanay skin,
Presently from it smoke will begin;
And everyone who shall take its smell
Shall be for ever healthy and well.

Here in the house-man's hand it goes,
Into the hearth he will place its nose;
Round the children sunwise he will go,
And seven times round the housewife so.

The housewife deserves it well to-day,
Her hand to dispense the Hogmanay,
Her hand to bestow butter and cheese,
The open hand and generous, please.

But since a drought has come on the land,
We do not hope for rarities grand;
Of summer's blooming a little dish
To go with the bread is what we wish.

But if so be there is no good cheer,
By your good leave detain us not here;
I am God's Son's gillie at the door,
Rise thyself, open to me therefore.
   Hogmanay, Hogmanay here once more!

367. *Hogmanay Night*   *Pabbay of Harris*

We are come to your door to stay, Ma'am,
To be better ere we away, Ma'am,
To all generous dames to say, Ma'am,
That to-morrow is New Year's Day, Ma'am.

O may God protect the house and bless,
Each stone, and rafter, and beam no less,
Each food, and drink, and the clothes in press,
Ever here be health and happiness.

O but if you turn us from the door,
All this you must hear from us before:

God's malison and of Hogmanay,
Wailing buzzard's harm on you to stay,
May raven and hen-harrier prey,
Sly fox and eagle your harm to-day.

Wild-dog and wild-cat-harm on you be,
Harm of boar, of badger may you see,
Of the hipped bear, of wolf of the scree,
Harm of the marten foul of the tree.

368. *The Coming of Spring*

A month of the Wolf, the wind greedy to kill,
Nine days of the Garron that gallops away,
A week of the Whistle-wind, piping and shrill,
A week of the Hag-breeze, when calmer the day,
Three days of the Broom-wind that sweeps with a will,
And then up with the Spring that is come to stay!

369. *The Birth of Spring*

On her Feast Day Saint Bride bending low
A finger dipped in the river-flow;
Off the cold-hatching mother did go;
   O feast of Saint Bride, feast of the maid,
   White-fingered Bride of the music played.

Bride warms with her hand, Mary with toe,
Though Patrick a cold stone doth bestow;
High sad-gillie notes Bride's page doth throw;
   O feast of Saint Bride, feast of the maid,
   White-fingered Bride of the music played.

On Saint Patrick's Day Bride bending low
Both her hands bathed in the river-flow;
Off the cold-bearing mother did go;
   The Night of Saint Bride supper and light,
   But sleep and light for Saint Patrick's Night.

As far as the wind indoors shall blow
On Saint Bride's Day, by Saint Patrick's so
In by the door shall enter the snow;
   The Night of Saint Bride supper and light,
   But sleep and light for Saint Patrick's Night.

On Saint Bride's Day o'er the moorland go
The flocks to the counting, while below
Garrons are led to the fields they know;
   O feast of Saint Bride, feast of the maid,
   White-fingered Bride of the music played.

On Saint Bride's Day the nests start to grow,
The building ravens fly to and fro,
And wheeling rooks activity show;
   O feast of Saint Bride, feast of the maid,
   White-fingered Bride of the music played.

370. *The May-Day Blessing*   *South Uist*

Bless, O Threefold true, unstinting-handed One,
Myself, my wife, children, or daughter or son,
My tender ones, ahead their mother adored,
On smooth fragrant field, on mountain shieling sward,
   On the fragrant field and mountain shieling sward.

Each thing in my dwelling, each thing that is mine,
Each flock and corn, and each crop and herd of kine,
From the Hallow Eve to Eve of Beltane Day,
With blessing gentle, good progress for the way,
From sea to sea, and mouth where stream-waters flow,
From wave to wave, and foot where fall-waters go,
   Sea to sea, wave to wave, and where waters go.

Take hold the Persons Three of all in my store,
My shielding aright be the Trinity sure,
To satisfy my soul the words of Saint Paul,
And 'neath thy glory's wing shield my dear ones all,
   Beneath thy glory's wing shield my dear ones all.

Give blessing to each thing and the persons all,
Who by my side compose this my household small;
With the power of love the cross of Christ at hand,
Till we come to see the happy joyful land,
   Until we behold the happy joyful land.

The hour when from the stall the cattle-stock wend,
The hour when from the sheepfold the flock I send,
The hour when the goats the mist-mountain ascend,
The Trinity's might be on their track to tend,
   The strong Trinity upon their track to tend.

Thou Being who at the first didst create me,
Hearken and attend me when I bend the knee,
Morning and evening as for me it is right,
O God of all living things, in thine own sight,
  Great God of all living things, in thine own sight.

371. *May-Day Prayer*   *Benbecula*

Mary, mother of saints and holiness,
Our calves in the stall and our litters bless;
Let no hurt or hatred come to us near,
Drive all the ways of wicked men from here.

Each Monday and each Tuesday watch with care
The calves in the stall, the queys that pair;
Take us along from the hill to the sea,
The flocks and the lambs thy gathering be.

Each Wednesday and each Thursday with them be,
Ever about them thy hand graciously;
The cattle tend down to the milking-floor,
Tend the flocks down to the shieling-fold door.

Each Friday, O Saint, be thou at their head,
The sheep from the mountain-face to be led,
With the little lambs innocent behind,
With God's encompassing compassing bind.

Be with them each Saturday as before,
Bring goats and young to a sheltering door,
Every kid and goat to the sea-lapped shore,
From the Rock of Eager towering high,
Where around its top the green cresses lie.

Might of the Triune our shield in distress,
The paschal Christ's might with his peace to bless,
Spirit's might, Healer of salvation's state,
The gracious King's might, precious Father great.

Might of Saint Mary, Saint Michael, Saint Bride,
The might of the twelve Apostles beside,
And of each saint who after them arose
And who earned the kingdom of God's repose.

309

Bless us ourselves, the children that we own,
Our generations bless that shall be sown,
Bless the sire who gave unto us our name,
And bless her, O God, from whose womb we came.

Each holiness, each blessing, and each power,
Each time be yielded to us and each hour,
In the name above of the Holy Three,
Father, Son, Spirit everlastingly.

The cross of Christ be our shield down to-day,
The cross of Christ our shield up on our way,
The cross of Christ round be our shield and stay,
Taking at our hands the blessing of May,
    At our hands blessing of the Beltane Day.

372. *The Shieling-Procession* *Barra*

White-horsed Michael of the heavenly war,
Who the Dragon of blood's homage inbore,
For love of God, for MacMary's great woe,
Spread thy wing o'er us, shield all as we go,
    Spread thy wing over us, shield as we go.

White-Lambed Mother, lovely Mary serene,
Aid us, pure Virgin, nobility's Queen,
And flock-shepherdess, O beautiful Bride,
Safeguard our cattle, both round by our side,
    Safeguard our cattle, together beside.

White-beached Columba, so friendly, benign,
In name of Father, Son, Spirit divine,
Through the Trinity, Three-in-One to fend,
Our own selves protect, our procession tend,
    Ourselves protect, our whole procession tend.

White-beamed Father, Son, Holy Spirit bright,
Be the Three-in-One with us day and night,
On the sandy plain, on the hill-ridge led,
Three-in-One with us, guide-hand on our head,
    Three-in-One our helmet-hand round the head.

White-sprayed Father, Son, Holy Spirit light,
Thou Three-in-One be with us day and night,
On the wave-crest as on the hill-side sped,
Our Mother with us, her hand 'neath our head,
    Borne on the wave as on the hill-side sped,
    Our Mother with us, hand beneath our head.

373. *Michaelmas-Cake*   *Benbecula*

    From my creels each kind of grain
I mix and bake and make the cake,
The name of God the Son to take
    Who gave growth and swelling rain.

    Milk and eggs and butter too,
The produce good of flock and earth,
That in our land there be no dearth,
    Nor at home the season through.

    In my loving Michael's name,
Who unto us did leave the power,
With Mary Mother's blessing dower,
    And of God's unblemished Lamb.

    At thy footstool set us low,
Round us thine own covering be,
Devil, demon, duress to flee,
    O defend, preserve us so.

    Our land's produce sacred be,
Prosperity and peace, o bring,
In the name of the Father King,
    Name of loved apostles three.

    Dandelion, foxglove spire,
Butterwort, greens, smooth garlic in,
With triple ribworts' grassy skin,
    And marigold yellowfire.

The beast-plant grey culled for cake,
The seven-pronged seven times due,
The ruddy heath, the mountain yew,
    And red madder do I take.

Water last upon them all,
In precious name of God's own Son,
In Mary's name, the gen'rous one,
    And on Patrick's name I call.

When we sit down at the board
Together to partake of food,
I sprinkle in the name of God,
    On the children all 'tis poured.

374. *Hymn of the Lord's Day*   *South Uist*

The hymn of the Lord's Day, O God so white,
The truth for ever 'neath Christ and his might.

Upon the Lord's Day was Saint Mary born,
Mother of Christ, hair of gold-yellow corn;
Upon the Lord's Day the Lord Christ was born
As an honour to men that winter's morn.

Sunday the Lord's Day is the seventh day,
On it God ordained the taking of rest,
The life everlasting with us to stay,
Not using ox or man at his behest,
Nor any creature at Mary's request;
No threads of silk or satin to be spun,
No sewing, no embroidering at all,
No sowing seed, harrowing, reaping done,
No rowing, games, fishing to befall,
No going forth into the hunting hill,
Nor any thorn-plashing on the Lord's Day,
No byre-scouring, no threshing for the mill,
No fire for kiln, no baking in the clay,
For God ordained a rest on the Lord's Day.

Whosoever would keep the Lord's Day best,
Quiet and long for him the day of rest,
From the Saturday setting of the sun,
Until Monday sunrise has begun.

Good recompense therefrom he will obtain,
Produce in the wake of the plough and rain,
Fish in pure salt-water of whiteness-gleam,
Fish excelling in watersmeet and stream.

The Lord's Day water sweet as honey-mead,
To him that drinketh refreshment indeed,
Consolation therefrom to him will go
From every affliction and every woe.

Hill river-water is full fresh to taste,
E'er down to Jordan wandering in haste,
Right well did it keep its worth on its way
Though great was its flood upon the Lord's Day:
But though pure its water never a drop
Shall run in the Red Sea channel and stop.

Too soon is the weeping of the Lord's Day,
And she who does it in time is astray,
Early on Monday let a woman weep,
But never a tear the Lord's Day to keep.

Too soon is the kindling of the Lord's Day,
In the pool it feebly smoulders away,
Although off in ashes should fall its head,
It would until Monday lie asleep dead.
For the wood of the Lord's Day now, ah me!
May lie in the channel of the Red Sea,
And although the head should tumble off red
It would be till Monday asleep and dead.
About the mid-day of the Monday's noon,
The wood will arise and will be too soon,
And by the great flood that without may swell
Will haste the tale of my trouble to tell.
To gather lamb, sheep, kid or goat no need
As a sacrifice to the King indeed.
Now is the time for the burning it due,
Unheeding the noise of a stranger's view,
Or of people blind with gossiping new.

'Tis lawful to save corn high on a hill,
Physician to bring to one sorely ill,
A cow to the mighty herd-bull to send,
With stray beast to go to the cattle penned.

313

Be it far, be it near the step to fare,
Each creature alive is in need of care;
To let a boat forth under sail from the land,
To her unacquaintance on a far strand.

And he who my hymn would think on and pray,
Who each Monday evening my hymn would say,
Upon his head Saint Michael's luck would dwell,
Nor ever would he see the straits of hell.
Let me not leave behind· me any trace,
To talk of my new covenant a space.

375. Sunday Hymn   *Barra*

On God's holy Sunday do thou mind
    To give thine heart to all mankind,
Love to father and mother to bring,
    More than other person or thing.

Despise not the weak or poor at all,
    Do thou not covet large or small,
For semblance of evil make no place,
    Give thou ne'er nor merit disgrace.

The ten commandments God-given of old
    Con and know early, proven gold,
Direct in the King of life believe,
    Idol-worship behind thee leave.

To thine own chieftain be clansman true,
    To thine own chief the service due,
True to thyself with a firm belief,
    True through each mood to thy High Chief.

On no man pass the sentence malign,
    Lest malison in turn be thine;
Take the step of God's Anointed-One,
    Journey by sea or land begun,
        The very step of God's own Son.

XXXIV. CLOTHING

The wool is carded, washed and dyed,
    And ready for the loom;
The ember heat and reeking peat
Pervade and cense the house inside,
    Wall-shadows in the gloom.

The threads of yellow, blue and green,
    The black, the red, the white,
By fingers deft in warp and weft
A criss-cross sett are laid between
    To form the cloth aright.

The fulling at the waulking-frame,
    The maidens all a-row
On either side sit well supplied
With love-songs ready to exclaim
    In movement to and fro.

God bless the wheel, the spinning hand,
    God bless the weaving through,
God bless the songs of rights and wrongs,
God bless the clothing of the land,
    The maker, wearer too.

376. *The Warping*   *North Uist*

Thursday excelling,
For warp and fulling,
Ten fifteens telling
    For pulling.

Finest blue thread-strand,
Two white surround it,
Madder with red band
    To bound it.

Warp even spreading,
God, give me blessing,
All in my steading
    Possessing.

Michael, might-sending,
Mary fair, over,
Christ, Shepherd-drover,
Blessing befriending
    Unending.

To each one resting,
God and Christ naming,
Spirit, investing
Peace from molesting,
    Grace flaming.

Like dew providing
Wise Lady-bearing,
The High King's guiding
    Her caring.

Evil repressing,
Eye and wish fended,
Warp and woof blessing,
    Thread tended.

Thine arm enfolding
Each fulling maiden,
In need her holding
    And aiding.

As once on Mary
Virtues did shower,
The High King's glory
    My dower.

God, to each living
Giving the growing,
Wool to us giving,
    Grass sowing.

Bless the flock grazing,
Bleating lambs singing,
Young for us raising,
    Herds bringing.

Wool for us bearing,
Milk appetising,
Clothes for our wearing
    At rising.

377. *The Loom*   *Benbecula*

Thrums and odds of thread they all must go,
My hand never kept them nor will keep;
All colours of the shower's arching bow
'Neath the cross-stretch through my fingers sweep,

Red and madder, white and black they go,
Green, dark grey, and scarlet in a row,
Colour of the sheep, and roan, and blue,
No ends wanting to the clothing due.

Calm Bride I pray, open-handed, kind,
Mary I pray, mild, the loving so,
The Christ I pray, Jesu of mankind,
That alone to death I may not go,
    That alone to death I may not go.

378. *The Sett* *Benbecula*

The black go by the white thread,
The white go by the black led.
The green go in between red,
The red between the black thread.

The black go in between red,
The red between the white thread,
The white between the green led,
The green between the white thread.

The white between the blue thread,
The blue between the bright red,
The blue, the scarlet-hue thread,
The scarlet true the due thread.

The scarlet to the blue thread,
The blue to scarlet-hue wed,
The scarlet to the black led,
The black unto the bright red.

A thread go to the threads two,
Of colours two, good and true,
The two the threads of black due,
The one the thread of white through,

    Seven threads to five be,
    And five be unto three,
    Three to two, two to one,
    In every border done.

379. *Loom Blessing*   *Benbecula*

My Chief of generous heroes, bless
My loom and all things near to me,
Bless me in all my busy-ness,
Keep me for life safe-dear to thee.

From every brownie and banshee,
From every evil wish and grief,
Being of aid, be aiding me,
While in this land of life I live.

In Mary's name, mild wondrous maid,
In just Columba's, who achieves,
My four-post loom keep holy laid,
Till my hand Monday ready weaves.

The pedals, to-fro shuttle, slay,
The reels, the warp, the cogs that wind,
The cloth-beam, thread-beam of array,
The thrum-ends and the thread-ply twined,

Each web of black, and pale, and white,
Of roan, and dun, and check, and red,
On each spot let thy blessing light,
Each shuttle going 'neath the thread.

And so my loom unharmed shall go,
Till Monday I arise from rest;
Mary mild-white her love shall show,
No hindrance that I shall not best.

380. *Prince Morag*

With a ho Mòrag,
Ho ro na ho ro sure-ag,
And a ho Mòrag.

Winsome Morag and curled your hair,
'Tis my intent to speak you fair.

With a ho Mòrag,
Ho ro na ho ro sure-ag,
And a ho Mòrag.

319

Y

If you are gone beyond the sea,
Hasten you homeward back to me.

With a ho Mòrag,
Ho ro na ho ro sure-ag,
And a ho Mòrag.

Mind, bring the troops of fairy-head,
Strong to full the cloth that is red.

With a ho Mòrag,
Ho ro na ho ro sure-ag,
And a ho Mòrag.

381. *Smoothing the Cloth*

O wear the cloth till the threads be bare,
The cloth until tattered do thou wear,
With food and music the wearing be
In every way we would wish for thee;

In health and modesty, friends and love,
In the grace of the Father above,
In the grace of the Son unto thee,
In the grace of the Spirit Holy,
And in the grace of creation's Three.

382. *Cloth-Folding Blessing*   Morvern

Good is the rune for me to say,
Descending with the glen away;
Rune one, rune two, I hold the cloth,
Rune three, rune four, and rolled the cloth,
Rune five, rune six, I fold the cloth,
Rune seven, half, half, all told the cloth.

No hurt for him who wears this garb,
Never the tearing of the barb;
In scene of fight or battlefield,
The Lord protecting him with shield,
  In scene of fight or battlefield,
  The Lord protecting him with shield.

No second-cloth, no begging's wear,
Nor is it priest's or cleric's share.

Green cresses picked, stone overhead,
A gift to woman, word unsaid;
Deer-shank in head of herring-fish,
In speckled salmon's fin-tail swish.

383. *The Consecration of the Cloth*   *Morvern*

My sun-turn is made
In the Father's aid.

My sun-turn is made
In God the Son's aid.

My sun-turn is made
In the Spirit's aid.

And each sun-turn made
In God the Three's aid,
And each turn it take
For God the Three's sake.
   And each sun-turn made
   In God the Three's aid.

384. *The Gaelic Shoe*

One awl one last, stitches two,
Two awls two lasts, stitches through,
Three awls three lasts, stitches six,
Four awls four lasts, stitches fix,
Five awls five lasts, stitches ten,
Six awls six lasts, stitch again,
Seven awls seven lasts, stitch between,
Eight awls eight lasts, stitches clean,
Nine awls nine lasts, stitch eighteen;

Awl, last, tallow, waxen thong,
Thrust through heel hen-feather-prong,
Stitches eighteen up from toe
Down to heel right round a row
In the Gaelic shoe they go.

Bonnet and feather with tartan and plaid,
Bonnet and feather with tartan and plaid,
Bonnet and feather with tartan and plaid,
The Clans of the Gael are swingingly clad.

See it and see it and see yet it cheers!
See it and see it and see yet it cheers!
See it and see yet its virtue appears,
The white and red ribbons round by thine ears!

XXXV. SAINT KILDA POEMS

Turf-green carpet to cliff-drop sheer
Slopes clett-studded 'neath mist-caps peer,
    Isle of the well
    And distance spell,
Farthest of all the Hebrides
    Girt by the seas,
    Nor stormless these.

Steeps with myriad gannets teem,
Bloom-white the settled fulmars gleam,
    Guillemots grace
    The waters' face,
Puffins unwise tunnel and fly,
    Rising on high
    Razorbills cry.

Pathless and straight tower the stacks
Lifting inhospitable backs
    Where on each ledge
    And rock-fall edge
Kittiwakes are in rows arrayed
    And nests are made
    And eggs are laid.

Sea-pink and primrose raise a head;
The wren within the wall-crack bred
    Doth peep forth shy
    Where meadows lie;
The sheep graze up where the winds soar
    Above the roar
    Of sea-wave floor.

Here the men of the ocean dwell,
Hemmed by the never-ceasing swell,
    Cliff-rockers they,
    The birds their prey,
An angel-watch'd mariner race,
    Born to the place,
    Full of God's grace.

386. God of the Moon

St Kilda

God of the moon and God of the sun,
God of the sphere and the stars each one,
God of the waters, the land, the skies,
God who the King of promise supplies,

It was Mary mild who kneeling went,
The King of life to her breast was sent,
The darkness and tears were set behind,
Up early the star of guiding shined.

It lighted the earth, lighted the place,
Lighted the doldrum and current race,
All grief was laid and all joy was raised,
And music with harp and pedal praised.

387. Saint Kilda Duet

St Kilda

Away bent spade, straight spade away from me,
Every goat and sheep and lamb away flee;
Up with my rope now, and up with my snare,—
I have heard the gannet on the sea there!

Thanks to the Being, the gannets are here,
And the great birds along with them are near;
Dark maid dusky dark, a cow in the stall!
A brown cow, a brown cow, a lovely brown cow,
A brown cow, my love, that would milk the milk all,
Ho ro ru ra ree, a playful maid thou,
Dark maid dusky dark, a cow in the stall!
The birds are coming, I hear their song-call!

Truly my sweetheart is the herdsman sweet
Who would threaten the staff and would not beat!
Dark maid dusky dark, a cow in the stall!
A brown cow, a brown cow, a lovely brown cow,
A brown cow, my love, that would milk the milk all,
Ho ro ru ra ree, a playful maid thou,
Dark maid dusky dark, a cow in the stall!
The birds are coming, I hear their song-call!

Mary, my dear love is the maid so meet,
Though dark be her locks her body smells sweet!
Dark maid dusky dark, a cow in the stall!
A brown cow, a brown cow, a lovely brown cow,
A brown cow, my love, that would milk the milk all,
Ho ro ru ra ree, a playful maid thou,
Dark maid dusky dark, a cow in the stall!
The birds are coming, I hear their song-call!

Thou art my pretty one, my lover true,
Fulmar honey-sweet from thee first I knew!
Dark maid dusky dark, a cow in the stall!
A brown cow, a brown cow, a lovely brown cow,
A brown cow, my love, that would milk the milk all,
Ho ro ru ra ree, a playful maid thou,
Dark maid dusky dark, a cow in the stall!
The birds are coming, I hear their song-call!

My turtle-dove thou, my mavis of the air,
Thou my music-harp in the morning fair!
Dark maid dusky dark, a cow in the stall!
A brown cow, a brown cow, a lovely brown cow,
A brown cow, my love, that would milk the milk all,
Ho ro ru ra ree, a playful maid thou,
Dark maid dusky dark, a cow in the stall!
The birds are coming, I hear their song-call!

My treasure thou art, my huntsman, my dear;
Gannet and auk from thee yesterday here.
Dark maid dusky dark, a cow in the stall!
A brown cow, a brown cow, a lovely brown cow,
A brown cow, my love, that would milk the milk all,
Ho ro ru ra ree, a playful maid thou,
Dark maid dusky dark, a cow in the stall!
The birds are coming, I hear their song-call!

When thou wast but a child my love I gave,
Love unabating till I lie in grave.
Dark maid dusky dark, a cow in the stall!
A brown cow, a brown cow, a lovely brown cow,
A brown cow, my love, that would milk the milk all,
Ho ro ru ra ree, a playful maid thou,
Dark maid dusky dark, a cow in the stall!
The birds are coming, I hear their song-call!

My hero thou, thou my shark of the sea,
Guillemot of ring, puffin-bird from thee.
Dark maid dusky dark, a cow in the stall!
A brown cow, a brown cow, a lovely brown cow,
A brown cow, my love, that would milk the milk all,
Ho ro ru ra ree, a playful maid thou,
Dark maid dusky dark, a cow in the stall!
The birds are coming, I hear their song-call!

Thou eye-twinkle mine and delight's heart-fire,
In the mountain of mist my singing lyre.
Dark maid dusky dark, a cow in the stall!
A brown cow, a brown cow, a lovely brown cow,
A brown cow, my love, that would milk the milk all,
Ho ro ru ra ree, a playful maid thou,
Dark maid dusky dark, a cow in the stall!
The birds are coming, I hear their song-call!

The Being to keep, the Creator to aid,
Behind thy rope the Holy Spirit laid!
Dark maid dusky dark, a cow in the stall!
A brown cow, a brown cow, a lovely brown cow,
A brown cow, my love, that would milk the milk all,
Ho ro ru ra ree, a playful maid thou,
Dark maid dusky dark, a cow in the stall!
The birds are coming, I hear their song-call!

388. *And O for the Ocean Calm*   *St Kilda*

And o for the calm of the ocean sea,
And o for the sailor, bonnie is he,
And o for the calm of the ocean sea!

I would make the white cloth, thine let it be,
Good as the thatch-rope and strong be the thread,
And o for the calm of the ocean sea!

Quill-sewn thy lace-brogue would be made by me,
Beloved of men and pressing to be wed,
And o for the calm of the ocean sea!

I would give the precious anchor to thee,
With forefathers' gear from grandfather's shed,
And o for the calm of the ocean sea!

Of the bird is my love the taker bred,
Who earliest crosses the misty sea,
And o for the calm of the ocean sea!

The sailor my love of the waves aspread,
And great the joy of his brow unto me,
And o for the calm of the ocean sea!

389. *The Earl from Islay*   *St Kilda*

Ian Macgillies was once my dear,
   Time and times he was wiling me,
But since the Earl from Islay is here
   He will cease beguiling me.

390. *The Cliff-Crest*   *St Kilda*

It were no grief that my laddie and I
Were astride of the Gādag Cliff-top high,
Would we were both there and under my eye
His well-founded tackle complete did lie.

391. *The Orphans*   *St Kilda*

Thou Being of great glory kind,
That the young orphan seed may live,
No prop, no cleft-rock theirs behind,
Thy cherishing and nurture give.

392. *No Crew of Landsmen*   *St Kilda*

It was not any landsmen's crew,
On Wednesday the ferry they crossed:
'Tis tidings of disaster true
   If you be lost.

What has kept you so long from me?
O does the sudden wind prevail?
For the high breakers of the sea
      Set you not sail?

It is an empty journey done
That took the noble man away,
From me, from Donald our one son
      Gone in a day.

My son is gone, my brothers three,
My mother's sister's only son,
And, hardest tale that comes to me,
      My husband gone.

What makes me draw the ashes out
And take a while at digging ground
Is that the men are hence without
      Word of them sound.

On the floor of the glen I sit,
Without smile or sport I am left;
My eyes are wet, oft tears are writ
      For the men reft.

393. *The Swan-Wort of Saint John*   *St Kilda*

O yellow swan, wort of Saint John,
Whoe'er has thee has my envy,
I pluck thee with my right-hand's hold,
And with my left I take and keep,
Who findeth thee in cattle fold,
Shall never want for kine or sheep.

XXXVI. TRAVELLING

Slow is the step of the going,
  Of the riding, or the rowing
To the glens and bens that are strange,
Or the exile's isles of exchange,
  The horizons of unknowing.

Swift is the step of returning
  With a heart brimming of burning
To the door and floor that is known,
Where the firelight brightness is shown,
  Where the loving needs no learning.

Sure is the step of wayfaring
  For those of the club-moss wearing,
And where bound and sound from all harm
A Gospel-text next to the arm
  For minch and sea gives the daring.

Sad is the step of migrating,
  Weary the storm unabating,
Long the way and day of no end,
But those afraid, strayed God befriend,
  God shorten the anxious waiting.

Sweet is the step of the sending
  To shepherd, save the offending,
To outseek the weak and the spent
In the despair where they repent,
  To guide when mist is descending.

Strong is the step of the ranger
  When God protects from the danger,
Who goes forth or north, east, south, west,
With naught to fear near, and he blest
  Though to the way he be stranger.

Safe is the step of ascending,
Of the path of God's intending,
Of the tossing, crossing of sound,
Of passhead drear sheer to the ground,
The highway of God unending.

394. *The Roadmaker*

God be shielding thee by each dropping sheer,
God make every pass an opening appear,
God make to thee each road a highway clear,
  And may he take thee in the clasp
  Of his own two hands' grasp.

395. *Travelling Prayer*   *Baleshare of North Uist*

Alive be all my mouth-speech,
  In what I say be sense,
Bloom-cherry on my lips each,
  Till I come back from hence.

Christ Jesu's love tide-welling
  Fill every heart for me,
Christ Jesu's love tide-welling
  My fill for each one be.

By fells, by forests shading,
  By long lone slopes afield,
Fair Mary white still aiding,
  Good Shepherd my foot-shield,
Fair Mary white mine aiding,
  Jesu good Shepherd shield.

396. *Afloat and Afield*

I pray to God my petition and rite,
To Mary's Son, to the Spirit of right,
In distress to assist afloat, afield:
The Three to give succour, the Three to shield,
The Three to watch me by day and by night.

God and Jesus and the Spirit so pure,
Possess me, and shield me, assist me sure,
Order my path and before my soul go
In hollow, on hill, and on plain below,
Afloat, afield, the assisting Three sure.

God and Jesus, Holy Spirit of right,
Give shielding and saving to me in might,
As Three and as One, the great Trinity,
By my back, by my side, and by my knee,
As through the drear world-storm my steps alight.

397. *The Journey Blessing*   *Benbecula*

O God, bless to me
The earth beneath my toe,
O God, bless to me
The path whereon I go;
O God, bless to me
The prayer of my desire to know;
O thou timeless Moon of moons the best,
Bless thou to me my rest.

The thing bless to me
Wherein my hope is met,
The thing bless to me
Which my love longs to get;
The thing bless to me
Whereon my every faith is set;
O King of kings, do thou sanctify,
Bless thou to me mine eye!

398. *Finding the Club-Moss*

O man so merrily journeying on,
To you nor hurt nor mishap shall arise
Nor in sunshine nor in the darkness gone
If the club-moss on your journey but lies.

399. *The Gospel of the God of Life*   *Coll*

The Gospel of the God of life sufficed
To shelter thee, aid with its word;
Yea, Gospel of belovéd Jesus Christ,
The holy Gospel of the Lord;

To keep thee from all malice and backbite,
From all disaster, harming pain;
To keep thee from all jealousy and spite,
From evil eye and piercing bane.

Thou shalt journey to, thou shalt journey fro,
Thou shalt journey headland and mound,
Thou shalt journey down, upwards thou shalt go,
Thou shalt journey ocean and sound.

Christ himself is shepherd o'er thee to stand,
Enfolding thee on every side;
He will not forsake thee or foot or hand,
Nor let evil nigh thee abide.

400. *Christ's Gospel*   *Tiree*

The keeping of Christ about thee I lay,
And the guarding of God with thee I lay,
To possess thee, and to shield thee alway
From drowning, from danger, from loss to pay,
From drowning, from danger, from loss to pay.

The Gospel of God so gracious I bring,
From thy head-top to thy foot covering;
The Gospel of Christ, our salvation's King,
To thy body be a plaid-wrapping thing,
To thy body be a plaid-wrapping thing.

O be thou not drowned when out on the sea,
Be thou not mourned when on land wand'ring free,
Nor ever a man thy vanquisher be,
Nor ever a woman to ruin thee,
Nor ever a woman to ruin thee!

401. *Protection Charm*

Unto God thou shalt be to take,
And God shall be taking to thee,
Thy two feet surrounding to make,
His two hands round thy head to be.

335

z

Amidst holly or bramble tree
A thick mighty oak thou dost stand;
A safe rock thou art in the sea,
A fortress thou art on the land.

Michael's buckler round thee to veil,
Christ's shelter is o'er fore and aft,
And Columba's coat of fine mail
Gives thee shielding from fairy shaft.

Charm against birds' call of the sheer,
Against the prey-birds on the wing,
Against the world's muddying here,
Against the yon-world's evil thing.

Turned back to the woman on knee,
To the woman who vents her spleen,
To the woman whose eye doth see,
To the woman with envy green;

To the woman herding her kine,
To the woman by her cows' young,
The woman at flocks' tether-line,
Till it reach her heart-muscles strung.

To the woman frowning too bold,
The woman who gives slander name,
To the woman out uncontrolled
Till she reach the place whence she came.

Each woman of spleen, envy filled,
Who sunders her blood, flesh and gore,
Spleen and scratch on herself be spilled,
From now till the end evermore.

402. *Fear by Night*

God before me, God behind,
God above me, God below;
On the path of God I wind,
God upon my track doth go.

Who is there upon the shore?
Who is there upon the wave?
Who is there on sea-swell roar?
Who is there by door-post stave?
Who along with us doth stand?
God and Lord on either hand.

I am here abroad, without,
I am here in want, in need,
I am here in pain, in doubt,
I am here in straits indeed,
I am here alone, afraid,
O God, grant to me thine aid.

403. *By Upland and Brae*

On every steep to thee God's shielding shade,
On every climb to thee may Christ give aid,
On every rise the Spirit's filling made,
Thy way by upland or by plainland braeed.

404. *A Mother's Blessing*   *Benbecula*

The great God between your two shoulders be,
Your defence for going and coming he,
Be near to your heart the MacMary-Maid,
And the perfect Spirit pour you his aid—
   O, the perfect Spirit pouring his aid!
Tascal, Torquil, Una and Hugh,
All light and health be unto you.

405. *The Mother's Farewell*

The blessing of God, be it thine,
The blessing of Christ, be it thine,
The blessing of Spirit be thine,
On thy children be it to shine,
On thee and thy children to shine.

The peace of God, may it be thine,
The peace of Christ, may it be thine,
The peace of the Spirit be thine,
Thy whole span of life to refine,
All thy days and life to refine.

Shield of God in the pass be thine,
Aid of Christ in the gorge be thine,
Spirit-water in stream be thine,
Every going thou dost design,
A land or an ocean design.

The Father eternal's shield thine,
Upon his own lit altar-shrine;
The Father's shield always be thine,
Eternal from his altar-shrine
Lit up by gold taperflame-shine.

406. *Mother Blessing*

Where you bring the crown of your head,
Where you bring your brow overspread,
O strength therein be to you shed,
Great grace to you the pow'rs there bred;
  O strength therein be to you shed,
  Grace be to you the pow'rs there bred.

Long life be yours in your down-lay,
Long life arise at morning ray,
Long life be yours by night and day,
Good to my dear be heav'n for aye;
  Long life be yours by night and day,
  Good to my dear be heav'n for aye.

God's face be to your countenance,
Christ's face the kindly you enhance,
Spirit's face, holy influence,
Each hour be your safe sustenance,
In danger, sorrow, your joyance;
  Each hour be your safe sustenance,
  In danger, in sorrow, joyance.

407. A Clanranald Farewell South Uist

The Michael kind-white, strong-white, red-white, beside thee,
    Preserve, protect, and provide thee,
With the might of his hand, with the point of his blade,
    'Neath his shimmering shield's sure shade.

408. By Mountain and Glen and Plain

The King to shield you in the glen,
The Christ to aid you on the ben,
Spirit to bathe you on the brae,
Hollow, or hill, or plain your way,
Be glen, or ben, or plain your way.

XXXVII. JUSTICE

To a place where triple waters meet
The suppliant goes with solemn feet,
    With his two hands he bathes his face
As the sunrise-beams spread ninefold grace,
        The sunrise-beams of grace.

Long days ago when "under the wood"
The Virgin she gave the pureness good,
    Washing in milk the Jesus white,
The innocence of the Egypt-flight.
        The innocence of flight.

O God, give the strength, the force to speech,
O God, give the love to all, to each.
    God, give the love returning back,
O God, supply each suppliant lack,
        The poor suppliant's lack.

Dark and strange is the town over there,
And dark the looks that the people wear,
    The swan is white, the oath is white,
A queen o'er all she prevails aright,
        Queen prevailing aright.

In the name of God the way is clear,
As horse's strength and as cautious deer,
    As subtle serpent, royal king,
The gifts of God all success shall bring,
        God's gifts success to bring.

Ingoing the staff is tightly held,
In this way each falsehood is repelled;
    The justice of God doth not fail,
Slander and evil cannot prevail,
        Evil doth not prevail.

And when at last to the Judgement-hall
The Christ doth enter and summon all,
At "the balancing of the beam",
The ill outweighed be God's verdict-deem,
The ill outweighed God's deem.

409. *Each Day and Night* *Barra*

Each day in justice let me speak,
Each day thy chastening marks, O God, display,
Each day in wisdom let me speak,
Each night at peace with thee, at peace each day;

Each day thy mercy's causes store,
Each day may I compose to thee a song,
Each day give heedance to thy law,
Each day string out, O God, thy praises strong;

Each day love let me give to thee,
Each night, O Jesu, grant I do the same,
Each day and night laud give to thee
Or dark or light, for goodness of thy Name,
Or dark or light,
Each day and night.

410. *For Justice* *South Uist*

God, I wash my face at the light
Of the nine rays of the sun,
Lo, as Mary washed her Son
In the rich milk seething and white.

Be love in my face to transcend,
Be my looks with kindness hung,
Dew-honey be in my tongue,
My breath as the incense ascend.

Over yonder black is the hall,
Black those against me gathered,
I am the swan white-feathered,
A queen reigning over them all.

In the name of God I will move,
Wary deer, strong horse to ride,
Serpent wise, king dignified,
And stronger than all shall I prove.

My face I wash at light
Of the nine sunbeams airy,
Her Son as washed Mary
In the rich milk white.

In mouth let honey be,
My face kind-approving;
Mary her Son loving
In all hearts for me.

May God all-seeing be,
All-hearing, and all-voicing,
Strengthening, sufficing,
'Gainst mine enemy.

Blind, deaf, and dumb be he,
My mocker and my scorner,
Drive him to the corner,
My dread enemy.

Columba's tongue imbued,
Columba's word my speeching;
Victorious Son preaching
Before multitude,
Composure of thy teaching
Be to me endued;
Composure divine,
O Christ, be mine.

412. *The Justice Purification*   *Benbecula*

I am laving my face to-day
In the mild fire of sunrise-ray,
As Mary laved her Christ and Son
In the rich milk Egyptian.

May sense be in my speaking placed,
Upon my lips the nectar's taste,
And in my mouth be force amain,
Till hither I return again.

Let sweetness all my sayings teach,
And wisdom be in all my speech,
Love for her Son of fair Mary
Be in the heart of all for me.

The love of Christ be in my breast,
Beauty of Christ protecting best,
In sea, on land, there is nothing
That can o'ercome the Sunday King.

About my neck the hand of Bride,
And Mary's hand by heart and side,
The hand of Michael laving me,
The hand of Christ, o saving me.

413. *Justice Invocation*   *Barra*

In Father's name I bathe my brow,
And in name of the Son again,
I bathe in name of Spirit now,
And in name of the Three, Amen.

In the name of God I will go,
Wary like deer, like horse so strong,
Wise like snake, like king royal so,
Than all persons am I more strong.

The hand of God is saving me,
The love of Christ within my pores,
The strong Spirit is laving me,
The Three to shield and aid my cause,
The Three to shield and aid my cause,
The Spirit's hand is laving me,
Mine aid the Three each step ensures.

Black and dark is the yonder town,
And blacker the men gathered there;
Above them a queen looking down,
The swan I am white-feathered fair.

345

414. *The Stream Bathing*

> In the name and the ordered rite
> Of the glorious King of life above;
> In the name and the ordered rite
> Of the all-sufficing Lord Christ of love;
> In the name and the ordered rite
> Of the perfect Spirit who guideth me;
> In the name and the ordered rite
> Of the might and the aiding of the Three;
> In the name and the ordered rite
> Of the might and the aiding of the Three :
> I am bathing, cleansing my face
> In the nine beam-rays of the sunrise light,
> As Mary bathed her Son of grace
> In the milk fermenting and seething white.

415. *Against Slander*   *South Uist*

> I will close my fist with fingers tight,
> Duly I hold my staff in hand;
> To be free of the injury-spite
> I have come now within to stand.

> All three of King Cluny's princely sons,
> And Manann the son of King Lear,
> The Green-robed King's young son, are the ones
> That this night shall have set me clear.

> Fionn the great prince of the hunting race
> From the falsehood shall set me free,
> Valiant Connell of fine-bladed grace
> With Goll of the blows shielding me.

> 'Tis Brian of song shall give me sain,
> Briais of virtue vantage bring,
> And Columcill the Clerk amain,
> And Alexander, 'gainst the sting.

> My shield shall be of the hunting race,
> The seven hosts with their fine blades,
> And the young son of the King of Greece
> The utter lies off me unlades.

346

Spirit Fite will go down with me,
    My head will Saint Bride raise on high;
From the infamy that I be free
    I am here, to outface the lie.

416. *High-Court Appeal*

Unto Mary I am appealing,
    The Mother who giveth men aid;
Unto Bridget I am appealing,
    The Lamb's mild-white Fostering-maid;

Unto Peter I am appealing,
    Apostle of fear and of sleep;
To Columba I am appealing,
    Apostle of shore and of deep;

To heaven I am appealing,
    That the city on high may know;
Unto Michael I am appealing,
    Arch-warman of dragon's o'erthrow;

To the Father I am appealing,
    Who did form all flesh that is born;
Unto the Christ I am appealing,
    Who suffered the pain and the scorn;

To the Spirit I am appealing,
    To make me as white and as pure,
My wounding so cleansingly healing,
    As white cotton-grass of the moor.

417. *God my Guide*   *South Uist*

O God with thy wisdom be my guide,
God with justice chastising provide,
O God with thy mercy be mine aid,
God my protection with might arrayed.

O God with thy fullness be my fill,
God with thy shadow-cloak shield me still,
God with thy grace my fullness be done,
For the sake of thine Anointed Son.

Jesu the Christ of King David's line,
Visiting One of the Temple shrine,
Sacrifice Lamb of the Garden pure,
Whose death did my salvation procure.

XXXVIII. BATTLE

God bless our body and our soul,
Protect and shield our persons whole,
Columba's arm and Michael's wing
Be our defence in everything.

We dedicate the arms we bear,
We dedicate the clothes we wear,
We dedicate the sword and shield
True-wielded on the battlefield.

God bless our chief and bless our cause,
Uphold thine everlasting laws,
Keep safe our folk, let right prevail,
Nor let our warring fingers fail.

And if the fatal arrow fly,
Or deadly wounding draweth nigh,
O God, make sure the voyage long
To the blest isle of hero-song.

And at the last, that we may live,
Do thou all cruelty forgive;
With honour at the judgement-seat
Stand we with single heart complete.

418. Christ's Safe-Guarding

O the Christ's guarding that it may
Safe shield you ever and a day.

419. The Charmed Life   *Morvern*

The charm on thy body I lay,
And on thy prosperity decked,
The God of life's charm there alway
    To protect.

The charm that dear Bride of the kine
Put round the fair neck of Whitehand,
That round her Son Mary did twine
    To withstand.

Between sole and throat, back and breast,
Mary Virgin laid the charm fair,
Between heart and knee, foot and chest,
    Eye and hair.

Beside Michael's song-host to fly,
Michael's shield o'er shoulder I place,
There is naught between earth and sky
To o'ercome the God upon high,
    King of grace.

By no spear shalt thou be riven,
And by no woman's wiles brought down,
By no wound shalt thou be driven,
    No sea drown.

Christ's own plaid about thee to go,
Christ's shadow above thee in heat,
From crown of thy head to the toe
    Of thy feet.

On thee now the charm of God came,
Thou shalt through the power of the same
    Know not shame.

Go forth in the name of thy King,
In the name of thy Prince thy recall,
To the God of life belonging,
   To Pow'rs all.

This charm Monday early I arm,
Rough bramble and thorn thy path near,
Go forth, on thy body the charm,
   And no fear.

The crest of the hill treading on,
Protected thou shalt be behind,
In the battle thou the calm swan
'Mid slaughter preserving shalt find,
'Gainst five hundred able to stand,
   Foes unmanned.

About thee, above thee, God's charm,
   And God's arm !

420. *The Son of God in Full Armour*   *South Uist*

Unto mine eye I will set thee this spell,
As the Being of life ordained it well,
From bosom of Peter and Paul 'tis done,
The third best spell it is under the sun.

A drop, O Mary, and a drop, O Bride,
King lawgiver Patrick, a drop applied,
A drop, O Columba kindly, I pray,
A drop, O Saint Ciaran of might's display.

For triumph in field, for hardness of hands,
In repulse or in onslaught, as he stands,
Upon every son that all may go well,
Son of God, in full armour with him dwell.

From the bosom kind of the Father One,
From the bosom kind of the blessèd Son,
From the bosom of the Holy Spirit,
So be it, amen, safety inherit.

The sain which Mary did set on her Son,
The sain from death, the sain from wounding done,
The sain between the breast and to the knee,
The sain from knee down to the foot for thee,
The sain of the three sains, of five, of seven,
Sain from thy crown to thy foot-sole be given.
The sain of each seven paters to thee,
The paternoster-sain one, two and three,
Four and five, six and seven paters be,
From brow-smile to coloured soles on the floor,
To preserve behind, to sustain before.

Salvation's helmet thy head to invest,
The covenant-corslet round thy throat go,
Be the priestly breastplate upon thy chest,
To shield thee in warfare and fight with foe.

O youth, if pursued from behind thy back,
Be the Virgin's power close-aid to thy lack,
To east or to west, west or east go forth,
Or to north or south, or to south or north.

422. *The Aiding*

Bridget defend me,
Mary defend me,
Michael defend me,
By land and by sea :
From all bitter cup-lees defend me
By land and by sea,
From all bitter cup-lees defend me.

Father attend me,
The Son attend me,
Spirit attend me,
By land and by sea :
The eternal Throne's fend attend me
By land and by sea,
The eternal Throne's fend attend me.

The Three befriend me,
Three after-tend me,
May the Three send me,
By land and by sea,
To the godly's Vine-garden send me
By land and by sea,
To the godly's Vine-garden send me.

423. *East or West*

May the everlasting Father throw
His shield to shade you
Every east and west that you may go,
His shield to aid you.

424. *MacCrimmon's Pipe*

Thy beauty and thy piping music here
Have brought to thee a fairy lover dear;
I hand thee now the silver chanter clear
Will 'neath thy fingers perfect sing to ear.

425. *The Making of the Bow*

The yews for the bow by the Esragan grow,
In Glenorchy's brown grove the birch for the shaft,
From the Loch Treig eagle the feather to wing,
Dunkeld's yellow beeswax and silk for the string,
The arrow-head from the Clan Paterson's craft.

426. *The War-Doublets*   *Uist*

O men of the limbs that grace a man,
To whom kilt is becoming and gay,
O men of the short red-coated clan,
And to me far too short is your stay,

O men of the short red-coated clan,
  Gleaming for war in the sunny day,
You gave your Bible-oath to a man,
  As you were marching down Auldearn way,
  That sheathed be no sword until the day
  When crowned King Charles was the King to stay.

427. *The Cat-Men*

The Cats are come, Cats upon us are come,
The Cats are come, Cats upon us are come,
They are come upon us, they come to-day.

In upon us to break and spoiling make,
To steal the kine and the cattle to take,
To whip off our horses, our homes to rake,
They are come upon us, they come their way.

They are come, they are come, they come, they scour,
They are come, they come, they come in ill-hour,
They are found amidst us cruel and sour.

The Cats are come, Cats are come on us near,
The Cats are come, Cats are come on us here,
The Cats are come, Cats are come on us sheer,
In the hour of evil the Cats appear,
Their stroke is upon us, their stroke of fear.

The sons of the wicked, by storm-wind drilled,
Are swarming the heather, hollowed and hilled,
Their blood on the meadow is warmly spilled,
Their shafts by their sides, their quivers a-filled.

The Cats are come, Cats upon us are come,
The Cats are come, Cats upon us are come,
They are come upon us, they come to prey.

For murder, for mauling, they come their way,
For wailing, for danger, they come to fray,
For pillage, for plunder, rain-windy day,
The kine and the calves for lifting away.

The Cats are come, Cats upon us arrive,
The Cats are come, and on us the Cats drive,
The Cats are come, and on us the Cats thrive,
In the hour of evil Cats are alive,
Their stroke is upon us, their stroke to rive.

For kine droving and calves, bustling the sheep,
For blood and for wrath, for moaning to weep,
For blood and for wrath, a Thursday they sweep,
They are come upon us a snowdrift deep.

428. *The Prince over the Water*   *South Uist*

There is many a haughty maiden found,
In becoming tartan mantled and wound,
From Balmeanach down to the Barra Sound
    Who for all her great love of thee sighs;

I must arise and arise and arise,
I must arise and arise and arise,
I must arise and arise and arise,
    To wield the claymore I must arise.

In Italy some, some in France away,
There are some in the Isle of Beagram grey,
Nor here is there ever a sermon day
    But in Kilpheder are our allies.

429. *The Son of My King*

Upon land and sea a cloudy day,
Who would not aid the son of my king?
For the silver flute now who would play,
In Scotland here the son of my king?

Like raven wise to a feast away,
In Scotland here the son of my king!
For the silver flute now who would play?
Who would not aid the son of my king?

Upon land and sea a cloudy day,
In Scotland here the son of my king!
Night of the seven elements' sway,
Who would not aid the son of my king?

No haze on the white moon's spotless ray,
In Scotland here the son of my king!
Upon land and sea a cloudy day,
Who would not aid the son of my king?

430. Battle Prayer

South Uist

Jesus MacMary, I call on thy name,
    Lov'd John the apostle's name for me,
Each saint's name in the red world who o'ercame,
    To protect in the battle to be,
        To protect in the battle to be.

When my mouth shall be closed and speaking done,
    When eye shall be shut nor beholds,
When breath stops rattling and blood does not run,
    When heart throbs no more and life withholds,
        When heart throbs no more and life withholds,

When awful upon the throne sits the Brieve,
    And full-heard has my cause been to plead,
Jesus MacMary, my soul aid, reprieve,
    Mild Saint Michael, my posting o lead;
Jesus MacMary, my soul aid nor leave!
O Michael mild, this my going receive!

431. The Might of River

Thine be the might of river going,
Thine be the might of ocean flowing,
    The might of vict'ry on the field.

357

Thine be the might of fire consuming,
Thine be the might of lightning dooming,
    The might of rock that will not yield.

Thine be the might of element biding,
Thine be the might of troop outriding,
    The might of heav'nly love God-sealed.

XXXIX. THE SEA

Angel of God who hast me in charge
From the dear Father of mercy large
With sea-wall for craft, of saintly might,
To fend me from storms throughout this night;

All that can tempt me or harm repel,
On the sea of evil plank me well;
In narrows or crooks or kyles or bays
Keep thou my coracle frail always.

Before a bright flame of pilgrimage,
Above a guide star of pilotage,
Below a smooth sea on which to sail,
Behind a steersman who cannot fail.

And when I am tired and stranger shy
Lead to the quay where I do not die;
If home it be time that I should go
To the cove of Christ where peace doth flow.

(This poem is based upon one of the originals of number 163.)

432. The Three Everywhere

The Three who are over my head,
The Three who are under my tread,
The Three who are over me here,
The Three who are over me there,
The Three who are in the earth near,
The Three who are up in the air,
The Three who in heaven do dwell,
The Three in the great ocean swell,
Pervading Three, o be with me.

433. The Kindly Lantern

The very self of the Mary Virgin's Son
To you a kindly lantern may he be,
Over your head a guiding, shining one
For the wide rough ocean of eternity.

434. The Lighthouse Prayer
Monks' Heiskir of North Uist

O God, who from last night's sweet rest dost me convey
To the light of joy of the day that is to-day,
From the new light of this day be thou bringing me
Unto the light of guidance of eternity,
From the new light to-day be thou bringing me
Unto the guiding light of eternity.

435. Sea-Prey   Skye

Seven herrings the salmon's meal;
Seven salmon the feast of seal;
Seven seals for the small sow-whale;
Seven small whales the big regale;
Seven big whales to kraken giv'n;
Leviathan has kraken sev'n.

436. *The Sea-Cows* *Harris*

In the Sea of Canna is heard a long lowing,
    A cow from Barra, and a cow from Tiree,
An Islay cow lowing, an Arran cow going,
    A cow from green Kintyre of the birchen-tree.

O lost and o lost and o lost will be Curly,
    O lost will be Giddy, and lost will be Prue,
Lost will be Sad-Eyes, and lost Shoulder-White burly,
    Lost will be brown Trim of the cattle-fold too.

I will go, go, go to Mull beyond the skerries,
    To Erin of the men of blood I will go,
I will go to little Man, the isle of wherries,
    And o'er to France I will go and safely so.

O lost and o lost and o lost will be Silly,
    O lost will be Darkie, and lost will be Slow,
O lost will be Fatty, and o lost Mule-Millie,
    And lost brown Lovey of the shaggy gold glow.

437. *The Uist Voyager*

Lift sails away from the Uist sand
Where the red shell-drakes settle and stand,
From the headland yonder set behind,
With the sweat of eyebrows pouring blind;
    Lift sails away from the Uist sand
        Where the shell-drakes land.

To brindled and low Uist of sand
Where the red shell-drakes for nesting land,
Going the way of the wild wild sea,
As trimly as could be wished to be,
    To brindled and low Uist of sand,
        To the shell-drake strand.

O may God bless thy cross
Ere thou go o'er the sea;
On thy way illness-loss
Shall not with it take thee.

O may God bless thy cross crucifying
   'Neath the roof where the Christ dwelleth here,
'Gainst drowning, 'gainst danger, 'gainst spell-dying,
   'Gainst sore pang, against sweating with fear.

As the King of kings stretched up beseeching
   To the pitiless, merciless tree,
To the leafy, brown, roped top-bough reaching,
   As Christ sinless triumphed in body,

As the lady blest-sevenfold showing,
   Who goes in at the head without fear,
God, bless all that before thee are going,
   And bless thee with them, voyaging near.

Grace of form, grace of voice thy part;
   Grace of lowliness of heart;
Grace of knoll-sense, grace loveliness,
   Grace of healthiness to bless;
Grace of the sea, grace of the land;
   Grace of music, guiding hand;
Grace of the war-cry, grace to win;
   Grace of life be thine within;
Grace of praise, of the loving heart;
   Grace thine of the dancer's art;
Grace of the lyre, the harper's song;
   Grace of neatness-skill belong;
Grace of reason, and grace of word;
   Grace of lovely story heard;
Grace of smooth peace be unto thee,
   Grace of God thine let it be.

Soft music-voice for thee I am praying,
   And a tongue that is loving and mild :
Two good things husband and wife arraying,
   Two things good for a girl and boy-child.

The joy of God in thy face reflected,
    And be joy to all who thee behold;
The circling of God keep thee protected,
    Shielding angels of God thee enfold.

        Nor sword shall give thee wound and pierce,
        Nor brand shall give thee burning fierce,
        Nor arrow shall thee tear and rend,
        Nor seas shall drown and under send.

Whiter thou art than the swan lake-nesting,
    Whiter than the fair gull of the tide,
Whiter thou art than snows mountain-cresting,
    Whiter than love the angels provide.

Thou art the gracious red rowan stanching
    The ire and anger that all men know,
From flow to ebb as a sea-wave launching,
    As sea-wave from the ebb to the flow.

The mantle of Christ for thine onlaying,
    From thy crown to thy sole to give shade;
The God of life's mantle safe thy staying,
    Thy champion and thy leader to aid.

Thou'lt not be left to the wicked's devising,
    Nor shalt be bent in the court of lies;
O'er them victorious thou shalt be rising
    As the arching waves victorious rise.

        Thou art the pure love of the cloud,
        Thou art the pure love of the sky,
        Thou art the pure love starry-browed,
        Thou art the pure love mooned on high,
        Thou art the pure love, sun above,
        Thou art the pure love heaven wings,
        Thou art the pure angelic love,
        Thou art the pure love Jesus brings,
Thou art the pure love of the God of living things.

O thou who dost dwell in the soaring sky,
On us thy tide-mark of glad blessing lie,
Carry us over the crest of the seas,
Carry us safe to a haven of peace,
Our shipmen bless and our ship fore and aft,
Our anchors bless and the blades of our craft,
Each stay, each halyard, each voyaging man,
Keep our tall-stepped masts with their mainsails' span,
O King of the elements, strong and taut,
That with good success we homeward make port;
Myself sitting down in the helmsman's seat,
It is God's own Son sets my course complete,
As he Columba the mild did avail
What time he did set his stay to his sail.

O Mary, and Bridget, Michael, and Paul,
Gabriel, Peter, belov'd John, we call,
Pour down upon us the dew from on high,
For our faith a growing to us supply,
In the Rock of rocks our sea-wall bestow,
In every law that love's warping doth show,
That we may reach to the glad country far,
Where peace and affection and loving are,
All unfolded by grace before our eyes;
Nor ever to us the canker-worm nighs,
But there to the ending our safety lies,
From the grapplings of death we shall be free,
Though of the sin-seed of Adam we be.

Michaelmas, Martinmas, Andrewmas three,
Be an anchor-chain of loving to me,
On Saint Bride's Feast Day, my dear day to keep,
Throw forth the old serpent into the deep,
That the swallowing waves over him sweep;
May Saint Patrick's Day, a powerful day,
Brighten the storm from the north under way,
Its fury to blunt, its wind-wrath allay,
Its fierceness to minish, its cold to slay.

The Three Kings aloft on Trinity Day,
The crest of the breakers o smooth away,
Hallowmas May-Feast give dew falling soft,
John Midsummer Day a gentle wind waft,

Great is her fame, on Saint Mary's Feast Day,
Set the westerly gale from us away;
Each day and each night, stormbound or becalmed,
O Chief of chiefs with us, be we unharmed,
Be thou thyself to us a compass-chart,
Hand on the rudder-helm, steersman thou art,
Thou God of the elements, thine own hand,
Early and late as befits let it stand,
    Thy very own hand for piloting stand.

440. *The Prayer at Sea*   *Tiree*

How many the dangers and perils feared,
  The pounding sea and the drowning sea,
From which, O my God, thou hast safely steered
  Through the Prayer of Distress on my lee.

441. *Sea Blessing*   *North Uist*

God the Father almighty, whose kindness cheers,
O Jesu the Son of the sorrows and tears,
O thine aiding aid, Holy Spirit, endears!

The Three-One e'er living, great, lasting, o'erhead,
Who across the Red Sea the Israelites led,
And Jonah to land from the sea-monster sped,

Who led Paul with his company setting sail,
Forth from the sea-stress, from the wave-torment's flail,
From the storm that was great, from foul-weather gale,

When the tempest poured on the Lake Galilee,
The disciples cried out in their misery,
And thou Jesu of sleeping didst still the sea.

O sain us, set us free, and sanctify best,
On our helm, O King of the elements, rest,
And steer us in peace to our voyage's quest.

Gentle winds, kindly, pleasant, fragrant to waft,
Not an eddy, nor swirl, nor whirl for our craft,
But safe let her ride and unscathed fore and aft.

All things of thy bounty, O God, we beseech,
For thy will so and word accordingly teach.

442. *The Ship*   *Lochalsh and Kintail*

The Children of Israel, God taking them,
    Through the Red Sea their path became land,
For the quench of their thirst God slaking them
    From a rock unhewn by craftsman's hand.

Who are they at my helm-tiller to steer,
    My eastbound boat to aid and to speed?
Peter and Paul and belovéd John dear,
    Three to whom substance and worth is meed.

Who are the ones at my helm-tiller near?
    Peter and Paul and John Baptist are they;
At my helm the Christ is sitting to steer,
    The wind from the south making our way.

Who makes the voice of the wind to grow faint?
    And who makes calm the strait and the sea?
It is Jesus Christ, the Chief of each saint,
    MacMary, Stem-Root of victory,
    MacMary, Stock-Shoot of victory,
    Ruler of land, wind, sky and of sea.

443. *Ship Consecration*   *South Uist*

HELMSMAN:	Be the ship blest.
CREW:	By God the Father blest.
HELMSMAN:	Be the ship blest.
CREW:	And by God the Son blest.
HELMSMAN:	Be the ship blest.
CREW:	By God the Spirit blest.

ALL:	God the Father,
	And God the Son,
	God the Spirit,
	Blessing give best,
	Be the ship blest.
HELMSMAN:	What can afear
	With God the Father near?
CREW:	Naught can afear.
HELMSMAN:	What can afear
	And God the Son is near?
CREW:	Naught can afear.
HELMSMAN:	What can afear
	And God the Spirit near?
CREW:	Naught can afear.
ALL:	God the Father,
	And God the Son,
	God the Spirit,
	Be with us here
	And ever near.
HELMSMAN:	What care is bred,
	Being of all o'erhead?
CREW:	No care is bred.
HELMSMAN:	What care is bred,
	The King of all o'erhead?
CREW:	No care is bred.
HELMSMAN:	What care is bred,
	Spirit of all o'erhead?
CREW:	No care is bred.
ALL:	Being of all,
	The King of all,
	Spirit of all,
	Over our head
	Eternal fall,
	Near to us sure
	For evermore.

444. *A Sailor's Prayer*

Thou Being who Jonah didst safely land
Out from the bag of the sow of the sea,
Bring thou myself to the beckoning strand
With lading and ship entrusted to me.

445. *The Macleods' Imprecation*
South Uist, Barra, and Kintail

The wind be from the west
And on the tooth of Neist,
The wind and more again,
The mist and drenching rain;
The sea concealing high
The coastline and the sky;
And the Clan Donald there
On broken boarding bare,
No shred of sense left by—
No worse I for their cry!

A skiff-boat's toss and fall,
And masts too stout and tall,
Bellying sails enfold,
Drained barrels in the hold,
The winnowed spindrift fly
From wave-top to the sky,
Blind them the salt, and free
To them the Strangers' Sea.

To thwarts bilge-water swill,
The breaking baler fill,
The sails to ribbons fly,
Fog blanketing to lie,
Snow fall with choking flake,
The sea with swelling break,
And men strain to escape,
And every hole agape.

A crew weak in the hand,
Who cannot understand,
Too proud, and big of speech,
But scant of reason each,

369

And small indeed of sense,
In action blind and dense,
Hideous to appear,
Nor God nor man revere!

446. The Norsemen's Captive

South Uist and Barra

All like a dreaming doth fade
Departure taking,
On the wave-face gently laid
A bubble breaking.

Torrarnis of barley-corn,
The sea impaling,
From the Bent-grass Land forlorn
No craft comes sailing.

Both father and mother mine
On the bier lying,
And sister and brother mine
Shrouded for dying.

447. The Angel Warder

O angel-guardian of my right hand,
Be thou attending me this night,
In the battling floods rescuing stand,
My nakedness clothe in linen white,
Succour me, feeble, forlorn my plight.

My boat in the boiling whirlpools steer,
In gap and pit guide thou my tread,
In the turnings sly watch o'er me near,
From scathe of the wicked safely led,
From scathe this night be I safely sped.

O banish from me defilement's brand,
Till Doom from ill encompass me;
O kindly angel of my right hand,
This night from the evil make me free,
Freeing this night and rescuing be!

448. *The Helmsman*

God of the elements, glory to thee
For the lantern-guide of the ocean wide;
On my rudder's helm may thine own hand be,
And thy love abaft on the heaving sea.

449. *Doxology*   *Barra*

As it was, as it is, and as it shall be
Evermore, God of grace, God in Trinity!
With the ebb, with the flow, ever it is so,
God of grace, O Trinity, with the ebb and flow.

XL. THE SKY

God of the heavens and aery space,
God beyond time and God beyond place,
O God of an everlasting grace,
       Thy blessing sending;

God of the clouds and the thunder noise,
God who didst speak with a thunder voice,
God who didst shew the Son of thy choice,
       The Dove descending;

God where the mountain-top meets the sky,
God of commandment on Sinai,
God of transfiguration on high,
       Cloud and voice blending;

God of sunrising and morning hour,
God of the seeing and warming power,
God of the sunset and folding flower,
       Shielding, defending;

God of the moon from wax to the wane,
God of her light over rock and plain,
God of the tides, the breakers, the main,
       Guiding, befriending;

God of the star-points peopling the night,
God of the airts, of turning aright,
God of the way beyond human sight,
       Lead us ascending.

450. *The Voice of Thunder*

O God of the elemental might,
O God of the mysterious height,
O God of the stars and cloudsprings bright,
    O King of kings to bestow !
    O King of kings to bestow !

Thy joy the joy of the raindrops' play,
Thy light the light of the lightning's spray,
Thy war the war of the heavenly fray,
    Thy peace the peace of the bow,
    Thy peace the peace of the bow.

Thy pain the pain of groaning and clash,
Thy love the love of the sudden flash,
That lasts for aye like the music's crash,
    Till the end of ends below,
    Till the end of ends below.

Thou pourest thy grace, refreshing shower,
Upon men in grief and duress hour,
Upon men in straits and danger's power,
    Without cease or stint to show,
    Without cease or stint to show.

Thou Son of Mary of Paschal feat,
Thou Son of Mary of death's defeat,
Thou Son of Mary of grace replete,
    Who wast and art, shalt be so
    With the ebb and with the flow;
    Who wast and art, shalt be so,
    With the ebb and with the flow !

451. *Sunrise*   *South Uist and Mingulay of Barra*

The eye of God, the God who is great,
The eye of the God of glory's state,
The eye of the King of hosts that strive,
The eye of the King of all alive,
Pour out as time and moments go,
Pour out on us thy gen'rous flow,
    On us thy gentle gen'rous flow.

375

Thou sun of joy, glory to thee,
To thee be glory, O thou sun,
Face of the God of life to see,
Face of the morning rising one,
    To thee be glory, O thou sun.

452. The Sun   *Barra*

A hail to thee, thou sun of each day,
    As the skies on high thou dost pass;
Strong on the wing on high is thy way,
    Thou glorious mother of stars.

In swallowing sea thy resting lies
    All scatheless and all unafraid;
On a wave of peace up thou dost rise
    In fresh bloom like a queenly maid.

453. Sunset   *Arasaig*

I am in hope that in its time due
    The God who is joyous and great
For me the grace-light will not abate
    As this night the sun leaves my view.

454. Moon Worship   *Eigg*

In holy name of the Father One,
And in the holy name of the Son,
In holy name of the Spirit Dove,
The holy Three of mercy above.

Glory for ever to thee so bright,
Thou moon so white of this very night;
Thyself for ever thou dost endure
As the glory-lantern of the poor.

455. The White One of Beauty Barra

Hail to thee, thou moon so new,
Jewel-guide of sky so bright;
Hail to thee, thou moon so new,
Jewel-one of grace so white.

Hail to thee, thou moon so new,
Jewel-guide of stars above;
Hail to thee, thou moon so new,
Jewel-one of my heart's love.

Hail to thee, thou moon so new,
Jewel-guide of clouds so clear;
Hail to thee, thou moon so new,
Jewel-one of heav'n so dear.

456. The Jewel-Moon of Guiding

Hail to thee, moon so new, so slender,
Gently floating jewel-guide!
I bend my knee, my love I tender,
Guiding jewel, gently ride.

Lo, I to thee my knee am bending,
My hand I give unto thee,
Mine eye I up to thee am sending,
New moon of the months to see.

Hail to thee, moon so new, so slender,
O darling maid of my love!
Hail to thee, moon so new, so tender,
The graces' darling above!

Thou goest in thy course quiescent,
Thou steerest the full tides true;
To us thou turnest thy face crescent,
O moon of the months so new.

Thou queen-maid of the night for guiding,
Thou queen-maid of joyful hue,
Queen-maid belov'd serenely riding,
O moon of the months so new!

457. The New Moon of the God of Life

New is the moon and she my love,
The life-God kindling her above;
Be mine good love and purpose weighed
To each life of creation made.

My prayer, O God, be lifted high
As thou indeed dost sanctify;
And be my heart, O God, set fair
As thou indeed dost love and care.

My doing on the land comply
As thou indeed dost satisfy;
My wishing on the sea affect
As thou indeed dost trim-direct.

My hoping to the height aspire
As thou indeed dost search-require;
Below my love and purpose ply
As thou indeed dost satisfy.

My longing, God, do thou dispose
That it seek after thy repose;
O God, be then my final rest
With God the Son reposing blest.

458. The Moon of Moons   *Barra*

When I see the new moon on high,
    It becomes to lift mine eye,
It becomes me to bend my knee,
    Head to bow becomingly,

Praise to thee giving, moonstar-guide,
    Now that I have thee espied,
That I the new moon have espied,
    Of the way the jewel-guide.

Many a one beyond has passed
    Between this moon and the last,
Though earth I yet enjoy no less,
    Moonstar of the moons to bless!

378

459. Rune of the New Moon

When I see the new moon her light upraise,
My rune it becomes to speak to her face;
To the Being of life I must give praise
For his kindness and goodness all my days;

For many a man and woman the flight
O'er the river black of abysmal night,
Since last thy countenance gave its light,
O thou new moon of the heavens so bright!

460. The Moon of the Ages

I am raising to thee my hands above,
I am bowing to thee my head,
I am offering thee my love,
Thou glory-jewel of the ages bred.

I am raising to thee mine eye up high'r,
I am bending to thee my head,
I am giving thee my desire,
O thou new-moonlight of the ages shed!

461. New Moon of the Pastures

See there, the new moon bright,
Blest with the life-King's light;
O fragrant be each night
Whereon shines her ray!

Full be her shining might
To each poor one a light;
Entire and good her flight
To each in stress-fray.

Above be she aright
To each one in his plight;
Below her guiding sight
To each poor astray.

The moon of moonstars white
Through thick clouds from the height
On me, on each alight
    Through dark tears her way.

God's hand on me alight
In each befalling blight,
Now and until death's night,
    Till my rising day.

462. *The New Moon Up*

The new moon, lo there, lo there!
The King of life making her bright;
    Be mine an intending fair
    To whose eyes look on her light.

Upward be lifted mine eye
To the Father to bless on high,
    Below my heart be to lie
    With Christ who dearly did buy.

My knee be abased down low
To the queen of the loveliness;
    My voice be lifted up so
    To him who did make and bless.

463. *The Lady Moon*

The new moon is lady of my love,
By the King of the elements blest;
    Be mine a good purpose of love
To'rds each thing of creation's behest.

Holy each thing on which her light steals;
Be kindly each thing which she reveals.
    On land may she guide all beset;
On the sea guide the straitened and let.

Moonstar of moons, come through the cloud-veil
To me, to each mortal in travail;
    My love's maid, come through dense bank-cloud
Unto me and to all travail-bowed.

The King of grace aid my hand amain
Now till the day when I rise again.

464. Queen of the Night

Hail to thee, so bright,
Jewel of the night!
Beauty of the height,
Jewel of the night!
Thou star-mother white,
Jewel of the night!
Thou sun-fostered light,
Jewel of the night!
Queen-star in thy might,
Jewel of the night!

465. Jewel of Virtues   South Uist

Hail to thee, thou jewel-guide,
New moon in the night espied!
Hail to thee, thou jewel-guide,
New moon o'er the waves to ride!
Hail to thee, thou jewel-guide,
New moon of the ocean-tide!
Hail to thee, thou jewel-guide,
New moon of the virtues tried!
Hail to thee, thou jewel-guide,
New moon in my love to bide!
    Jewel of the heavens wide!

466. The Lantern of Grace

Be thy shining to me white!
Smooth to me thy journey's flight!
If thy starting good doth send,
Better seven times thine end,
   O new moon of time and space,
   O thou lantern great of grace!

Who created thee is he
Who likewise created me;
Who gave light and shape to thee
Life and death he did decree,
Seven joys all filling me,
   O thou lantern great of grace,
   O white moon of time and space.

467. The New Moon   *Barra*

O moon of the seasons, shining and bright,
New moon of the months and the tides so white,
  In name of the Holy Spirit of grace,
    In Father's name, of the City of peace,
  In our Jesu's name, who did death displace,
    In name of the Three, our shield without cease,
If well thou hast found us to be to-night,
O seven times better, when waned thy light,
Safe leave us, unharmed, season-moon so bright,
O moon of the seasons, shining and white.

XLI. CREATURES

Wild are the creatures of the bound,
Free the taking and living theirs,
      Seal of the sea,
      Marten of tree,
Badger, fox, serpent of the mound,
Live creatures of the God who cares.

Water-dog, bear, or ranging deer,
Great is the skill of man in chase,
      Swift is the hound
      Coursing the ground,
Yet safe the calves and mother here,
The cubs or young of moorland place.

O keep from preying's savageness,
And keep, O God, from bog and mist,
      A foothold sure,
      A path secure,
Invisibility to bless,
A "fāth-fīth" change of magic whist.

Grant we be loyal and be fair,
Steadfast, O God, and with no fear,
      Respecting life
      Though sure with knife,
The hunting hands' unfailing care,
Unerring through our sojourn here.

From my loins, O my son, thy life was born,
Fair let me steer thee the way of true game,
In the eleven Apostles' holy name,
In the Son of God's name, thy wounded One.

In Saint James', Saint Peter's, Saint Paul's good name,
Baptist John, and Apostle John on high,
Luke Physician, galled Stephen first to die,
Muriel mild, Mary mother of Lamb.

In Patrick's name of deeds holy and fine,
And Cormac the saint of the tomb and cause,
Columba beloved, Adamnan of laws,
Calm Fite, and Bride of the milk and kine.

In Michael's name warring, the hosts' archpeer,
In Ariel's name, youth of colour fair,
In Uriel's name, of the golden hair,
And Gabriel's name, the grace-Virgin's seer.

When closed is thine eye and silent thy tongue,
Then bend not thy knee nor move thou thy limbs,
Nor be wounding the duck as off she swims,
Nor ever be spoiling her of her young.

From the white swan of the sweet gurgling note,
From the dun-spotted cormorant tufted brown,
Till doom cut no feather off from their down,
While out on the crest of the wave they float.

Upon the wing let them always uplift
Ere thou draw back thine arrow to thine ear,
And the fair-white Mary will thee endear,
The lovely Bride of her kine will make gift.

Thou shalt not eat fallen fish, fallen flesh,
Nor single bird not brought down by thy hand,
Be thou thankful for the one on the land,
Although nine away should be swimming fresh.

The swan the fairy of Bride of the kine,
The mallard, Mary of peace, fairy thine.

469. Chase Consecration

In the name of the Trinity, as one,
    In word, in deed, in thought aright,
I bathe mine own hands in the water's run,
    'Neath the powers of the sky and light.

For not to return in my life my vow
    Without fishing or fowling good,
Without game or venison from the hill brow,
    Without a plump spoil from the wood.

Mary soft-white, kind-white, loving-white, blest,
    Silver salmon dead on the sea,
Or duck with brood on her water's edge nest
    Where it dries not, keep them from me.

The grey heath-hen on the crag hillock-crown,
    And the blackcock of the hoarse cry,
After the strength of the sun has gone down,
    Let the sound of them pass me by.

Mary sweet-fragrance, Mother of my King,
    The crown of thy peace on my brow,
My shield thy royal gold robe covering,
    With Christ's aiding be mine aid now,
    With the aiding of Christ aid thou.

470. The Hind

Saint Peter and Saint Paul were faring by,
A hind in fawn-birth on the path did lie;
Saint Peter said, "A hind is bearing, lo!"
Saint Paul said, "I can see that it is so.

"As down the leaves will fall from off the tree,
So her placenta gently falling be,
Through the radiant Father, Son of grace,
The Spirit of the wise and loving face;
    Radiant Father's name, Son's name of grace,
    In Spirit's name of wise and loving face."

Ossian's Mother
North Uist, Glencoe and elsewhere

Ah mother mine and thou that art a deer,
　　Give me hoirion ho a hau,
Arise ere the sun rises on thee here,
　　Give me hoirion ho a hau,
　　　Eho hir ir i-ivag o,
　　　Na hao hi ho a ro hau.

Ah mother mine and thou that art a deer,
　　Give me hoirion ho a hau,
Ere comes the chase-heat be o'er the hills clear,
　　Give me hoirion ho a hau,
　　　Eho hir ir i-ivag o,
　　　Na hao hi ho a ro hau.

Ah mother mine and thou that art a deer,
　　Give me hoirion ho a hau,
Beware thou the Fiann men a-hunting near,
　　Give me hoirion ho a hau,
　　　Eho hir ir i-ivag o,
　　　Na hao hi ho a ro hau.

Ah mother mine and thou that art a deer,
　　Give me hoirion ho a hau,
Beware thou the Fiann hounds as they career,
　　Give me hoirion ho a hau,
　　　Eho hir ir i-ivag o,
　　　Na hao hi ho a ro hau.

Be thou to corries of mishap away,
Beware thou the deeds of the hounds that bay,
The hounds of confusion, wrath-hounds that slay,
And they before thee in fury of fray.

Avoid Slender-one, and Swiftie evade,
Avoid darkie Paddler of banks assayed,
Avoid the she-hound with black tail arear,
Bran son of Yellowy, foe of the deer,
Of stag-pressing Sharpie be thou afraid.

Shouldst thou go down to the low-lying glen,
Do thou beware the Flash-Glint clan of men,
For the Flash-Glint clan and their hounds do stand
A twelve-hundred regiment of numbered men,
His very own blade in each hero's hand,

Each hound to his man, each man with his hound,
Each one of them on the MacLennan's thong,
And a wee little man in rocky ground,
While upon his leash he has twelve dogs strong,
And he fears he will miss the hunting sound.

Shouldst thou go up to the great massive ben,
Do thou beware the Great-Deed clan of men,
For the Great-Deed clan and their hounds do stand
A twelve-hundred regiment of numbered men,
His very own blade in each hero's hand.

Shouldst thou go up to the towering ben,
Do thou beware the Brave-Heart clan of men,
For the Brave-Heart clan and their hounds do stand
A twelve-hundred regiment of numbered men,
His very own blade in each hero's hand.

To the forest mist-land shouldst thou go then,
Do thou beware the Sight-Eyed clan of men,
For the Sight-Eyed clan and their hounds do stand
A twelve-hundred regiment of numbered men,
His very own blade in each hero's hand.

472. *Fàth-Fìth*   *North Uist and Glencoe*

Magic invisibility,
Its change I'll make on thee nor fail,
By Mary of the augury,
By Bridget of the mantling veil,
From sheep, from ram (they cannot spy),
From buck, from goat of shaggy coat,
From fox, from wolf (safe from their eye),
From boar, from sow (full hidden now),
From dog, from cat ready to spring,
From great-hipped bear that shambles there,
From dog of the wild, ravaging,
From watching eyes and preying sight,
From cow, from horse of angry force,
From heifer, bull of rushing might,

From daughter and from son who pry,
From bird on wing, from creeping thing,
From fish of sea, from every eye,
From imp of storm (covered to lie),
Hey presto, changed invisibly!

473. *The Spell of the Fox*   *Appin*

The spell of the wolf of the wood to hold
The sly padded thief who would reive the flocks,
To hold the desire and greed of the fox,
His gluttonous throat, sharp-toothed as the rocks,
His belly capacious in ample fold.

The charm of the Lord be on the sheep all,
The charm of Christ kind-white, gentle-white fall,
The charm of Mary mild-white, tender-white,
Against dogs, against birds, 'gainst men alight,
'Gainst dogs of fairy, and world dogs below,
Of the world to come, of the world to go.

474. *The Serpent*

The serpent shall come from her nest
On Saint Bride's morn early shall she,
The serpent I will not molest,
Nor shall she be molesting me.

The catkin will shoot forth its head,
The queen from the hill will appear,
Ivor's daughter from her hill-bed
With a tuneful whistle is near.

Stacks and hills on Saint Bride's Day white,
The serpent will come from the mound,
Though three-feet of snow should alight
And cover the smooth-mantled ground.

475. Little Beetle   *Melness*

Little beetle, little beetle,
Do you remember yesterday?
Little beetle, little beetle,
Do you remember yesterday?
Little beetle, little beetle,
Do you remember yesterday
The Son of God went by this way?

476. Omens   *Lismore*

Before my breakfast the cuckoo I heard,
I heard the stock-dove on the tree-top tall,
Beyond in the wood I heard the song-bird,
And I heard the barn-owl's night-hooting call.

I saw the lamb, his back turned to me here,
On a bare flagstone I saw the snail crawl,
I saw the foal with his quarters at rear,
I saw the wheatear on a drystone wall,
The snipe as I sat at ease I did see,
And I knew the year would go ill with me.

477. Easter Holidays   *South Uist*

Easter Monday early light,
I saw on the wave a-brim
A duck and a swan all white
And together did they swim.

It was Tuesday that I heard
A clear bleating in the sky,
For the snipe, the season's bird,
Was calling aloud on high.

And on Wednesday it would be
With my seaweed-cutting o'er,
That then I did see the three
As on the wing they did soar.

I knew then immediately
There was a going-away,
And no blessing there would be
In the wake of that to stay.

Bride the calm defending hold,
Mary mild defending hold,
Michael of war fending hold,
Round me and round mine enfold,
   Round me and round mine enfold.

XLII. BIRDS

The bird of the open, Saint Mary's lark,
 Soars rising high o'er the sea-girt meads;
As the morning light doth part from the dark
 Its quivering note God's worship leads.

The pyet, the pipit, the gull, the dove,
 The birds of the rock and of the shore,
O'er the surf wheeling, their cries above
 Sound calling beyond the breakers' roar.

The jackdaw and crow of Iona tower,
 The wheatear sained of the drystone wall,
The corncrake of field from its stalky bower,
 Make matin praise with the sparrow's call.

The swan and the goose are in from the sea,
 The long-tailed duck of MacAndy clan,
O'er the sound their sad and their glad notes flee
 As the racing currents and tides they span.

The birds of the hill, the birds of the sea,
 The diver, the shepherd of the deep,
The birds of the forest and of the tree,
 Awake all the world to prayer from sleep.

The eagle, the buzzard, the falcon grim,
 The brindled lanner of deadly flight,
God's avenging wrath is their quiet hymn
 As they swoop down silent from the height.

The raven-bird will return to its nest,
 The cuckoo flies back and brings the spring,
The petrel comes in from the sea for rest,
 Back to God the soul of man will wing.

478. *The Swan-Call*

Guiliog i! guiliog o!
Guiliog i! guiliog o!
Guiliog i! guiliog heard!
Call of the swan, call of the bird!

Call of the swan and she in mist,
Call of the swan and she forlorn,
Call of the swan in early dawn,
Call of the swan, the mere-face kist.

Call of the swan and she at sea,
Call of the swan and coldness there,
Call of the swan and biting air,
Call of the swan and she at sea.

My one foot black, my one foot black,
My one foot black with marching track;
My one foot black, where stream-mouth flows,
My other wounded plashing goes.

479. *The Swans*   *Benbecula*

I heard the swans how they sweetly sing,
As the day departed from the night,
Gurgling they were on the travelling wing,
Setting forth all their strength in the height.

I quickly stood still, and made no move,
But my two eyes were gazing at yon,
For who before should my guiding prove,
But the queen of the luck, the white swan?

Now this on a Friday's eve did fall,
And my thoughts on Tuesday all did stay—
My means and my folk they left me all
A year from that Friday's eve for aye.

But shouldst thou a swan on Friday see,
In the good morning joy of the day,
Increase to thy means and folk shall be,
And safe from dying thy flocks shall stay.

480. Consumption Charm *Tiree*

I tread upon thee, thou wasting rife,
    As a swan doth tread on the brine,
Wasting of back, chest-wasting of life,
    Wasting foul of the throat and spine.

May Christ's own Gospel bound to thee near
    Cure thee and all thy health replace,
The Healer of healers' Gospel dear,
    The Gospel of the God of grace,

To destroy from thee thy sickness dread
    In the pool of troubling that heals
Down from the topmost crown of thy head
    Unto the soles of thy two heels,

Forth from thy two loins thither to go,
Unto thy two loins hither to flow,
    From the kind God of love's embrace
And from all the Powers together so—
    Unto thee be the Love of grace!

481. *The Mavis*

FIRST MAVIS: O little red one!
                    O little red one!
                        Come away, son!
                        Come away, son!
                        Come away, son,
                    Home to your dinner, dear!

                        What is here?
                        What is here?

                    Worm and shell-sticker!
                    Worm and shell-sticker!

                        Quicker! quicker!
                        Night is looming!
                        Night is looming!
                            Dark glooming!

396

Poor Donald Mor!
Poor Donald Mor!
In jaw!
In jaw!
Swallow it!
Swallow it!
Every bit!
Every bit!
O Donald Mor!

And who made your knickers?
And who made your knickers?
They are too spare!
They are too spare!

The tailor MacLucas!
The tailor MacLucas!
Marred the pair!
Marred the pair!

THIRD MAVIS: Poor Donald Mor!
Poor Donald Mor!
Poor Donald Mor!
Your thirsty maw!
Your thirsty maw!
Swallow it!
Swallow it!
Every bit!
Every bit!

482. *The Corncrake*

O great God amain!
O great God amain!
Set food in the plain!
Set food in the grain!

483. The Crow

"Heart gnawing, flesh gnawing,
Wee black Robbie!" crow a-cawing.
"Heart gnawing, flesh gnawing,
Wee black Robbie!" crow a-cawing.

"Heart eating, flesh eating,
Bonnie little Donald sweeting!
Heart eating, flesh eating,
Bonnie little Donald sweeting!"

484. The Pigeon

Gu-roo! gu-roo! gu-roo!
Not of my clan are you!
Not of my clan are you!
My clan is good and true!
Gu-roo! gu-roo! gu-roo!

485. The Long-Tailed Duck   Berneray of Harris

Clan MacAndy!
Clan MacAndy!
Kinsmen weedy!
Kinsmen weedy!
Vioch! voch! vuch!
Uv-uv! uv-uv! uv-uv!
O! u! o! u!
U! o! u! o!
Ur! ur! ah!

Clan MacAndy!
Clan MacAndy!
Tribesmen greedy!
Tribesmen greedy!
Vioch! voch! vuch!
Uv-uv! uv-uv! uv-uv!
U! o! u! o!
O! u! o! u!
Our o! Our a!

Clan MacAndy!
Clan MacAndy!
Sowens handy?
Sowens handy?
Vioch! voch! vuch!
Uv-uv! uv-uv! uv-uv!
O! u! o! u!
U! o! u! o!

Grub! grub! grub!
Vioch! voch! vuch!
Uv-uv! uv-uv! uv-uv!
Uv-uv! o! u!
O! u! o! u!
U! o! u! o!

Ye sea-birds of sea-sigh,
That from the sea fly,
Sweet the sea-cry,
Sea-singing a vu!
Sea-singing a vu!

On the strand now what is new?
Sea-singing a vu!
Sea-singing a vu!
Swelling-singing! sea-singing! spray-singing vu!
Sea-singing a vu!
Sea-singing a vu!

Love's friendly heart is for you,
Sea-singing a vu!
Sea-singing a vu!
Swelling-singing! sea-singing! spray-singing vu!
Sea-singing a vu!
Sea-singing a vu!

Wind on lea, calm on the sea,
Sea-singing a vu!
Sea-singing a vu!
Swelling-singing! sea-singing! spray-singing vu!
Sea-singing a vu!
Sea-singing a vu!

Ye sea-birds of sea sigh,
That from the sea fly,
Sweet the sea-cry,
Sea-singing a vu!
Sea-singing a vu!

486. The Black-Throated Diver

Uist, Harris and Lewis

Slake! slake! slake!
The loch forsaking!
Slake! slake! slake!
The loch betaking!
Lake! lake! lake!
My heart is quaking!
Lake! lake! lake!
My strength is breaking!

Drink! drink! drink!
The water shrinking!
Drink! drink! drink!
The water slinking!
Brink! brink! brink!
Brink! brink! brink!
Brink! brink! brink!
My strength is sinking!

487. The Diver and the Rising Water

My woe! my woe!
My birds and my eggs.
My woe! my woe!
My birds and my eggs.
My oh! my oh!
My young with wet legs.
My oh! my oh!
My young with wet legs.
O my brood!
O my food!
My birds!
My eggs!
My dears!
My fears!

XLIII. PLANTS

Over the nine waves of the breaking sea
           Amid the sands
           On distant strands
           The figwort stands,
Saint Ternan's emblem of fertility,
White-flow'ring large, of healing property.

Beside the sands on emerald stretching plain
           Its double roots
           For seed and fruits
           The carrot shoots;
Saint John's wort bright and shamrock green are lain
With fairy flaxes, blue and white the twain.

Beyond the meads where sedgy lochans lie
           White tansy blows,
           Marsh-violet grows,
           Bog-myrtle shows
Its candle-branches to the reeds' wind-sigh,
With sticky butterwort of purple eye.

In hollows and the brakes of straggling trees
           The aspen quakes,
           The willow shakes;
           The bramble snakes
Where black-thorn blossoms; ivy-twine doth seize
The tasselled birch-trunks, catkins in the breeze.

Up from the rowan tree beside the door
           Wood-sorrel white,
           The primrose bright,
           The pearlwort slight
Bespread the spring-time shieling pasture-floor
Where folded glen gives place to tufted moor.

The club-moss covering drapes the soaring hill;
           The yarrow tough
           Doth grace the rough;
           On rocky bluff
The juniper to life doth cling, and still
From these the herbal virtues will distil.

The shield and warding from the Three-in-One—
The Father's dower,
The Son his flower,
The Spirit's power—
The plant-gathering in their name is done,
Produce, increase and safety to be won.

488. Saint Mary of the Flowers
Lochaber and Barra

Flower-crowned one of the ocean face,
Flower-crowned one of the earthly place,
Flower-crowned one of the heav'nly space,
Mary Mother of the God of grace.

Flower-crowned one of the land corn-sown,
Flower-crowned one of the wide sky-throne,
Flower-crowned one of the angels known,
Mary Mother of the God foreshown.

Flower-crowned one of the palaces,
Flower-crowned one of the star-filled skies,
Flower-crowned one of the paradise,
Mary Mother of the God so wise.

489. The Sure Yarrow
Skye and North Uist

I will pluck the yarrow sure,
That more kind my look endure,
That more might my hand may know,
That more swift my foot may go,
That more warm my lips may be,
That my speech show modesty,
Be my speech by sunbeams fed,
And my lips by strawberry red.

Island in the sea be I,
Hill on shore commanding lie,
Waning moon, a star in sky,
To the weak a staff to be,
Wounding able to give free,
No man able to wound me.

490. The "White-Joy" Plant
North Uist

I place the "white-joy" plant on me,
To ebb and drain all wrath and strife,
Safe-keeping for my fame to be,
Throughout the span of earthly life.

O Michael, take my hand in thine,
The love of God smoothe unto me,
If foe's ill-will or wish be mine,
'Twixt him and me Christ do thou be,
   O Christ, 'twixt him and me!

Ill-will or wish concerning me,
'Twixt it and me Christ do thou be,
   O Christ, 'twixt it and me!

491. *The Red-Stalk of Saint Bride*　　　　　*Barra*

So sure the red-stalk is for me to find,
The lint the gentle Bride found with her hand,
For the sake of health, and for friendship kind,
And for sake of sweet content to stand;
For sake of overcoming evil mind,
And evil eye, and witching to withstand,
For sake of evil deed, and doing planned,
For sake of overcoming when maligned,
For sake of evil tale, and talk behind,
For sake of bliss the red-stalk in my hand—
For sake of bliss the virtue I will bind.

492. *The Figwort*　　　　*Baleshare of North Uist*

I will pluck the figwort from the strand,
With the fruitfulness of sea and land.
As tide ebbs not but inflows o'er sand,
O Saint Mary gentle, with thy hand.

Columba kind, navigator mine,
Oran holy with his shielding sign,
Bride of women virtuously fine
Virtue-seed shall set within the kine.

As the King of kings ordained and blest,
To put milk within the flesh and breast,
As the Sovereign of life ordained best,
In gland, in udder the sap to rest.

In the udder of the badger slow,
In the udder of the reindeer flow,
In the udder of the whale below,
In the udder of the mare to go.

In the udder of the sow to show,
In the udder of the heifer so,
In the udder of the goat to grow,
Of the sheep and ewe, of cow and roe.

With milk, with cream, and with butter sent,
With pair, with mate, and with increment,
With she-calves surpassing excellent,
With young, and with fortune, with content.

No man evil-wishing to be there,
No woman with evil eye to scare,
No malice, no jealousy to bear,
Nor one single evil thing to snare.

In the twelve Apostles' saintly name,
In God's Mother Mary's name the same,
In the very Christ's own self-same name,
And Saint Patrick's of immortal fame.

493. *The Figwort Gathering*   *Benbecula*

I will pluck up the figwort of the beach,
Of blessings, of virtues, a thousand each,
Calm Bride endowing it unto my reach,
Mary the mild enriching, I beseech,
Mary the great, the people's Mother-leech.

Nine were the joys that traversed to the land,
Nine were the sea-waves that broke on the sand,
To pluck the figwort growing on the strand,
A thousand its blessings, virtues, to hand—
O a thousand blessings, virtues, to hand.

The arm of Christ encircle me around,
The face of Christ ahead to scan the bound,
The shade of Christ defending o'er me crowned,
My noble plant surpassing plucked from ground—
O noble plant surpassing plucked from ground.

In the holy name of the Father wise,
In the Christ's name, of Paschal sacrifice,
In Holy Spirit's name who grace supplies,
Who in a death's debating never flies,
Who will not leave me till a moonday nighs—
　　Who in a death's debating never flies,
　　Who will not leave me when the Doomday nighs.

494. *The Fairy Wort*   *Skye and North Uist*

I will pick the fairy wort,
Hoping, from the fairy bower,
To suppress confusion, hurt,
While it be the fairy wort.

Fairy wort, O fairy wort,
Envy I a maid thy power,
Nothing by the sun engirt,
But to her victory sure.

I will pick mine honoured plant,
Mary-picked, man's Mother-aid,
Silly scandal scathe to daunt,
Bad life, bad love, bad luck laid,
Hate, lie, fraud, and vexing stayed,
Till beneath the sod my haunt.

495. *Saint Columcill's Wort*

O arm-worn wort of Columcill,
　　I searched thee not nor sought!
Please God and Christ for this year still
　　I die not ere I ought.

O wild and lordling wort of gold,
　　My envy who have thee;
Who has thee in his cattle-fold,
　　Kineless shall never be.

496. *The Bog-Violet* *Benbecula*

    I will pluck up the friendly plant to-day,
    As plucked the world-King, victor in the fray;
    In Father's, Son's, and Spirit's name for aye,
    Bride, Mary, Michael, my true vanguard they.

    I in the field of danger and red fight,
    In which doth ebb each wrath and raging might,
    The cause of every joy and each delight,
    The Lord's o'ershadowing my shield aright.

497. *The Sandwort* *Benbecula*

    The little flower I will gather now,
    Nine plants for joining to make the ring,
    And I will gather and make my vow,
    To noble Bride and her Fosterling.

    The little flower I will gather now,
    As did the King of the powers ordain,
    And I will gather and make my vow,
    To Mary great and her Son who reign.

    The little flower I will gather now ,
    As did the King of all life ordain,
    To rise above each oppression-brow,
    And the spell of evil eye restrain.

498. *The Butterwort*

    I will cull the flower a-blowing
    Beneath a Sunday's white sunlight,
    Beneath the Virgin's hand pure-white,
    In the Trinity's name and sight
      Who bestowed on it the growing.

      While I keep the flower of knowing,
    No evil be within mine eye,
    No hurting in my mouth to lie,
    No sadness for my heart to sigh,
      Be my death a guileless going.

> Myself I pluck the catkin's woolly strand,
> The lint the gentle Bride plucked through her hand,
> For virtue, for kine, for increase to grow,
> ·For pairing, for udder, for milking's flow,
> For placid female calves all bellied white,
> As in the prophecy foretold aright.

500. *The Silverweed of Spring*

> The silverweed blest that grows in the spring
> Is of the seven breads of the Gael;
> The silverweed root that is nourishing
> Is of the seven foods without fail
> That most excellent
> Through the ground are sent.

501. *The Primrose*

> Primrose, pretty primrose,
> Wood-sorrel shyly shows,
> Free food for children grows
> Ere summer sunshine goes;
> But fettered, fettered, bound,
> With wine and plovers round,
> Rich food of men is found
> The winter-snow on ground.

502. *The Mountain-Yew*

> I will gather the juniper of joy,
> One sprigged-rib lovely for the Jesus Boy,
> In name of Father, Son and Spirit wise,
> Against all storm and stress and weary sighs.
>
> I will gather the juniper of joy,
> Three sprigged-ribs lovely for the Jesus Boy,
> In name of Father, Son and Spirit's grace,
> Against all hardness, pain and heartbreak-trace.

I will gather the juniper of joy,
Nine sprigged-ribs lovely for the Jesus Boy,
In name of Father, Son and Spirit's grace,
Against all drowning, fear, in danger's face.

503. The Bog-Myrtle

I pluck thee for the bonnet of my head,
Thou plant of readiness bog-myrtle red,
In name of Father of the virtues bred,
In name of Son my sweet worshippéd,
In name of God's eternal Spirit shed.

I pluck for virtue of good man's estate,
For virtue of good life-race dedicate,
For virtue of good woman to create,
For virtue of good life to consecrate,
For virtue of good step and journey great.

I pluck for virtue of good love at heart,
For virtue of good leap and venture's part,
For virtue of good cause, faith to impart,
For virtue of good lifetime, living's art,
Reproachless be it and no peril's smart.

504. The Double Carrot

A fork! a fork! a·forked and twofold root!
    Best carrot of the gladness for me!
A fork! a fork! a forked and twofold fruit!
    Best carrot of increase let it be!

Michael of war will give me fruit and seed,
    Calm Bride will give the love to the maid,
Fāth-Fīth will give wine, milk and honey-mead,
    And Mary mild will give me her aid.

O shamrock so leafy,
    O shamrock of power,
O shamrock so leafy,
    Of Mary's bank-bower,
O shamrock, I love thee,
    Of beauteous green,
For death's grave above me
    My choice be thy sheen,
For death's grave above me
    My choice be thy sheen.

XLIV. EVENING

At eventide the embers' heat
Is smoored by heaped-up glowing peat,
An unseen steady watch all night,
An angel flame within alight.

An angel takes the soul in dream
Through the wide realms of starry gleam,
The City walls that distant lie,
The gates eternal to descry.

An angel stands upon the floor,
A sentinel without the door,
A keeper stands beside the bed,
A tender guards the sleeper's head.

And so the household safe doth rest
To rise again with safety blest,
By the power of the Holy Three
Kept as the Holy Family.

For the Chiefs divine condescend
To lodge the night with clansman friend,
The Father, Son, and Holy Ghost
Sleep as the clansman-sinner's host.

The holy Three
For saving be,
To act as guard,
To aid and ward
The hearthstone fire,
The house entire,
The household all
As eve doth fall,
And night enthrall,
This evening light,
And o this night!
Each evening light,
Each single night.
So may it be,
O holy Three,
Amen to me.

507. *The Compassing of the Smooring*

This night I smoor my fire its flame to keep
As would the Son of Mary smoor ere sleep;
God's compassing for me and fire aglow,
God's compassing for me and everyone;
God's compassing for me and hearthstone done,
God's compassing for me and floor-pit low,
And on each flock and on each cattle herd,
Upon the household all in sleep unstirred.

508. *The Night Smooring*

I smoor the fire this night in portions three
As would the Son of Mary smoor the fire;
God's compass on the peats and fire to be,
God's compass on the company entire.

God's compass be about ourselves to hold,
God's compass be about us all in sleep,
God's compass be upon the flock of fold,
God's compass be upon the hearth to keep.

Who keeps the night-watch now and over mine?
Who but the Lord Christ of the poor is there,
The mild-white Bride, the maiden of the kine,
The mild-white Mary of the curling hair?

Sound be the house and sound the herd around,
Sound be the son and sound the daughter dear,
Sound be the wife and be the houseman sound,
And sound be all the household that is here.

509. *Sleeping Prayer*   *South Uist*

My soul and my body this night I place
On thy sanctuary, O thou God of grace,
On thy sanctuary, O Jesus Christ, here,
On thy sanctuary, Spirit true and clear,
    They who would stand to my cause, the Three,
        Nor coldly turn their backs on me.

Thou Father, righteous and kind one who art,
Thou Son, who o'er sin didst play victor's part,
Thou Holy Spirit of the mighty arm,
Give keeping to me this night from all harm;
    They who would my right uphold, the Three,
        This night and always keeping me.

510. *Resting Blessing*   *South Uist*

In name of Rabbi Jesus of avail,
And of the Spirit of the balm so blest,
In the name of the Father of Israel,
        I lay me down to rest.

If any trick or evil threat there be,
Or secret that on me fate doth contrive,
May God encompass me and make me free,
        Mine enemy forth drive.

In the name of the Father richly dear,
And of the Spirit of the balm so blest,
In name of Rabbi Jesus who is near,
     I lay me down to rest.

O God, encompass me and give me aid,
From this hour till my death the hour invade.

511. *The Sleep-Prayer*   *Benbecula*

I am going now into the sleep,
    Be it that I in health shall wake;
If death be to me in deathly sleep,
    Be it that in thine own arm's keep,
O God of grace, to new life I wake;
     O be it in thy dear arm's keep,
    O God of grace, that I shall awake!

Be my soul on thy right hand, O God,
    O thou King of the heaven of heaven;
Thou it was who didst buy with thy blood,
    Thine the life for my sake was given;
Encompass thou me this night, O God,
    That no harm, no mischief be given.

Whilst in the sleep the body doth stay,
    The soul in heaven's shadow doth stray,
Red-white Michael to meet by the way,
    Amen, early, late, night and day,
    Early and late, and night and day.

512. *The Gifts of the Three*   *South Uist*

Spirit so rich, of thy richness give,
Father so wise, give wisdom to live,
Son, to me in deficiency yield
'Neath the shelter, Jesus, of thy shield.

I lie me down to sleep for this night,
With the great Trinity of my might,
With the Father, with the Jesus Son,
And with the Spirit of great deeds done.

513. Sleep Sanctification   Benbecula

Down to-night my body I lay,
With the Father, and with the Son,
With the Spirit of truth to stay,
Who to shield me from harm are One.

With evil I will not lie down,
Nor shall evil lie down with me,
But with God I will lie me down,
God himself will lie down with me.

God and Christ and the Holy Ghost,
And the cross of white angels nine,
As Three and as One my shield-host,
From brow-tablet to foot-tip mine.

King of glory and of the sun,
Jesu, Son of the fragrant Maid,
Keep us from the glen where tears run,
From the house of sorrow's black shade,
  Keep us from the glen where tears run,
  The grim house of sorrow's black shade.

514. Bed Protection   Benbecula

Now in my bed down I lie
As I would lie when in the grave,
  'Neath my neck thine arm is by,
Virtue-MacMary born to save.

Angels wake and cover me
While I lie down in slumber deep,
  And angels watch over me
While in the grave I lie in sleep.

At my feet be Uriel,
At my back shall Ariel stand,
  At my brow be Gabriel,
Raphael shall be at my hand.

Michael shall be with my soul,
Strong buckler that I long to get!
Son of Mary, making whole,
The salve unto mine eye shall set,
Son of Mary, making whole,
The salve unto mine eye shall set!

515. *Night Prayer* *South Uist*

In thy name, O Jesu who wast crucified,
Down I lay myself for my repose;
In sleep far-away do thou watch by my side,
In thy one hand do thou hold me close;
In sleep far-away do thou watch by my side,
In thy one hand do thou hold me close.

Thy blessing, O my Christ, be upon me laid,
Unto me a buckler shielding be,
In the sinking bogland to my steps give aid,
To eternal life be leading me;
In the sinking bogland to my steps give aid,
To eternal life be leading me.

In the face of God o keep me, Son so fair,
Virgin's Son so good to whom I pray
Urging thee to grant thy strong unceasing care
From lie-down dusk till I rise at day;
Urging thee to grant thy strong unceasing care
From lie-down dusk till I rise at day.

516. *Sleep Invocation*

Down on my bed this night I lie,
With Bridget of the veils nearby,
Mary of peace upon the floor,
And with the Jesus of the poor.

Down on my bed this night I lie
With Saint Bridget the meek nearby,
With Mary whom we all revere,
With Michael of my wishing here.

Down on my bed this night I lie,
The King of life is lying nigh,
Christ of the naked lying near,
Nigh is the Holy Spirit here.

Down on my bed this night I lie,
With the nine crosses bright nearby,
From the top-crownings of my head
To where my soles are lying spread;
 From the top-crownings of my head
 To where my soles are lying spread.

517. *The Trinity at Night*

With God will I lie down this night,
And God will be lying with me;
With Christ will I lie down this night,
And Christ will be lying with me;
With Spirit I lie down this night,
The Spirit will lie down with me;
God and Christ and the Spirit, Three,
Be they all down-lying with me.

518. *Quietude of Sleep*   *Kintail*

  O God of life, this night
O darken not to me thy light,
  O God of life, this night
Close not thy gladness to my sight,
  O God of life, this night
Thy door to me o shut not tight,
  O God of life, this night
Refuse not mercy to my plight,
  O God of life, this night
Quell unto me thy grieving slight,
  O God of life, this night
Crown thou to me thy joy's delight,
O crown to me thy joy's delight,
  O God of life, this night.

519. Repose

Of virtues thou Being,
　　Shield me with thy might,
Thou Being decreeing
　　And of the starlight.

This night be my compass,
　　For body and soul,
This night be my compass,
　　Each night compass whole.

Aright be my compass
　　'Twixt earth and the sky,
Law-light be my compass
　　And for my blind eye;

That eye-caught belonging
　　And that unread here;
That clear to my longing
　　And what is unclear.

XLV. DEATH

So silently the sunshine falls and lies,
          The air is still
          O'er sea and hill,
And no bird sings or hovers in the skies;
          For all is peace
          As breath doth cease
And up the golden butterfly doth rise.

So quietly the soul doth make its prayer,—
          O Lord, forgive,
          Repentance give;
And happy death with shriving be it there,
          The dear soul-friend
          Close at the end
As forth the soul doth heavenward repair.

So shieldingly the angels spread a wing
          As by the gates
          Saint Michael waits
For the soul at the beam's fair balancing;
          And joy doth rise
          Beyond the skies
While the good outweighs and the harpers string.

So lovingly the Lord Christ on his throne
          The soul doth greet,
          As at his feet
Trembling the little draggler stands alone;
          And rest and peace
          Shall never cease
For one that he is not ashamed to own.

520. *The Golden Butterfly*

Butterfly, O butterfly!
Whose soul didst thou take and fly,
Butterfly, O butterfly!
Yesterday beyond the sky?

521. *The Rowan-Tree*

Before the door thou berried rowan tree,
'Neath me go thou to the burying place,
Then toward Dundealgan shall they put my face,
And a fair bier thou shalt be made for me.

522. *The Day of Death*

The black wrath of the God of life doth lie
As forth the soul of shadow-woe doth fly;
The white wrath of the King of stars doth snow
As forth the silent-hiding soul doth go.

A hush of birds is on the land and sea,
And peace comes down on moor and meadow-lea,
The twinkling look and smile of the King's grace
To the weak one downshine on ocean's face.

A day of peace, a day of joy inspire,
A day of brightness be when I expire;
For my salvation may Saint Michael's hand
Seek me when sunny whiteness bathes the land.

523. *A Last Prayer*

To Saint Peter, Saint Paul I pray my request,
To the Virgin I pray, I pray to the Son,
And I pray to the Twelve Apostles of rest
That I go not this night to ruin undone.

When the soul parts and goes from the body sly,
From mortal frame up in bright puddles of light,
Holy God of eternity from on high
Come to seek me, to find me, save me outright.

May God and may Jesus give aid unto me,
May God and may Jesus defending me be;
May God and may Jesus everlastingly
Seek for me and find me and save me wholly.

524. Death's Ford

O may the Father clasp you in his hand,
His fragrant loving clasp bring you to land,
Across the flooding torrent when you go
And when the stream of death doth blackly flow.

525. The Soul-Leading   South Uist

Lay this soul, O Christ, within thine arm,
    Thou King of the heavenly city;
Since thou, O Christ, didst redeem from harm
    This soul, keep it peaceful in pity.
And Michael of war, the angels' king,
    For this soul a crossing make steady;
O Michael of war with peace greeting
    A path to the kingdom make ready.

526. The Death-Blessing   South Uist

O God, this thy servant now in thy sight
Do not from thy covenant-grace omit,
For the sins which the body doth commit
That cannot be all accounted to-night,
O God, this thy servant now in thy sight,
        This thy servant now in thy sight.

Be this soul, O Christ, laid on thine own arm,
O thou King of heaven's city of dream,
And since it was thou didst this soul redeem,
The time of the balancing of the beam,
The time of the giving the judgement calm,
Be this soul, O Christ, laid on thy right arm,
    This soul now upon thy right arm.

And be holy Michael, the angels' king,
Forth coming to meet the soul as it wends,
Bringing it home as it upward ascends
To the Son of God's heavenly dwelling;
The holy Michael, the angels' archking,
Forth coming to meet the soul on the wing,
And bringing it homeward led by the hand
Into the Son of God's heavenly land,
    The Son of God's heavenly land.

527. *Soul Peace*   *South Uist*

Since thou Christ by purchase the soul didst get—
At the time when the life is paid away,
At the time when bursts forth the body's sweat,
At the time when up is offered the clay,
At the time when away the blood is shed,
At the time when the beam doth truly weigh,
At the time when the upcaught breath is fled,
At the time of the given judgement's say,
Be the peace of the soul thine own to keep;
Jesus Christ Son of Mary gentle Maid,
Be the peace of the soul thine own to keep,
    O Jesu, in thine own keeping laid.

And may Michael the white and kindly one,
The high king of the holy angel-host,
Of the soul beloved possession won,
Shield it to the Three of lovingness most,
    O unto the Three of lovingness most.

528. *Passing*

> The miserable soul doth freely flee,
> Out from its shrine it ascends above,
> O kindly Christ of the blessings free,
> Enfold in time the one of my love.

529. *The White Purifying*   *Barra*

> Till whiter than the singing swans so white,
> Till whiter than the wave-kist seagulls go,
> Till whiter than the snows upon the height,
> And whiter than the white love heroes know
>   Shall be the good men who on earth have died,
>   By white-winged angels fanned and purified.

530. *Going Home*   *Lewis*

> I am going home with thee
>   To thy home, to thy home!
> I am going home with thee
>   To thy home, winter come.
>
> I am going home with thee
>   To thy home, to thy home!
> I am going home with thee
>   To thy home, autumn come.
>
> I am going home with thee
>   To thy home, to thy home!
> I am going home with thee
>   To thy home, springtime come.
>
> I am going home with thee
>   To thy home, to thy home!
> I am going home with thee
>   To thy home, summer come.
>
> I am going home with thee,
>   Little child of my love,
> To thy bed eternally,
>   Long thy sleep lasts above.

I am going home with thee,
Little child of my love,
To the dear Son blessing thee,
To Father's arms above.

531. *Death Dirge*

Thou goest home this night unto thy winter's home,
To thy home of autumn, of spring, of summer-clime;
Thou goest home this night to thy perpetual home,
To thine eternal bed, thy lasting slumber-time.

O sleep thou, sleep, with thy sorrow away and sleep,
O sleep thou, sleep, with thy sorrow away and sleep,
O sleep thou, sleep, with thy sorrow away and sleep;
O sleep, thou sweet one, the Rock of the fold thy keep.

O sleep thou this night in thy Mother Maiden's breast,
O sleep, thou darling one, she soothing thee in bliss;
O sleep thou this night on the Virgin's arm at rest,
O sleep, thou belov'd one, while she herself doth kiss.

The great sleep of Jesus, the sleep surpassing deep,
The sleep of Jesu's wound, of Jesus sorrow-pressed,
The young sleep of Jesus, Jesu's restoring sleep,
The kiss-sleep of Jesus with peace and glory blest.

Darling, thine be sleep of the seven lights that shine,
Darling, thine be sleep of the seven joys the best,
Darling, sweet be sleep of the seven slumbers thine
On blessing Jesu's arm, the virtue-Christ's, to rest.

Death's shadow, O my dear, upon thy face doth lie,
But the Jesus of grace about thee hath his hand;
To thy pains be health from the Trinity anigh,
Calm is in Christ's mind as before thee he doth stand.

Tranquil be thy sleep, the sleep of tranquillity,
Guided by thy sleep, the sleep of the guided way,
Loving be thy sleep, the sleep of loving for thee;
In the Lord Chief of life, o sleep, my love, for aye,
And in the God of life, o sleep, my love, for aye.

532. The River Hard to See

Each saint of the host in the heavenly land,
Each holy woman of the heavenly band,
Each wingéd angel that in heaven doth stand,
May their arms outstretched to thee in welcome be,
May they smooth the way and clear be it for thee,
At the hour when thither beyond thou dost go
Across the dark river that is hard to see;
At the hour when thither thy home thou dost know,
    O across the river hard to see.

533. Saint Oran

Holy Saint Oran in the grave interred
Opened his eyes and uttered forth this word.

"The heav'n is not as they averring claim,
Nor is the hell as they asserting say,
The good is not for ever bliss the same,
The bad is not a misery for aye."

Columba listening stood beside the grave,
And wise the answer that straightway he gave.

"The earth, the earth on Oran's eye be laid,
Ere keen confusion's striving he awake,
Lest men of faith too open-eyed be made,
Lest brother-men too open-eyed mistake."

534. The Judgement Flood   North Uist

The great storm will come when Monday's a day,
    All the world of the air will outpour,
And through all its lasting we shall obey,
    We whose ears will be filled with its roar.

The freezing will come when Tuesday's a day,
    All pain to the heart and piercing fine,
Flecking from the cheeks, though pale of array,
    Blood as red as the red-pouring wine.

The wind it will blow when Wednesday's a day,
    Sweeping bare down the strath and the plain,
Sharp-showering the gusts that cut and slay,
    Thunderclaps and mountains split in twain.

The rain it will pour when Thursday's a day,
    Driving men into blind rushing flight,
Faster than leaves which scurry from the spray,
    A-shake like Mary's plant-leaves in fright.

The dark cloud will come when Friday's a day,
    The direst dread that ever was known,
Multitudes left with their reason astray,
    Grass and fish underneath the one stone.

The great sea will come Saturday's a day,
    Moving with a river's flowing might,
Each and every one with a smile away
    As they hasten to a hill's safe height.

My King will arise when Sunday's a day,
    Full of anger, full of sorrow's pain,
As he hears the bitter words all men say,
    A red cross on each right shoulder lain.

535. Iona

A seven years it is before the Judgement Ides,
The sea in single tide over Ireland strides,
And all Islay's greens and grassiness it hides,
Iona still, Columba's church, serene yet rides.

EPILOGUE

O Father almighty, of kindly face,
O Father mighty, creator of space,
O Father almighty, giver of grace,
        O be thine all my praise.

Thou didst set mountain and water-fringed sand,
Thou didst set grasses and streams in the land,
Thou didst set creatures, thou the townlands manned,
        O be thine my heart-raise.

Thou didst throw breezes across sand and plain,
Thou didst show cloudmists indriving the rain,
Thou didst sow sunlight with growth-force amain,
        O be thine my voice-lays.

O Christ, Son of Mary, born holy night,
O Christ of the cradle, so snowy white,
O Christ of the temple, inquiring, bright,
        Do thou heed me my days.

O Christ of the river and Holy Bird,
O Christ of the Father's heavenly word,
O Christ of the desert, the tempter heard,
        Do thou lead me my ways.

O Christ of the lakeside, summoning thine,
O Christ of the wedding, producing wine,
O Christ of the mountain, teacher divine,
        Do thou plead with thy gaze.

O Christ of the healing, fever's allay,
O Christ of the shieling, finding the stray,
O Christ of the kneeling alone to pray,
        Tend thy servant who prays.

O Christ of the feeding, multitudes there,
O Christ of the heeding to every prayer,
O Christ of the leading, transfigured fair,
           Friend thy servant who strays.

O Christ of the riding, welcomed with palm,
O Christ of the striding, whip to thine arm,
O Christ of the biding 'neath olive calm,
           Fend thy servant who lays.

O Christ of the life-bread in upper room,
O Christ of the cup shed, faithful bridegroom,
O Christ of the night tread to garden gloom,
           Guard thy sheep as they graze.

O Christ of the kissing, force-led away,
O Christ of the hissing, the buffet-play,
O Christ of the missing witnesses' say,
           Pardon him that betrays.

O Christ of the hall of the ruler's state,
O Christ of the call for crucified fate,
O Christ of the pall, man indicate,
           Harden, stablish always.

O Christ of the crown that the soldiers made,
O Christ, falling down 'neath the cross-piece laid,
O Christ of the gown for which guardsmen played,
           Of thy passion's delays;

O Christ, foemen forgiving, as they nailed,
O Christ, paradise living, as they railed,
O Christ, mother-son-giving, as light failed,
           God's forsaken amaze,

O Christ of the thirst, outstretched on the tree,
O Christ finished, curst for the sake of me,
O Christ's spirit burst and commended, he
           To the Father's hands pays;

O Christ of the side that was pierced and driven,
O Christ crucified, and thy heart was riven,
O Christ, the tomb's bride of the garden given,
            O Christ, lying three days,

O Christ of the rising, of Mary seen,
O Christ so surprising, the locked room's scene,
O Christ supervising the water's sheen
            As the fishing boat weighs,

O Christ ascending to Father's right hand,
O Christ outsending the missionary band,
O Christ attending the prayer, by me stand
            All my nights and my days.

O Spirit of power and the double flame,
O Spirit of power, to the Twelve who came,
O Spirit of power and baptism name,
            Compass me with thy rays.

O Spirit of wisdom, Spirit of might,
O Spirit of counsel, strength for the fight,
O Spirit of fear, understanding's sight,
            And where godliness stays;

O Spirit of faith, the descending dove,
O Spirit of hope outpoured from above,
O Spirit infusing and breathing love,
            Lighten, set me ablaze.

O Trinity ever for come and go,
O Trinity ever for to and fro,
O Trinity ever for ebb and flow,
            Where the ocean wave plays;

O Trinity, lengthen my days, protect,
O Trinity, strengthen me and direct,
O Trinity, chasten me and correct
            In my each wayward phase.

O Trinity, singular and complete,
O Trinity, Father, Son, Paraclete,
O Trinity, lantern unto my feet,
       Guide to paradise braes.

NOTES TO POEMS

The notes to the poems are numbered according to their arrangement in this book. Immediately following comes the reference to the original in the *Carmina Gadelica* volumes and pages, and the name of the reciter, if known.

1   i. 230-1. *Mary Maclellan (Macdonald), crofter's wife, Howgarry, North Uist.*
The first work of the day was kindling the fire (kept in all night) by "lifting" the peats. Nearly all tasks were, when suitable, performed ceremonially, if simply. Angel and fire ("his ministers a flame of fire") are synonymous in Gaelic. Cf. 169.

2   iii. 40-7. *Mary Gillies, crofter, Morar.*
This is a morning prayer; there is no other like it in the collection. Is it possible that there might be some portions of a creed-hymn (repeated in the Celtic Church services) remembered and handed down as a private devotion? There is a break in the text at the introduction of baptism owing to the reciter becoming confused at being delayed by transcribing.

3   iii. 64-7. Cf. 91.

4   iii. 314-15. *Malcolm Macmillan, merchant, Monkstown, Benbecula.*

5   iii. 316-17. *Malcolm Macmillan, merchant, Monkstown, Benbecula.*
Sometimes a Eucharistic feature (in the Anglican liturgy the prayer for the Sovereign) attached itself to this moment. In Skye, says Martin, "The islanders have a great respect for their chiefs and heads of tribes, and they generally conclude grace after every meal with a petition to God for their welfare and prosperity" (p. 248).

6   iii. 178-9. *Dugal Macaulay, cottar, Creagorry, South Hacklett, Benbecula.*

7   iii. 230-3. *Mary Mackintosh (Smith), tailor's wife, Garrynamonie, South Boisdale, South Uist.*
This is a woman's prayer for the men of the house. There is a gap in the text at the end of the power (*feart*) lines, while the Fiann have melted into "power on land". "Pillow-death" was rare among fishermen and rock-climbers or "rockers".

8   iii. 202-3.

9   i. 240-1. *Catherine Macpharlan (Pearson), soldier's wife, Kenntangaval, Barra.*
As "lifting" the peats was the first household duty, "smooring" or smothering them (to keep them in) was the last. Cf. 175, 506ff.

10   iii. 344-5.
The words *todhar* and *todhraich* are of manuring or of bleaching and "making white".

435

11   iii. 356-7.

12   i. 66-7. *Archibald Currie, shoemaker, Ardnamonie, Iochdar,
     South Uist.*
     Highland people believed that each person was attended by an
     angel (good or bad), who, during sleep, would conduct the soul
     heavenwards or otherwise. The cross of the nine angels is a
     technical term (explained by Dr Douglas Hyde, ii. pp. 32-3); two
     angels moving outwards in each direction in the form of a cross
     from a central figure: ....:.... thus.

13   i. 88-9. *Archibald Currie, shoemaker, Ardnamonie, Iochdar,
     South Uist.*
     The "lying down" theme is discussed in the introduction. Cf. 50,
     256, 513, 516f.

14   i. 176-7. *Janet Campbell (Mackinnon, from Skye), nurse, Loch
     Skiport, South Uist.*
     St Bridget or St Bride of the Isles, patroness of spring and of birth,
     by tradition was the aid-woman in the stable at Bethlehem and
     the fostermother of Christ.

15   i. 166.
     This verse was part of the ritual attending childbirth. The midwife
     (or another woman), standing on the doorstep, made the petition
     before beginning her task.

16   iv. 192-3.
     This conversation motif was a favourite form of healing prayer.
     The kidney-nut of Mary (an Atlantic nut or bean with a natural
     cross-marking) was used as a talisman and was held tightly by the
     mother.

17   iv. 192-3.

18   iv. 16-17.
     The two sleep lines are inserted.

19   ii. 301-2.
     A shepherdess nursing her child heard a fairy singing this to her
     changeling in the bower. Lismore in Loch Linnhe (both a royal
     and holy place) was the boyhood home of Dr Alexander Car-
     michael.

20   ii. 194-201. *John Ewen Macrury, farmer, Griminish, Benbecula.*
     A woman with a sickly child found a wounded swan on a frozen
     lake. She cared for the bird, and her child grew well also. There
     is a break where the second person changes to the third.

21   i. 60-3. *Janet Campbell (Mackinnon, from Skye), nurse, Loch
     Skiport, South Uist.*

22   iii. 370-1.
     These lines come from Barra, the second referring to Purgatory.

23   i. 44-5. *Flora Macdougal (from Moran), cottar, the Glen, Barra.*
     There are sun- and moon-prayers, but no star-prayers; the stars,
     however, are in force on the night of Christmas, reinforced for
     the Hebridean by the Northern Lights.

436

24 ii. 172-5. *Mary Macrae (from Kintail), dairywoman, North End, Harris, and Alexander Matheson, shipmaster, Dornie, Lochalsh.*
This is a portion only of what was recited as one; a further portion forms 99. Cf. the Cornish carol, "Righteous Joseph" (*Oxford Book of Carols*, 41).

25 ii. 162-5. *Malcolm Macmillan, crofter, Griminish, Benbecula.*
This is a Gaelic version of the "Cherry Tree Carol" and a legend of the Coventry Plays.

26 iii. 110-13. *Roderick Macneill, cottar, Island of Mingulay, Barra.*
Christmas Eve was a night of bannocks and gifts; there was a little ceremony of mothers giving their girls the bannock-stone to nurse, as St Bride was the first to receive the Son of God into her lap. Mingulay (contracted for pronouncing into Mewlay), like so many islands, is now uninhabited.

27 i. 126-31. *Angus Gunn, cottar, North Dell, Ness, Lewis.*
This carol for waits or guisers is in two parts, the first a house-greeting and blessing outside, the second an inside Christmas prayer.

28 i. 132-3. *Angus Gunn, cottar, North Dell, Ness, Lewis.*
Guisers wore white shirts for surplices and tall white hats for mitres. Near the Butt of Lewis (the source of the carol) the mountains lie well to the south, a distant gleam; those of Skye and the mainland can also be seen far over the Minch.

29 i. 134-7. *Angus Gunn, cottar, North Dell, Ness, Lewis.*
When they entered a house guisers took up a child or a doll and processed round the hearth three times, carrying the baby on a sheepskin and singing the carol. Afterwards they feasted.

30 i. 138-9. *Roderick Macneill, cottar, Island of Mingulay, Barra.*
A bull's hide was carried round sometimes on the Night of the Gifts, sometimes on Hogmanay. Dr Johnson refers to this custom in Coll (p. 120). But the "little Christ" is also here.

31 i. 140-1. *John Macdiarmaid, crofter, Island of Scalpay, Harris.*

32 i. 142-3. *Kirsty Gillies, crofter, Dungannachy, Benbecula.*
Monday after Christmas was in some districts Cake or Bannock Monday. The song-man or wait-leader came to the house as the "little Christ", a custom analogous to that of Connemara of leaving the door on the latch so that the Christ, in the form of any poor man in need, might enter if he wished. The cross on the right shoulder appears elsewhere also; the right is free, but the left shoulder is taken up with the plaid and its pin or buckle.

33 i. 144-5. *Donald Macdonald, crofter, Stoneybridge, South Uist, and Donald Johnson, catechist, Island of Eriskay, South Uist.*

34 i. 146-7. *Ewen Wilson, crofter, Griminish, Benbecula.*

35 iii. 114-15.
In the Roman Catholic islands Christmas breakfast is a meal of mutton cooked the night before and eaten on return from the midnight mass. It is still usual to kill a sheep (sacred to Christ, the Lamb of God) for the first food of Christmas Day in South Uist (M. F. Shaw, *Folksongs and Folklore of South Uist*, p. 15).

36 ii. 168-9. *Ann Currie, crofter's daughter, Iochdar, South Uist.*
This was a church hymn or prayer recited or sung by the priest in procession round his oratory or chapel, or while making a circuiting out of doors. Cf. 386.

37 iii. 116-17.

38 i. 318-21. *Angus Maclellan, cooper, South Hacklett, Benbecula.*
The Christmas ritual here began with a lustration and a circuiting of the isleman's boat and tackle. The young fishermen went out to catch for the widows, orphans, and poor. Traditionally St Peter was required to row seven hundred and seven strokes before catching the tribute-fish (a haddock); the Uist boats went out for this number of strokes before the lines were cast.

39 i. 28-9. *Duncan Maclellan, crofter, Carnan, South Uist.*
The word rendered beam by Dr Carmichael is *lub*, bend or fold, and it is repeated with the silk. Perhaps bundle would be right. Further Christmas poems are 159 and 225.

40 iii. 200-1.
Every Highland child was set by baptism under the protection of the Holy Trinity by the grace of the Holy Spirit at the very earliest possible moment lest the fairies take him or her away. This blessing seems to be of the baptismal grace, or was uttered by a witness to the child's baptism and reception in church, when all bystanders took the baby in their arms in turn.

41 iii. 10-11.
A nurse's or midwife's (knee-woman's) baptism of a child, which was done at once, was known as birth baptism. This is a formalized version—of three threes.

42 iii. 16-19. *The wife of Donald, son of Ewen, crofter, Island of Berneray, Barra.*
The more remote the situation the greater was the significance of this ceremony (here in an enlarged form); for a priest's visits were few and far between. Children indeed could be some years old before a priest's baptism was administered. This poem comes from another now non-existent community, that of Barra Head, the home only of lightkeepers to-day.

43 iii. 20-3. *The wife of Donald, son of Ewen, crofter, Island of Berneray, Barra.*
This second poem follows on from the preceding. The custom of birth baptism was dying out in Dr Carmichael's day; these three prayers preserve it.

44 iii. 6-9. *Catherine Macneill, cottar, Breivig, Barra.*
Hebridean baptism was threefold—of the midwife (at birth), of the nurse (at the first washing), and of the priest (if possible on the eighth day of the tradition of the Circumcision). Here the first and second baptism are coupled together in one poem of two parts.

45 iii. 12-15. *Mary Macneill, crofter.*
The child was usually given a temporary name at birth baptism and washing (a boy Ludovick, tonsured of the Lord; a girl Gertrude, beloved). The location of this prayer is not recorded,

but is almost certainly Barra, where the people were, of old, conspicuous for the way in which they hung upon their chief in the matter of marriages or disasters such as cattle-loss (Martin, pp. 161-2); similarly baptism was a fealty for life.

46   i. 114-15. *Roderick Maccormick, crofter, Dungannachy, Benbecula*
In church the temporary was superseded by the permanent Christian name. Certainly baptismal assurance was made trebly sure; it was necessary to qualify for the right of burial in consecrated ground, and to ward off evil spirits and fairies. There is no specific reference to godparents, although all present in church acted as sponsors with their benedictions. The word *tiur*, imprint, is of the mark left by the receding tide on the sandy western shores of the Outer Isles.

47   iii. 200-1.
There can be few, if any, parallels to this baptismal Sacramentary of the Outer Hebrides.

48   iii. 52-3.
Riaradh, sufficing, has the technical meaning of the distribution of the Sacramental Elements; *suain* is of the slumber of death, which is shown below in the "happy death" poems. That Communion in both kinds was a practice of the Celtic Church is demonstrated by the Hymn of St Sechnall in praise of St Patrick (l. 67) in the Irish *Liber Hymnorum* (Bernard and Atkinson, i. p. 11 and ii. p. 103).

49   iii. 312-13.

50   i. 82-3. *John Macinnes, crofter, Stilligarry, South Uist.*
Cf. 13, 256, 513, 516f.

51   iii. 370-3.
"Happy death" denotes that a dying person is shriven and anointed, and that the soul-peace or death-hymn has been chanted. Cf. 52ff and 167.

52   iii. 376-7. Cf. 51, 53f, 167.

53   iii. 392-3. Cf. 51f, 54, 167.

54   iii. 386-7. *Malcolm Macmillan, crofter, Griminish, Benbecula.*
Cf. 51ff, 167.

55   iv. 1.

56   iv. 1.

57   iv. 1.
The original lines have effective alliteration. The goldfinch (*carduelis carduelis britannica*) "was once common in the Central Highlands and Moray Basin. Its extinction in the third quarter of the 19th century was caused by excessive bird catching for the dealers . . ." (Darling, p. 77). It was rare previous to 1892, but was recorded in Eigg, Glen Coe, and Benderloch (J. A. Harvie-Brown and T. E. Buckley, *A Vertebrate Fauna of Argyll and the Inner Hebrides*, p. 70).

58 iv. 248. *Dugal Macaulay, cottar, Creagorry, South Hacklett, Benbecula.*
After this verse the child with the "prickly sleep" in the foot would tramp and tramp, and no doubt get some milk as well.

59 iv. 248. *Dugal Macaulay, cottar, Creagorry, South Hacklett, Benbecula.*
These lines are for soothing, and for wishing and rubbing away a hurt.

60 iv. 18-19.
The fairy mouse brings the coin to the chink in place of the milk-tooth. Normally the field-mouse was considered a bad influence. The Hebridean long-tailed field mouse (*apodemus sylvaticus*) is a relic of lost woodland. It "is often the only mouse to come indoors" (Darling, p. 210).

61 iv. 120-1.
The voice of a dead mother comes to the aid of her child against a stepmother. Ragwort (*senecio jacobaea*), a plant of river flats and sandy soil, and a prolific denizen of the machair, was used for keeping away mice from stored grain (with tansy), and for creels and switches.

62 ii. 247.
This is a Highland boy's promise in play. It comes from the story of the fox who ate the grey goat's kids, but protested innocence to the returning mother.

63 ii. 301.
This was for a game of "tig". King Geigean is the grave king, the president of death revels.

64 ii. 210-11. *John Stewart, merchant, Bachuill, Lismore.*
This was for a swinging, bumping funeral game of Dr Carmichael's own boyhood. Kill is used in its embracing sense of church and burial ground. St Moluag is the patron of Lismore and its see of the Isles. Martin gives a most curious parallel custom of divination from Kilmartin in Trotternish of Skye (p. 172).

65 iii. 204-5.
This is the only short blessing that couples together sea and land travel. Cf. the travelling prayers, 394ff, for this section.

66 i. 198.

67 iii. 48-9.
Known as "The Path of Right" or "The Just or True Way", this was a song of going out to work, crooned or uttered aloud, or hummed in an undertone if strangers were about.

68 iii. 194-5. *Mary Macdonald, crofter, Stoneybridge, South Uist.*
This was a farewell blessing, a God-speed from the door.

69 iii. 250-1. *Sarah Maclellan (Morrison), Beoraidmore, Morar.*
This was the hymn for the farewell ceremony for a member of the family leaving home. The ritual included washing the face in milk from a tradition that so was the Christ-child washed on the

Flight into Egypt. There is a close similarity to the justice prayers (409ff). Cf. also 108, 404ff.

70   iii. 62-3.

71   iii. 50-1.
This is a poem of itinerancy—of the travelling steward or chief or missionary, of riding, journeying and dues, of the cross of repentance and the court of justice. Certain families had hereditary itinerant tasks and rights, and the representative usually carried the staff that denoted the office.

72   iii. 170-1. Cf. 163, 447.

73   iii. 84-5.

74   iii. 70-1. *Little Catherine Macdonald, cottar, Borve, Barra.*

75   iii. 176-7.

76   iii. 322-3.
The embers of an open-air supper fire (*riaraich*, rear, sustain, nourish, satisfy) die away behind these words.

77   iii. 320-1.
"I am the door" of the sheep.

78   iii. 202-3.

79   iv. 130-1. *Isabel MacEachainn, cottar, Bunessan, Mull.*
The smooth *monalan* is an unidentified plant; it was worn by the Blessed Virgin as she escaped into Egypt.

80   iv. 208-13. *Isabel MacEachainn, cottar, Bunessan, Mull.*
This poem for sprain was accompanied by embrocation (an extract of St John's wort—St Columba's flower—or other prescription) and massage. The final stanza is a variant. Cf. 97, 224, 331ff.

81   iv. 256-7. *Isabel MacEachainn, cottar, Bunessan, Mull.*
This was a poem of vigorous and exhausting rubbing and massage for the "chest-seizure". Cf. 154, 332ff, 480.

82   iv. 180-3. *Isabel MacEachainn, cottar, Bunessan, Mull.*
There is unfortunately a break in the text in the Killarney stanza. The poem is full of particular significances. The drop is of lustration and salving. Bunessan lies both on one of the main migration routes from Iceland to Africa, and on the pilgrim highway along the length of the Ross of Mull. The Manx shearwater (*procellaria puffinus*), for example, has been proved to have flown a distance of seven hundred and thirty miles from the Faroe Islands to Skokholm of Pembrokeshire, passing over Mull. The largest serpents in Scotland were at one time in Mull also. The connection with Killarney is Columban, St Cummain the Tall having his cell there; he was recommended to an Irish king as a confessor or soul-friend by St Columba himself. Cf. 139, 150, 155, 216, 220f, 420, and the eye poems 342ff.

83   iv. 288-91. *Isabel MacEachainn, cottar, Bunessan, Mull.*
The story of this poem is local, set in Loch Scridain, where St Columba and his twelve disciples were rowing home in their

curachan to Iona; it concerns a widow woman of Tavool in Ardmeanach on the shores of the loch, whose only cow was suffering from surfeit. The Saint was summoned, the boat put in, and he applied his veterinary skill. Cf. 243, 245f, 315, 359 for the legend, and 245f, 315, 358f for the surfeit.

84 iv. 86-7. *Isabel MacEachainn, cottar, Bunessan, Mull.*
Cf. 247 and the dairy poems 261ff.

85 iv. 122-5. *Isabel MacEachainn, cottar, Bunessan, Mull.*
The third stanza is incomplete, the third line being interpolated, as also "the men of false gain" in the fouth stanza. The root is not identified, but the provenance is of the dairy (cf. St Bride in 271 and 363). The "root of joy" may be the box (*buxus sempervirens*), known as the white joy, which was much regarded. The heath-grass is of the genus *trioda*, but *ciob* is also used of the club-rush (*scirpus caespitosus*).

86 iv. 132-5. *Isabel MacEachainn, cottar, Bunessan, Mull.*
The disputed *mothan* is here identified as the pearlwort. Cf. 230, 269, 496ff.

87 iii. 28-9.

88 ii. 289.
These lines are really a riddle to which the answer is night and day.

89 iii. 30-1.

90 i. 98-9. *Mary Macinnes, cottar, Tighary, North Uist.*

91 iii. 34-9. *A narrator from South Uist.* Cf. 3.

92 iii. 24-7. *Catherine Maclennan (Macdonald), crofter, Achadh nam Breac, Moydart.*

93 iii. 56-7.

94 iii. 58-61.
There is one break, the fourth line of the third stanza being interpolated.

95 iii. 54-5. *Dugal Macaulay, cottar, Creagorry, South Hacklett, Benbecula.*
The reciter received this prayer from an old man named Somerled Maccalman, who "was always crooning these little hymns to himself". He called it Somerled's Petition.

96 ii. 104-5. *Neil Macdonald, mason, Torlum, Benbecula.*
The aspen tree (*populus tremula*) and aspen-wood were "crossed" or forbidden. One tradition was that this was the wood of the Cross of Christ; another, that alone of the trees it refused to bow as the King passed to Calvary. Aspens were therefore abhorred, and the wood could never be used. This poem of the Cross comes from treeless Benbecula. Another version, set to an Eigg air, appears in the *Songs of the Hebrides* (M. Kennedy-Fraser and K. Macleod, iii. pp. 27-31). Cf. also 162.

97 ii. 18-19. *Mary(?) Mackenzie, crofter's wife, Island of Berneray, Lewis.*
This is a charm for sprain. Cf. 80, 224, 331.

98 i. 160-1. *Duncan Maclellan, crofter, Carnan, South Uist.*
Similar in language to many of the Christmas carols, this poem has its surprises. One is the introduction of the Celtic figure of Cairbre, the heavenly charioteer, who transports heroes to the world beyond. For other such introductions and juxtapositions cf. 140, 261, 277, 281. The knoll is normally the place of court and meeting; here it must be Jerusalem and Golgotha. The priestly chorus has been expanded. Easter Sunday was known also as Crucifying Sunday, when the sun was reputed to dance for joy as it rose.

99 ii. 172-7. *Mary Macrae (from Kintail), dairywoman, North End, Harris, and Alexander Matheson, shipmaster, Dornie, Lochalsh.*
These stanzas were recited with others—the first two at the beginning, and the last at the end. Most of the poem in between is given above (24).

100 iii. 366-7.
There is one lacuna in the third line of the third stanza which has been filled with a variant reading. It was probably a ceremonial hymn for a circuiting and blessing of a new house, carried out by a priest or a minister.

101 iii. 72-5. *Roderick Macdonald, Manal, Tiree.*
Special names were applied sometimes to both spells and prayers. One of these is the Prayer of Distress, which has here a maritime particularity.

102 iii. 262-3. *Marion Macneill, cottar, Castlebay, Barra.*
What were called "crosses of prostration" were common throughout the Highlands and Islands. They were usually at a spot where the first sight could be had of a place of worship. A traveller or pilgrim would kneel or prostrate himself, sing his hymn, and proceed to church. Cf. Martin, pp. 155 and 106-7.

103 iv. 234-5 and 244-5. *Isabel Calder, crofter, Tulloch, Bonar Bridge, and Peggy Maclean (Ross), crofter's wife, Achnagart, Strath Kyle, Kincardine, Easter Ross.*
This is a blending and abbreviation of two eye charms for the removal of motes, an operation which was often achieved at a distance. Cf. 347ff.

104 iv. 126-7.
The reed (*phragmites communis*) had a similar signification to the aspen (v. *supra* 96). In South Uist the occupants of a cottage at Ceannlangavat walled with turf and thatched with reeds, regarded the latter as a misfortune. The reed is a plant which soon fills lochans and contributes to their disappearance.

105 iii. 336-7.
This was a little ritual prayer of barring the door and putting out the light.

106 i. 76-7. *Sarah Macisaac, crofter's wife, Stoneybridge, South Uist.*
It was of ill omen to see anything dead when setting forth on a

fishing, shooting, or hunting expedition, and even sick or elderly persons were avoided. A woman with red hair caused consternation, it being the colour of Judas Iscariot.

107 ii. 114-15. *Christine Macvicar, cottar, Moor of Aird, Benbecula.*
The passion-flower or crucifying-tree is a plant of the genus *passiflora*, to which it gives its name. The usual variety is *passiflora coerulea;* it may, however, be a species of sorrel or dock, such as *rumex patientia* (passion), once used widely as a laxative. The lines come from a wise herbwoman.

108 iii. 254-5.
Poems of farewell to members of the family leaving or emigrating were used in conjunction with a ceremonial encircling or encompassing (*caim*), accompanied sometimes by the gift of a talismanic keepsake. Cf. 404ff.

109 ii. 154-7. *Isabel Chisholm, tinker, temporarily of Lochmaddy, North Uist.*
This remarkable poem of malediction—equal to the worst that a fairy could spell—has many obscurities. It is a kind of chest charm in reverse. Tinkers were a feature of the Highlands; and this is an interesting revelation of the inner feelings sometimes harboured by such separatists.

110 i. 294.
The *ceilidh* (where world-affairs came up) was the one relaxation from the busy activity of repairing, wool-working, and educating.

111 iv. 320-1. *Ian Morrison, Rucaidh, North Uist.*
MacShiamain, the Man of Straw or Rope, is an imaginary Highland character—the typical handyman, and a sort of Robin Goodfellow. The second verse, though in character, possibly does not belong, and may be part of a hunting poem.

112 i. 164.
This is a short prayer before going to a *ceilidh*, or for other occasions.

113 ii. 282-3. *Farquhar Beaton, shepherd, Coradale, South Uist.*
This is a fragment of an old poem of geological interest. All the places are in South Uist. Coradale provided a refuge cave for the Young Chevalier for several weeks. There are two points of Thor (Torrarnis), both famed for bere-crops; but there are not many nuts anywhere now. Sgoth is "a place-name in Uist and Harris" meaning "a steep rock, an abrupt hill, a bank of cloud, an overhanging haze". An t'Ionaire Mor is a stream flowing north from the slopes of Hecla into Loch Druidibeg. Loch Darkhead is Loch-a-Cheann-dubhain. Dulse (*rhodomela*) is still consumed; garlic (*allium*) is found as an occasional survivor of lost woodland.

114 ii. 310. A poem of *Rob Donn of Reay.*
This is a version of a self-description by a famous Gaelic poet of the years immediately following the "Forty-five". Tiriodh (pronounced Tiree, as the island) means cornland; there are several Tiriodhs in the Gordon districts of Sutherland. Cataibh (the Cat country) is applied to the whole county, Caithness having the same origin. The high summer pastures of Reay Forest contain a lake known as Loch Airidh a'Bhaird, the loch of the bard's

444

shieling. Traditionally the bard is the hunter and shieling love poet, Rob Donn.

115 iv. 102-3.

116 ii. 343.

117 i. 42-3. *Ian Cameron, crofter, Borve, Barra.*
The *Carraig nan al* is really the Rock of the generations, or perhaps "the rock whence we are hewn". Fittingly the crest of the Macneills of Barra is a rock proper as anciently borne (R. R. Stodart, *Scottish Arms*, ii, p. 43). Cf. 439.

118 iii. 200-1.

119 iii. 78-83.
Alla, Lord, and *Maighistir*, Master, only occur here; but *alla* is also jewel or beauty, and a form of it is used in the new moon poems below.

120 iii. 98-101. *Mary Cameron, cottar, Borve, Barra.*

121 iii. 104-5.
A *caim*, encompassing, together with its invocation, was performed sunwise round a person by the right forefinger extended; the invisible circle enclosed and protected the subject (whether another or the person himself), and accompanied him as his shadow. This was done by Protestant and Roman Catholic alike.

122 iii. 206-7.

123 iii. 102-3.

124 iii. 76-7. *Alexander Macdonald, crofter, Borve, Barra.*

125 iii. 106-7.
For the nine angels see below (156).

126 iii. 244-5.

127 iii. 108-9. *Ann Livingstone (Maccallum), crofter, Bay, Taynuilt, Lorne.*
The protecting influences of the mantle of St Bride and the linen of St Mary are those of the wrapping at Bethlehem and the shrouding at Calvary. Shelter-houses (apart from shieling huts) were sometimes constructed in the Highlands for distant expeditions.

128 iii. 94-7. *Catherine Macneill, Kenntangaval, Barra.*
This charm required "a right heart and good thoughts and a clean spirit" for efficacy; where these were present it was invincible. There are two gaps (in the middle of the third, and before the last stanza).

129 iii. 208-9.

130 iii. 206-7.

131 iii. 208-9.

132　i. 30-1. *Rachel Macpherson, cottar, South Hacklett, Benbecula.*
Practically the whole hierarchy of fairies (perhaps dethroned
heathen gods and goddesses) are here: the *gruagach*, brownie of
dairy and fold, Celtic sun-god, beneficent if propitiated: the *ban-
sith*, banshee, queen of wisdom: the *glaistig*, a vicious nymph,
half-woman, half-goat: the *fuath* (hatred, wrath), troll, another
water-fiend: the *greann* (rough, grim), siren: and the *uruisg*,
ghoul also half-human and half-goat, terrifying, but not otherwise
unfriendly. Cf. also 234. Shrews had a connection with paralysis
and were dreaded, whether the grass-mouse or common shrew
(*sorex vulgaris*) or the fairy mouse or lesser shrew (*sorex pyg-
maeus*). Cf. 60. 379. Presumably the evil influence of mice and
shrews was proximity out of doors to fairies and dwarfs—a sound
practical tradition, for they were no doubt carriers of more than
magical influences.

133　ii. 232. *Catherine Mackintosh, cottar, Stilligarry, South Uist.*
The reindeer (*rangifer tarandus*) once existed all over the High-
lands; the "little people" were the companions of these hill
rangers.

134　ii. 266-7.
The spirit hosts of the departed (*sluagh*) on a hunting expedition
in the sky were heard calling to their hounds in these words by
some of Clanranald's men at Nunton in Benbecula.

135　ii. 306-8. *A woman, West Bennan, Arran.*
A *gruagach* at East Bennan in Arran herded the cattle of the town-
land with this song; but she became offended and left when
offered a garment and sandals by the grateful population. The
historical allusion in the poem is interesting. Pennant records:
"In the year 1558, the English fleet under the Earl of Sussex, after
ravaging the coast of Cantyre, at that time in possession of James
Macconnel, landed in this bay" (Lamlash), "and burned and de-
stroyed all the neighboring country: proceeded afterwards to
Cumray, and treated it in the same manner" (p. 214).

136　ii. 320-1. *Mary Macinnes, cottar, South Hacklett, Benbecula.*
The *loireag* is a water-fairy not unlike the brownie. Both ex-
pected to receive libations of milk. This is the song of a *loireag*
enraged at being driven away from a cow by a "little cross carle"
in Benmore Uist, the means used being an invocation of St
Columba. The places in the song are all in the wild hilly pastures
of eastern South Uist. The red broomrape (*orobranche rubra*) can
be found in Coradale and also in Fuday of Barra, growing from
thyme.

137　ii. 254-6. *Lachlan Macdonald, crofter, Griminish, Benbecula, and
another.*
This is a poem of the *cnoc*, mound, the *grianan*, bower or sun-
garden (of the heroic tales), and of the single tree (a survival of
tree-worship). Part of it comes in a beautiful description of the
fairy-queen offering wisdom in a cup to womankind; those who
scorned or came late obtained none.

138　iii. 182-3. *Malcolm Sinclair, fisherman-cottar, Balephuil, Tiree.*
Both the blue or common flax (*linum usitatissimum*)—an escape
usually from cultivation—and the purging flax (*linum catharti-
cum*), with white flowers, were much prized, and might not be
stolen.

446

139   iv. 156-7.   *Catherine Macneill, cottar, Breivig, Barra.*
      Cf. other "evil eye" poems, 82, 150, 155, 216, 220f, 342ff, 420.

140   iii. 152-3.

141   iii. 206-7.

142   i. 164-75, iii. 154-9, and 160-3. *Donald Macdonald, crofter,*
      Griminish, Benbecula, and Peggy Maccormick (Macdonald), crofter
      and nurse, Ard Bhuidhe, Loch Boisdale, South Uist.
      Three variants have here been conflated and combined. Genealo-
      gies were learnt by heart, and it was one of the duties of a sean-
      nachie to compile them; at installations the lineage of a candi-
      date was proclaimed. An Iona tradition of St Bride takes her back
      through a druidic father to an Irish royal house. St Bride's
      (1 February) was the early spring festival. The mantles will be
      monastic veils, the peat-heap is characteristic of both the High-
      lands and Ireland, the sight is divination or augury, the twining
      hair is of the figure decorated by girls for the festival. Cf. 14f, 85,
      112, 127, 271, 290f, 363, 369, 474.

143   iv. 138-9.
      St Patrick (17 March) is not confined to Ireland as a Celtic
      tutelary; and he is closely connected with St Columba. "The
      relics of Patrick were enshrined sixty years after his death by
 · Columcille" (The Annals of Ulster from the *Book of Cuana*). His
      Gospel Book, known as St Martin's Gospel (given to him by St
      Martin of Tours, commemorated by the High Cross of Iona),
      became St Columba's (Reeves, p. 326). Cf. 236, 369, 505.

144   i. 178-81. *George Gunn (from Kildonan, Sutherland), peasant*
      proprietor, St Ola, Orkney.
      St Magnus of Orkney (14 April) was a great peacemaker, but was
      martyred by his brother, Earl Haakon, in Holy Week, 1115, in the
      island of Egilsey. Norse and Celtic influences are here fused. Both
      the water-vole or water-rat (*arvicula amphibius*), and its black
      Scots variety (*arvicula atra*), together with the field-vole (*arvicula*
      agrestis) are very destructive, particularly of young tree life.

145   ii. 235-7. *Malcolm Maclean, smith, Kenntangaval, Barra.*
      St Brendan or Brandon (16 May) is the Columbus of the Celtic
      Church, a tremendous missionary, sailor and explorer, who is
      reputed to have crossed the Atlantic Ocean, and had a seven
      years' maritime search for the "Fortunate Isles". Like St Brendan
      of Birr and St Cormac he was one of the twelve apostles of
      Ireland. It is thought that Hinba may be his Hebridean cell (W. J.
      Watson, *The History of the Celtic Place-Names of Scotland*, p. 81).
      According to Pennant, Bute derives its name from *Bothe*, a cell of
      St Brendan, and the inhabitants of Arran were called Brandani
      (p. 187). It was claimed that "from the time he took piety he had
      never gone over seven furrows without his mind on God" (Ber-
      nard and Atkinson, ii, p. 196). He was buried beside his soul-friend
      St Moluag in Lismore. Black Donald was a local farmer of Vater-
      say or Barra, who disapproved of Saints' days and not working on
      them. But his garrons were successively transformed in the hollow
      where he wished to plough on St Brendan's day into donkeys and
      rabbits, with corresponding changes to his plough and himself,
      until he showed repentance. A similar tale with a poem is told of
      Black Donald and St Patrick.

146 i. 194-7. *Sarah Gillies, cottar, Moor of Aird, Benbecula.*
The Feast Day of St Mary the Great is not Lady Day, but a
Lammas 15 August. It was observed with ritual; bere (usually) was
plucked, dried, husked, winnowed, ground, kneaded, and made
into a bannock, which was then toasted and shared round by the
man of the house. Circuitings indoors and out were then made by
the family, as they sang the hymn. Cf. also 160.

147 i. 108-9. *Isabel Galbraith, crofter's wife, Skallary, Barra.*

148 i. 110-11. *Isabel Galbraith, crofter's wife, Skallary, Barra.*

149 iii. 126-33. *Mary Maclellan (Macdonald), crofter, Beoraidh Mhor,
Morar.*
In this long poem one small lacuna has been filled in the sixth
stanza. The Saving (or Kidney-nut) of Mary was a special prayer.
There are two examples above (16f).

150 ii. 66-7. *Donald Macpherson, shoemaker, Griminish, Benbecula.*
This is an eye spell, but, as is often the case, it also contains a
catalogue of ills and diseases, some of which are not known. Cf.
82, 139, 155, 216, 220f, 342ff, 420. The main-land, coast-land, lake-
land, and ocean are the four chief geographical features of Ben-
becula.

151 iii. 144-7. *Ann Livingstone (Maccallum), crofter, Bay, Taynuilt,
Lorne.*
The greatest day of the whole year was Michaelmas (29 Septem-
ber). Sea, horses, and war are St Michael's provinces. Michaelmas
Eve saw the bringing in of carrots, the baking of the cake (*struan*),
the killing of the lamb, and the keeping, obtaining, or stealing of
the horses for the feast-riding. Michaelmas itself was a day of
early mass, of lamb and cake (which were also distributed out-
side), of a pilgrimage and service and mounted circuiting of the
local burial-ground, of presents of carrots, and of the *oda* or
sports, with a great dance in the evening. Other Michaelmas
poems are 182, 288, 373, 504.

152 iii. 148-9.

153 iii. 143.
For St Michael's horse Brian, or Brianag, cf. 66, 174.

154 iv. 252-3. *Ewen Maclennan, farmer, Achadh an Tobair, Resolis,
the Black Isle.*
The favourite Celtic trio—St Mary, St Bride, and St Michael—are
invoked in one of many charms for the *glacach*, chest-seizure. Cf.
81, 332ff, 480.

155 ii. 64-5. *Rachel Stewart, cottar, Island of Baleshare, North Uist.*
Cf. 82, 139, 150, 216, 220f, 342ff, 420.

156 iii. 204-5.
This is a brief *caim*, encompassing, blessing. The nine angels
correspond to all the Saints, there being both nine archangels and
nine orders of angels (in hierarchies of three). Greek Liturgies
name them Angels, Archangels, Powers; Thrones, Dominions,
Principalities; Authorities, Cherubim, Seraphim. There are seven
archangels from scriptural sources, to whom the Celts seem to

have added two. But only four of the names are biblical—Michael (who like God), Gabriel (the man of God), Raphael (the cure of God), and Uriel (the flame of God). The three others—Chamuel, Jophiel, and Zadkiel—are of Jewish or legendary authority only. To these were added Ariel, the angel of youth, and Muriel, both of whom figure in these poems. Cf. 72, 125.

157 i. 2-3. *Ann Macdonald, crofter's daughter, Bohuntin Edge, Lochaber.*
"Nature's tincture" renders *gne*, a word which denotes expression, complexion, tinge, sort, or nature; but perhaps Dr Carmichael's "Spirit" is better, although distinct from the *Spiorad*. Other Lochaber poems are 251, 322, 488.

158 i. 96-7. *Mary Macdonald, crofter's daughter, Greater Bohuntin, Lochaber.*
There is a gap in this poem in the last two lines of the second stanza.

159 i. 26-7. *Ann Macdonald, crofter's daughter, Bohuntin Edge, Lochaber.*

160 iii. 118-25. *Mary Macdonald, crofter, Greater Bohuntin, Lochaber.* Cf. 146ff, 215, 488.

161 i. 102-3. *Isabel Mackintosh (Kennedy of Lianachan), crofter's wife, Ionnaruay, Lochaber.*

162 i. 46-7. *John Fraser (from Lochaber), street porter, Frederick Street, Edinburgh.*
This prayer is not quite complete. Cf. 67, 96ff.

163 i. 48-9, and 92-3. *Isabel Mackintosh (Kennedy of Lianachan), crofter's wife, Ionnaruay, Lochaber, and Ann Macdonald, crofter''s daughter, Bohuntin Edge, Lochaber.*
Two similar Lochaber prayers (the Guardian Angel and the Soul-Shrine) are here conflated. Cf. 72, 447.

164 i. 70-1. *John Macdonald, shepherd, Keppoch, Lochaber.*

165 i. 90-1. *Mary Macdonald, crofter's daughter, Greater Bohuntin, Lochaber.*
The Soul-Shrine is a retiring prayer; during sleep angels hold sway over the soul.

166 i. 100-1. *Isabel Mackintosh (Kennedy of Lianachan), crofter's wife, Ionnaruay, Lochaber.*

167 iii. 388-91. *Ann Macdonald, widow, Lochaber.*
Cf. 51ff.

168 i. 104-5. *Catherine Maccuithean, cottar, Clachanagluip, North Uist.*

169 i. 232-3. *Catherine Macdonald, crofter's wife, Smiorasary, Glen Uig, Moydart.*
Cf. 1.

170 iii. 350-5. *Catherine Macphie, cottar, Ardmore, Iochdar, South Uist.*
The firestone (flagstone or hearthstone), upon which the peats were raised, was almost the altar-stone of the household.

171   iii. 358-9.

172   iii. 360-5.   *Alexander Maclean, Manal, Tiree.*

173   iii. 264-5.
The chief means of daylight illumination in the black house was often the chimney, or rather smoke-aperture. The walls being double were of considerable thickness, and any windows were very deeply set and correspondingly diminished of light-giving property ("upon each hole that lets in light").

174   iii. 168-9.
This is a prayer (of encompassment) for Highland girls going out in the dark to draw water. Brianag, little Brian, is St Michael's horse, and clearly a star traversing the sky. Cf. 66, 153.

175   i. 236-7.   *Patrick Smith, crofter, Lethmeanach, Stoneybridge, South Uist.*
The fires of the townland were never extinguished except for the annual rekindling from the common neid-fire of Beltane or May Day. Cf. 9, 506ff.

176   iii. 338-9.   *Dugal Macaulay, cottar, Creagorry, South Hacklett, Benbecula.*

177   ii. 40-1.   *Ian Pearson, cottar, Kenntangaval, Barra.*
This love-charm is full of obscurities and lost significances. The capillary attraction of drawing water through a straw may simply be symbolic of magnetism. For the rest, it is composed of an aromatic herbal concoction and ritual circuiting (a relic of fertility rites). The foxglove (*digitalis purpurea*) is only of inferred identification; other possibilities are the blue aconite or monkshood (*aconitum napellus*), the poisonous wolfsbane (*aconitum anglicum*), and the meadowsweet (*filipendula ulmaria*), or a plant of the genus *spiraea*. Similarly the butterbur (*petasites vulgaris*) is doubtful, and may be the coltsfoot (*tussilago farfara*). The three old man's bones are probably sprigs of southern-wood (*artemisia abrotanum*), which in the west of England is known as Boys' Love. The purpose of the royal fern (*osmunda regalis*) is not known. There is a similar South Uist poem.

178   ii. 280-1.   *Kenneth Morrison, cottar, Treen, Minginish, Skye.*
This is a fragment of a love poem, with the perennial theme of a duel between suitors.

179   ii. 229.
These lines are two stanzas of old songs. The "mount of mist" is a common Gaelic poetic term.

180   ii. 348, 286, 365, 278, 231, and 230.
This poem is compounded of separate couplets and stanzas. The second stanza is from an Arthurian romance, a version of the whole of which appears in the fifth volume of the *Carmina Gadelica*.

181   iv. 350-1.
It is only in Scotland that the red deer (*cervus elaphas*), the largest surviving British wild animal, has remained continuously in its natural state; but it needs continual checking if arable farming is to be pursued.

182 i. 206.
Presents and promises were exchanged at the Michaelmas Night Ball. Cf. 151ff, 288, 373, 504.

183 iv. 366-7.
A trout in a holy well was thought to possess something of the wisdom and sanctity of the original consecrator, usually a Saint. It could therefore be consulted in difficulty. The cairn maiden is a *gruagach* (v. 135). The Isle of Youth and the back of sun are a Celtic paradise and heaven of perpetual youth, life, and love. The champions of old are Oscar, son of Ossian, Connlaoch, son of Cuchulainn (slain by his father), and Fraoch (for whom all the fairy women of Ireland made lamentation).

184 iii. 204-5.

185 i. 6-11. *Duncan Maclellan, crofter, Carnan, South Uist, Margaret Macdonald, Tiree, and others.*
Martin records that at marriages "epithalamiums and panegyrics" were made "which the poet or bard pronounced" (p. 176). The "seven elements" are particularized in the rendering. The "dark townland" lines appear also in the justice poems. Fann is the Fairy Woman and Queen of Wisdom; faithful Penelope, queen to Ulysses, is the woman of Greece; Eimir was wooed by Cuchulainn, as told in the Red Branch cycle; Darthula is Deirdre, who eloped to Glen Etive from Ireland; Maeve is the Amazon Queen of Connaught who instigated the Cattle-spoil of Cooley; Binne-bheul, the mouth of melody, caused all living things to stand still when he sang.

186 iii. 212-15, and 216-25.
Two versions are conflated, the longer second incorporating the first. The poem is for a princess; Gillian is a near assonance to *Gile-Mhin*, white-mild, one of the stock epithets applied to St Mary.

187 iii. 210-11.

188 ii. 212-15. *Peggy Macaulay (Robertson, from Skye), crofter's wife, Houghmor, South Uist.*
The kertch or coif was the head-dress of the married woman; it was ceremonially substituted for the snood on the morning after marriage.

189 ii. 279.

190 iii. 226-7.

191 iii. 228-9.

192 iii. 210-11.

193 iii. 206-7.

194 iii. 234-5. *Mary Macmillan, crofter's daughter, Liniquie, Iochdar, South Uist.*

195 iii. 204-5.

196   iii. 238-9.

197   iii. 204-5.

198   iii. 238-9.

199   iii. 204-5.

200   iii. 240-1.
It is hard to see who the son of the stars can be other than the Saviour, although Professor Watson does not render him so. Is he a Celtic personification of the "music of the spheres"?

201   iii. 204-5.
Seven, the holy number *par excellence*, is of perfection and a common term of benediction.

202   iii. 240-1.

203   iii. 210-11.

204   i. 4-5. *Mary Macrae (from Kintail), dairywoman, North End, Harris.*
There is some expansion in this rendering.

205   iii. 236-7.
Cuchulainn (of the Coolin Hills), and the Fiann were the standing army of the Gael of distant history—in later medieval language, the knights. War and hunting were their occupations; but from the stories they were seamen also.

206   ii. 233.
The badger (*meles meles*) is the mammal of the Highland oak wood, while the red deer (*cervus elaphas*) is of the altitudes. The otter (*lutra vulgaris*) is plentiful in the Western Isles; the reindeer has appeared above (133). Duntulm Castle was the northern seat of the Lords of the Isles, several of whom were poets; these lines are probably from one of their compositions. The one hundred badgers, otters, and stags, the hundred steeds, reindeer, and hinds, may well match the hundred ships of John of Islay when he wooed Margaret, grand-daughter of Robert Bruce.

207   iv. 352-5. *The wife of Angus, son of Lachlann, Acha-da-Dheardail, Eigg.*
This is possibly a matriarchal poem; in the days of St Donnan himself Eigg was ruled by a queen. Three warrior sons occur more than once in Highland history.

208   ii. 202-7. *Malcolm Maclellan, crofter, Griminish, Benbecula.*
There is one lacuna, the petrel and the fulmar having been brought in to fill it. Under the title "At the Wave Mouth" a version of a small portion of this song is set to music (Kennedy-Fraser and Macleod, iii, pp. 5-7). A shipwrecked princess from Ireland is found on the shore with her little son by two of the nuns of Benbecula.

209   ii. 208-9. *Malcolm Maclellan, crofter, Griminish, Benbecula.*
This is a second poem on the theme above.

210 iv. 316-19. *Ian Pearson, cottar, Kenntangaval, Barra.*
This is a poem composed, as like as not, for the baby son of a chief of the Mackinnons of Strath in Skye, who were of the seed of Alpin; Blaaven is the landmark of their country.

211 iv. 70-1.
Three of the great chiefs of the Outer Isles were Macdonald of Clanranald, Macneill of Barra, and Macleod of Macleod. This is a milking song of an annual sporting or hunting gathering.

212 i. 268-9. *Neill Macneill, herdsman, Eoligarry, Barra.*
This is a poem of the chief's herd; it comes from the steadings of Macneill of Barra. It revolves around the substitution of a dummy for a dead calf so that the cow may continue to supply milk, the dummy being covered with the calf's hide.

213 iv. 74-5. *Mary Macneill, head milkmaid, Eoligarry, Barra.*
The milking croons of the great herds lack the religious element.

214 iii. 346-7. *The daughter of John Macneill and Mary Maclean.*

215 ii. 332, 255, 287, 222, 303, and 372.
A number of couplets and lines are here set together. The Celtic tradition of the colouring of the Virgin is of a gold brown, rather than fair or dark; the Grecian woman is here Helen of Troy (and of the Renaissance). The figwort (cf. 275, 492f) is a symbol of fertility; the three little maidens are Faith, Hope, and Charity (as below).

216 ii. 52-3. *Donald Macpherson, shoemaker, Griminish, Benbecula.*
This is a spell for the evil eye. Cf. 82, 139, 150, 155, 220f, 342ff, 420. The spells of white or good, as distinct from black or evil, magic were used alike sometimes for humans and cattle stock. The names of the three virtues are interpolated. The first half of the final stanza is obscure.

217 ii. 192-3. *Sarah Mackay, cottar, Island of Heisgir nan Cailleach, North Uist.*
"Under the wood" is the normal Gaelic term for fugitives; the legend is of the Flight into Egypt. There are similar legends elsewhere. For the beetles cf. 475. The poem comes from the Monach group of islands, now uninhabited, off North Uist, from a cottar woman living on the site of the ruined nunnery.

218 iv. 184-7. *Margaret Macdonald, cottar, Obbe, Harris.*
See below for the erysipelas of the breast and cf. 226f, 328f, 355. Again this is a tradition of the Flight into Egypt, upon which the Christ and his Mother healed a poor woman of this disease. The element of a spiritualized transference of the disease to the Holy Family has become merged in the healing power of Christ.

219 iv. 226-9.
This is a prayer against blindness, perhaps strictly against cataract (cf. 313). The tradition says that Christ requested his Mother (as they walked by a river in the Holy Land) to restore the sight of a salmon, blind in one eye. The second and third stanzas are conjectural.

220 iv. 172-5. *Mary Mathieson, cottar, Malacleit, North Uist.*
The apocryphal story of Christ and the fruit is here combined with the healing of the centurion's boy or the nobleman's son. The seven fairies are the proverbial complete number of them. Cf. 82, 139, 150, 155, 216, 221, 342ff, 420.

221 ii. 70-1. *Sarah Maclellan, crofter's wife, South Boisdale, South Uist.*
This is of the Bethlehem stable and of the byre, though whether the yarrow was plucked by the infant or the healing Christ is not stated. For the yarrow see below 489. Cf. 82, 139, 150, 155, 216, 220, 223, 230, 232, 235f, 238, 242, 249f, 342ff, 420.

222 iv. 198-9.
St Columba's friend is an unidentified Maoliodha. He (or she) may be an aboriginal of Iona (tonsured of the yew-tree), either druid or monk, or perhaps a Columban Saint. Another possibility is Maelcobha, King of Ulster; one authority transcribing Reeves calls him Maeleobha—more likely a misprint than a correction (J. F. S. Gordon, *Iona*, p. 62). He granted the bards a respite from exile upon St Columba's plea (Bernard and Atkinson, ii, p. 226), the place of meeting between the poets and the king being "to the north-west of the Yew" (ibid., ii, p. 55); he was besides related to the Saint, and his grandson, Dunchadh, was the eleventh Abbot of Iona. Cf. 330.

223 ii. 116-17. *Borgach Macleod, servant-maid, Island of Eithisey, Harris.*
This plant is not identified, "red-palmed" has the variant reading "red-stalked", and both may be "red-rooted" or "footed"; it is probably of the machair.

224 ii. 20-1. *Mary Macdonald, shepherd's wife, Caim, Arasaig.*
This is a charm for sprain. Cf. 80, 97, 331.

225 ii. 166-7. *Mary Macdonald, crofter's daughter, Island of Mingulay, Barra.*
Cf. the Christmas poems, 23ff, 159. In a land of little pictorial art and of no written literature, word pictures such as this hold the place in devotion occupied elsewhere by the creations of the master-painters. Other poems from Mingulay are 26, 30, 234, 307, 451.

226 ii. 2-3. *Una Macdonald, herdsman's mother, Island of Fuday, Barra.*
Cf. 218, 227, 328f, 355.

227 ii. 4-5. *Ann Macleod, crofter's wife, Island of Scarp, Harris.*
Cf. 218, 226, 328f, 355.

228 ii. 76-7. *Mary Mackinnon, shepherd's wife, Island of Sandray, Barra.*
Ivy (*hedera helix*) is one of the Celtic sacred shrubs; it is connected with the byre (as here), the flocks, and with faithful love (cf. 178). Triple-twined rings of it would be hung over the cowhouse lintel and with the milking vessels. It is, however, a relatively uncommon plant, and the reference may be to the woodbine or honeysuckle (*lonicera periclymonum*), which occurs as far out as St Kilda.

229 i. 266-7. *Catherine Macleod, shepherd's wife, Island of Hellisay, Barra.*
The Herdsman is Isaiah's little child, leading the animals. Storm-staying, with its accompanying anxieties, was and is a frequent experience of Hebridean life. All the islands of the Sound of Barra are particularly beautiful at the time of the spring flowers.

230 ii. 114-15. *Mary Stewart, crofter's wife, Island of Grimisey, North Uist.*
This is another *mothan* poem, not certainly identified in Dr Carmichael's original volumes, but apparently the pearlwort in the later publications. Cf. 86, 269, 496ff. The poem has a lacuna, filled by the repetition of the opening couplet.

231 i. 36-7. *Matili Campbell (Morrison, from South Uist), crofter's wife, Island of Pabbay, Barra.*

232 ii. 100-1. *The wife of Slaine, shepherd's wife, Island of Vatersay, Barra.*
The yellow flower is St John's wort. Cf. 238, 242, 249f, 393, 495.

233 ii. 60-1. *Hugh Macintyre, crofter, Island of Eriskay, South Uist.*
This is a fierce poem to counteract any masculine or feminine spells. Eriskay was the scene of Prince Charles Edward Stewart's first landing in Scotland in 1745; he brought the seeds of the sea convolvulus (*calystegia soldanella*) with him (which grows now in Vatersay of Barra as well) when he set foot on what is still called the Prince's Strand.

234 ii. 352-3. *Roderick Macneill, cottar, Island of Mingulay, Barra.*
The origin of the fairies (in Mingulay at least) is that in following after Lucifer when he was shut out of heaven, they were left between the upper and the lower world. They must live underground and may not emerge on Sunday (the Lord's Day), on Thursday (St Columba's), on Friday (the Son of God's Day), nor on Saturday (St Mary's). They are sometimes heard exclaiming in the first person words similar to those of the second stanza.

235 ii. 116-17. *Sarah Macqueen, cottar, Island of Taransay, Harris.*
The fir club-moss is a much-worn plant. Cf. 398. The yew is used of both the bow and the arrow; the water-nymph is the *glaistig*, the most inimical of the water spirits with the exception of the water-horse. Taransay is the island of St Ternan, who was a Celtic sailor-missionary.

236 ii. 106-7. *Margaret Macpherson, shepherd's wife, Island of Fuday, Barra.*
Cf. 143, 505. This is not St Patrick's shamrock, but some other four- or five-leafed clover. This is given by Dr Carmichael as coming from Fuidhey of Benbecula, a misprint from the line preceding in his list; possibly Flodday of Benbecula is meant, an island by the North Ford; but Fuday, a sheep island of Barra Sound, is much more likely. In winter it is the home of great flocks of barnacle geese (*branta leucopsis*); in summer it is the only Outer Island habitat of the fragrant (*gymnadenia conopea*), and the pyramidal orchid (*orchis pyramidalis*).

237 i. 34-5. *Catherine Macintyre, crofter's wife, Island of Berneray, Barra.*

238 iv. 116-17.
This is another St John's wort prayer. Cf. 232, 242, 249f, 393, 495.
Ales were sometimes spiced with worts.

239 iv. 28-31.
St Columba's solicitude for living things is famous. The incident
of the crane similar to this of the swan is recorded in Adamnan's
Life, bk. i, cap. 48. Cf. 20, 478f.

240 iv. 10.
In the original only the words of the flounder and of the saint are
in verse. The flounder (*platessa flesus*) is a small flat fish of British
waters resembling the plaice. The Strand of the Sand-Eels or Small
Fry is on the eastern shore of Iona, to the south of the landing
place.

241 ii. 126-7. *An old man, Tiree, taken down by the Reverend John
Gregorson Campbell.*
Strangles is a horse disease, though not confined to them; it con-
sists of an abscess between the branches of the lower jaw. This
conversation-charm is obscure, though a well-healing is indicated.
Martin uses one of his favourite phrases to describe the healing-
well of Tiree "called Toubir in Donich" whose waters were "by
the natives drunk as a catholicon for diseases" (p. 296). A possible
explanation is a use of well-water and the juice of the St John's
wort (St John the Baptist).

242 iv. 116-17.
Cf. 232, 238, 249f, 393, 495. The "lifting" of the first stanza is of
the spirits or host, a much-dreaded occurrence.

243 iv. 54-61. *Catherine Macneill, Kenntangaval, Barra.*
This poem is attributed to St Columba; it is in three parts, com-
posed for a widow woman in distress. The first is the rune, the
Charm of the Wild Heifers (an additional fragment has been incor-
porated in the rendering)—its effect was to cause the cow to take
to her calf and to give her milk; the second is the woman's
thanksgiving, the Milkmaid's Blessing; the third (the last two
stanzas) is the Correction. Cf. 83.

244 iv. 46-7.
Between them, St Mary the Mother, St Bride the milkmaid, and
St Columba the herdsman, keep the cattle safe.

245 iv. 290-1. Cf. 83 which clearly forms the background.

246 iv. 292-3. *Roderick Macleod, shepherd, Culnacraig, Coigach.*
This charm of cleaving and transference suffers from two lacunae
—the veins break off with the kidneys, and the sword couplet
hangs poised in mid-air. The anatomy of the twenty-four veins
is probably symbolic.

247 iv. 82-5. *Kate Macneill, cottar, Breivig, Barra.*
Of their many patrons St Columba most entered into the High-
landers' pastoral life, the friend particularly of animals and of
the poor. Indeed St Adamnan inserts no less than three incidents
concerned with dairy-work in his *Life* (bk. ii. caps. 16 and 38,
and bk. iii. cap. 23), besides mentioning the bestowal of the Saint's
blessing upon the milking and dairyman of Iona before his de-
cease. An incident in character must lie behind this charm. Cf. 84.

248   i. 162-3.   *Finlay Maccormick, cowherd, Grogarry, South Uist.*
St Columba's Day is 9 June, but the Thursday of the second week in June is also his, and all other Thursdays as well (except a Beltane Thursday), making that day propitious in every way. The tradition (resting on a gloss to the *Amra*) is that "his spirit used to go to heaven every Thursday" (Bernard and Atkinson, ii, p. 62). The poem is of Thursday-luck.

249   ii. 98-9.   *Ann Macphie, crofter's daughter, Carnan, South Uist.*
The St John's wort was reputedly worn by St Columba because of his admiration for the life and preaching of St John the Baptist. Cf. 232, 238, 242, 250, 393, 495.

250   ii. 96-7.   *Sarah Macisaac, crofter's wife, Stoneybridge, South Uist.*
Cf. 232, 238, 242, 249, 393, 495.

251   i. 12-13.   *Mary Macdonald, crofter's daughter, Greater Bohuntin, Lochaber.*
Cf. the Lochaber poems 157ff.

252   iii. 28-9.

253   iii. 88-91.
The attribution of Fatherlike and Sonlike qualities here to the Holy Spirit is not so much a confusion as a tribute to the Oneness of God and the all-sufficiency of each Person in himself: "The Holy Ghost is of the Father and of the Son: neither made, nor created, nor begotten, but proceeding."

254   i. 106-7.   *Angus Mackintosh, crofter, Dungannachy, Benbecula.*
Benbecula, like South Uist and the Barra isles, is still a Roman Catholic area, due to the adherence of Macdonald of Clanranald and Macneill of Barra.

255   i. 68-9.   *Ann Macisaac (Maclellan), cottar's wife, Ceannlangavat, South Uist.*

256   i. 80-1.   *Christina Macinnes, cottar, South Hacklett, Benbecula.*
Cf. 13, 50, 513, 516f.

257   iii. 348-9.
A long tradition of efficacy is here. Part of the preface to St Columba's Latin hymn *Noli Pater* (MS. of the Franciscan convent in Dublin) in translation is as follows: "And it is sung against every thunder; and whosoever recites it at lying down and at rising up, is freed from all danger by fire or lightning flash, as (also) the nine persons dearest to him of his folk" (Bernard and Atkinson, i, p. 87 and ii, p. 28).

258   ii. 186-7.   *Duncan Cameron, constable, Lochaline, Morvern.*

259   iii. 374-5.   *Barbara Macphie, cottar, Dremisdale, South Uist.*
This prayer makes ready for the last journey.

260   iii. 86-7.
This poem is a fragment and suffers from a lacuna after the first stanza; only the three final lines of the second stanza are in the original.

261　i. 262-3.　*Margaret Macrae, crofter's wife, Tiobartan, South Uist.*
St Columba and the druids whom he defeated (like Moses before
Pharaoh), stand side by side as equally beneficent. Cf. 98, 140,
277, 281. The bramble bush protected from the evil eye. Sprigs of
it hung over byre lintels, here perhaps two woven circlets; it was
combined often with ivy and rowan. It is sacred from being used
by Christ as a riding switch when entering Jerusalem, and a whip
when cleansing the Temple. The moorhen (*gallinula chloropus*)
breeds in Hebridean swamps and marshes. For other dairy poems
v. 85, 211ff, 229, 243.

262　i. 258-9.　*Margaret Macrae, crofter's wife, Tiobartan, South Uist.*
St Brendan and St Ternan were both sailor Saints—this is a poem
of shore, machair, and moorland shieling. The dove (cf. 484) seems
here to be the wood-pigeon (*columba palumbus*) or the stock-
dove (*columba oenas*)—another relic of lost woodland. The torsk
or tusk (*brosmius brosme* or *vulgaris*) is of the *gadidae* family, like
the cod; it comes to land from the deep Atlantic early in the year
to spawn in the seaweed; its flesh, dried and salted, forms the best
stock fish.

263　i. 260-1.　*Mary Stewart (from Skye), dairywoman, Malacleit,
North Uist.*
For open-air milking a tether was necessary and usual. For a
musical version of part of this song v. Kennedy-Fraser and Mac-
leod, i, pp. xxv and 70-1.

264　i. 264-5.　*Roderick Maclachlan, gardener, Balnabodach, Barra.*

265　i. 270-1.　*Christine Macdonald (Macneill), crofter's wife, Ersary,
Barra.*

266　iv. 62-7.
Minnie is a transliteration of *Mineag*, a pet-name meaning little
gentle one.

267　iv. 72-3.　*Mary Macrae (from Kintail), dairywoman, North End,
Harris.*

268　iv. 76-7.
Hummelled cattle are not infrequent in the Highlands and are
sometimes reckoned the best in the byre. There are no strains in
the Outer Isles; the Skye district of Strath (of the Mackinnons)
comprises Strath Suardal, Strath Mor and Strath Beag, and
Strathaird. The drovers' road to the mainland through Glen
Arroch and across Kyle Rhea to Glen Elg traversed the Mackin-
non country.

269　iv. 78-81.
This poem certainly has a "fourth flow" not recorded, and perhaps
more, which would range over daughters, the house-woman her-
self, calves, produce, and so on. For the *mothan* v. 86, 230, 496ff.

270　iv. 82-3.　*Kate Macneill, cottar, Breivig, Barra.*
The staff-churn (*crannachan*), which superseded earlier types, is a
cylindrical vessel of staves, with a detachable lid, holed for the
plunger which has a perforated disc at the bottom.

271　ii. 152-3.　*John Macdonald, tailor, Garrynamonie, South Boisdale,
South Uist.*

The nun (*caillich*) is St Bride, a conflation having taken place with St Bridget of Kildare (v. Bernard and Atkinson, i, pp. 112-16, ii, pp. 40-1 and 194-5). Cf. 85, 142, 363.

272 ii. 142-51. *Mary Maclellan, crofter's wife, South Hacklett, Benbecula.*
Conditions for the rendering of this churning song are difficult; its point is largely in its metre. (Cf. Kennedy-Fraser and Macleod, i, pp. 40-1). The blackcap (*sylvia atricapilla*) breeds in Scotland.

273 iv. 68-9.
This small charm is for reconciling a beast to new surroundings.

274 iv. 68-9.
Not only did particular cows show preference for their own favourite songs, but there were particular ties between milker and beast.

275 ii. 78-85. *Flora Macleod (from Lewis), cottar, Clachan-reamhar, South Uist.*
This is a charm of the *torranan* or figwort, which in the Isles is for milking. Cf. 215, 492f. The borderland beast (*scan foirinn*) is unidentified; it appears in 472 below.

276 i. 278-9. *Angus Macdougal, cattleherd, Liniclett, Benbecula.*

277 i. 272-3. *Angus Maceachain, cattleherd, Stoneybridge, South Uist.*
There were several Irish Saints of the name of Cormac (notably the King-bishop of Cashel of the Gaelic Glossary); in addition Cormac MacArt (under whom the Fiann reached their greatest influence) is reputed to be buried in Iona. But the Saint of the poem is another great Celtic navigator, who penetrated to Greenland; St Columba obtained conduct for him to sail to Orkney, and he was one of the four to visit the apostle at Hinba in the Garvellach Isles. For Cairbre v. 98. Cf. 140, 261, 281.

278 i. 274-5. *Donald Macdonald, cattleherd, Nunton, Benbecula.*

279 i. 276-7. *Somerled Macdonald, cattleherd, Balranald, North Uist.*
This herding song is from the extensive North Uist pastures of the big house of the island, Balranald House; it was anciently of Donald Gormesone and of the Macdonalds of Sleate, normally regarded as the senior branch of the clan.

280 iv. 40-1.
V. 277 for St Cormac, and 145 for St Brendan. A mental conflation may have taken place with St Maol Duinne. Second only to St Brendan's, the voyage of Maildun was a famous Irish Odyssey. But Pennant writes that Iona "was rebuilt by *Malduinus*, in the seventh century" (p. 291); he came to the Scottish throne in 664 and was buried there. But in 1055 Maelduin mac Gillaodhran, "bishop of Alba, and the glory of the clergy of the Gaedhil, rested in Christ" (Reeves, p. 400).

281 iv. 42-5.
St Oran of Latteragh may have preceded St Columba to Iona and the Hebrides; his name is in places both in Mull and Tiree; but he is more usually identified with St Columba's first follower of the Reilig Oran (v. 533). St Dermot is one of four of the name; in 831

he took the books and papers of St Columba to Ireland for safety. Fionn, Cormac, Conn, and Connall (Cool) were all kings and princes of Ireland in heroic times. St Maoloran was a Scot connected with both St Ciaran (v. 420) and St Donnan. St Maoldomhnaich was a Barra anchorite whose island cell was commemorated in Macneill of Barra's deer park, the island of Muldoanich near the entrance to Castle Bay.

282   i. 282-3. *Murdoch Maccuis, cattleherd, Griminish, North Uist.*
The terrain is of the Machair Leathann, broad machair, a two-mile stretch of duned peninsular shoreland with a burial-ground at each end; it is in the north of North Uist. Cf. Kennedy-Fraser and Macleod, iii, pp. 36-9. Another herding poem is 244.

283   ii. 32-3. *Flora Macleod (from Lewis), cottar, Clachan-reamhar, South Uist.*

284   ii. 132-5. *Ian Macinnes, crofter, Stilligarry, South Uist.*
The pastures of Uist are everywhere surrounded and intersected by water—the sea, the wide water-lily lochs, the soft hill-foot ground, the marshy stretches and islets amid sheets of lake water, the many streams and cuts of the meadows. Art and artifice are necessary to cause cattle to make crossings—this is done by throwing down a wand before the beast to simulate a path and bridge, with its accompanying hymn. St Raphael has been substituted for the *Muirinn* of the text; the latter might be a water-angel. There was, however, a saintly Irish princess of the name Muirenn who died in 748, but her possible significance here is unknown.

285   iv. 52-3.
The indigenous breeds of cattle in Scotland are the West Highland, the Galloway, the Angus, and the Shetland. The Ayrshire may not be originally of pure blood.

286   ii. 130-1. *Ian Macinnes, crofter, Stilligarry, South Uist.*

287   ii. 136-7. *Flora Macleod (from Lewis), cottar, Clachan-reamhar, South Uist.*
The apostles are naturally regarded as not only shepherds, but herdsmen and drovers.

288   i. 198-211. *Janet Macisaac (Currie), crofter's wife, Stoneybridge, South Uist.*
This is a Michaelmas circuiting hymn for a croft or farm. Cf. 151ff, 182, 373, 504.

289   i. 280-1. *Donald Macinnes, crofter, Balgarva, Iochdar, South Uist.*
St Modan is another form of St Aidan; sixteen Saints bore this name, the most well known now being St Aidan of Lindisfarne (W. J. Watson, *The History of the Celtic Place-Names of Scotland*, p. 289). St Maolruan is Irish, but he left a rule which became the basis for Culdee monastic life in the Celtic Church, a copy of it being in the Dublin *Leabhar Breac*. St Donnan is the martyr of the Celtic Christians—on Easter Day, 617, in Eigg. St Moluag is the patron of Lismore. St Maolrubha (v. also 281) was a most popular Saint in northern Scotland; he gives his name (contracted) to Loch Maree, and he is the tutelary of the sanctuary of Applecross; his death took place at Urquhart in the Black Isle at the hands of Norwegians.

290 iv. 50-3. *Archibald Currie, shoemaker, Ardnamonie, South Uist.*
For St Bride cf. 14f, 85, 112, 127, 142, 291.

291 ii. 34-5. *Mary Currie, crofter's wife, South Lochboisdale, South Uist.*
There is a break in the text before the final couplet. The white-tailed sea-eagle (*haliaëtus albicilla*) has become extinct in the Highlands; but the mountain golden-eagle (*aquila chrysaëtus*) is still found. The peregrine falcon (*falco peregrinus*) or lanner (*falco lanarius*) abounds in the Torridonian Highlands; the sparrowhawk (*accipiter nisus*) is the predator of the pine forest, but the goshawk (*accipiter gentilis*) has gone thence.

292 ii. 245-6.
The poem has lost one line in the middle. Horses, in the Islands especially, were much used and bred; Islay was particularly famous for them. But they have gradually diminished and there are few poems here for them. Rowan berries were a favourite safeguard for animals and animal-motherhood.

293 iv. 48-9.
The old Highland sheep proper does not exist now, the only similar specimens being the Shetland breed and the Soay sheep from St Kilda.

294 i. 288-91. *Lachlan Macdonald, crofter, Griminish, Benbecula.*
This poem is of two parts, the first for the clipping of the ears of new lambs, the second a general livestock protection prayer. The marking was done on a Thursday (St Columba's).

295 i. 292-3. *Malcolm Macpherson, shepherd, Bagh nam faoilean, South Uist.*
The shearer said this prayer as he freed a sheep.

296 ii. 304.

297 i. 284-7. *Donald(?) Maclean, farmer, the Small Isles, home from Canada, from Clara Macdonald, crofter, Ormacleit, South Uist.*
This is the only poem of the farmyard proper; it has dropped a couplet (the second of the first egg stanza). Twelve is a complete brood; middle finger and thumb are used for lifting eggs, those set being marked with soot.

298 ii. 118-19. *John Beaton (from Skye), shepherd, Aird nan laogh, South Uist.*
The catkin (flower of the birch, beech, willow, and other trees) was triply twined (for the Trinity) and made into a circle (for eternity) for the milk vessels and for protection of stock. Cf. 499.

299 ii. 263.

300 i. 162-3.
It was the custom on Maundy Thursday in Iona, Lewis, and elsewhere to enter into the sea and pour a libation of gruel or ale to the god of the sea with these words. Cf. Martin, pp. 107-8. Manure is the chief use of seaweed, but as kelp, the calcined ashes of seaweed, it brought an all too brief a burst of prosperity in the latter eighteenth and early nineteenth centuries.

301 iv. 32-3.
The task of soil-renewal in the Hebrides by means of seaweed manure is tremendous. St Patrick is a variant reading for *Connan*, whose precise identification is doubtful.

302 iv. 34-5.

303 i. 242-5. *Lachlan Macdonald, crofter, Griminish, Benbecula.*
Seed-corn was carefully prepared and moistened, everything being done with strict ritual. The sheaf-hag—a straw old woman deposited in the last field of the district to be reaped—was not confined to the Highlands. She symbolized a burden in the winter to the tardiest farmer.

304 iv. 118-19.
For the silverweed v. 500.

305 i. 246-7. *Angus Macdonald, crofter, Garrynamonie, South Boisdale, South Uist.*
A hymn was sung in the presence of the whole family or household at the cutting of the first sheaf. This is a Lammas fertility rite, the corn-spirit being usually regarded as the Corn-Mother in northern Europe, while the last sheaf sometimes represents her old age and death (the *cailleach*), sometimes her continuing life (the daughter or Maiden).

306 i. 248-9. *Donald Wilson, crofter, Ardmore, Iochdar, South Uist.*
The poem has a gap in the last stanza after the invocation. In Raasay, says Dr Johnson: "I saw the harvest of a small field. The women reaped the corn, and the men bound up the sheaves. The strokes of the sickle were timed by the modulation of the harvest song, in which all their voices were united." (pp. 55-6).

307 i. 250-1. *Neill Campbell, crofter, Island of Mingulay, Barra.*
Parched grain or graddan was one of the specialities of the Highlands—resulting from a swift method of producing meal from the newly reaped harvest. Though wasteful, it had an attraction in districts where meal was not plentiful, and the harvest was long anticipated for the replenishment of stores.

308 i. 252-7. *Two crofter women, Breivig, Barra.*
Corn-grinding at home was carried out at the quern. As with churning, the metre is important. The flute has been inserted in the rendering.

309 iii. 242-3.

310 iii. 32-3. *Catherine Maclean, crofter, Naust, Gairloch.*

311 iv. 194-7. *Catherine Maclean, crofter, Naust, Gairloch.*
This is a breast charm for a feeding mother, similar in background to the rose or erysipelas charms. Infection of the breast is a not uncommon complaint of maternity. Cf. 218, 226f.

312 iv. 270-1. *Catherine Maclean, crofter, Naust, Gairloch.*
Colic (*colica Pictonum*), a complaint of the intestines unaccompanied by fever, has causes such as spasm, obstruction, overdistension, or inverted action. Usually there is vomiting and wind, and the pain is severe. This rune was said by a stranger over the

man of the house who was struck by colic; the wife had refused, but the husband had proffered the hospitality of a bed of barley awns in the barn. A point of interest is the Gospel identification of the Lord Christ with a chance stranger.

313   iv. 222-5.   *Isabel Chisholm, crofter, Melvaig, Gairloch.*
This poem is called the Charm of the Scales; it incorporates a piece of delicate surgery. Cataract is of two kinds, hard and soft, the former affecting the old, while the latter is more obvious externally and affects a person of any age. The cataract resembles a herring-scale. A basin of running stream-water is fetched with the first part of the charm. Three blades of grass are also brought, and a gold or silver coin is set in the basin. The blades are dipped one by one in the water with a further part of the rune. In the name of each Person of the Trinity the three blades are drawn softly one by one over the affected eyeball. And so the cataract is cut.

314   iv. 302-3.   *Alexander Cameron, the Bard of Turnaig, Gairloch.*
The fleshworm (*fiollan fionn*) is a small worm which causes great pain by moving between the flesh and the skin. It comes sometimes through sleeping in the open air. The cure was again three blades of grass, put in a bottle and shaken up well with water, which was then poured on the painful spot, the rune being said. Near the entrance to Inverewe, now a Scottish National Trust property, a memorial cairn is raised to Alexander Cameron.

315   iv. 298-9.   *Catherine Maclean, crofter, Naust, Gairloch.*
This charm is incomplete, a break coming after the St Columba couplet. The disorder *muatan* is not known—sickly cow is a substitution. Cf. 83, 245f, 358f.

316   iii. 266-7.   *Mary Macleod, Naust, Gairloch.*
In the west of Scotland partnership and neighbourliness were necessary conditions of life; small teams were made for ploughing, fishing, waulking the cloth, and so on.

317   iii. 200-1.
When a man entered a house he uttered a prayer for peace and prosperity—usually in verse.

318   i. 14-17.   *Donald Monro Morrison (from Harris), physician, Edinburgh, from Kenneth the Carpenter and his wife, Obbe, Harris.*
Day and night are alternatives in this poem, depending upon when it was used.

319   i. 18-21.   *Donald Monro Morrison (from Harris), physician, Edinburgh, from Kenneth the Carpenter and his wife, Obbe, Harris.*

320   i. 22-5.   *Donald Monro Morrison (from Harris), physician, Edinburgh, from Kenneth the Carpenter and his wife, Obbe, Harris.*
These three poems from Harris are Protestant; the references are not to the Saints but to the Atonement. The hinterland of Obbe, and the way to the Forest of Harris and the slopes of Clisham are rough going. The great relief is the "down of the mountains", and the "lily of the lake"—the bog-cotton or cotton-grass (*eriophorum*), a sedge-whiteness of blowing adornment, with shallow lochans partly mantled with white or yellow water lilies (*nymphaea alba* and *lutea*), which spring from the peat beneath.

321 iii. 206-7.

322 iii. 256-9. *Ann Macdonald, widow, Lochaber.*
This Lochaber poem, in contrast to the Harris forgiveness poems immediately above, yet close to them in spirit, deals directly with the Sacrament of Penance; it is the only poem to do so. It is not quite complete, the "Good Shepherd" couplet being inserted. It was used, either individually or by the family, before going to Confession.

323 iii. 206-7.

324 iii. 268-9.
The intrusion of fairy bowers is apparent, not real. They are the greenest spots of a district. The *Sithean Mor*, big fairy mound, in Iona is the same as the *Cnoc Aingil*, knoll of the angels; it was there that St Columba had his angelic visitations.

325 iii. 208-9.

326 i. 38-41. *Mary Ferguson, cottar, Obbe, Harris.*
This poem was composed by a Harriswoman afflicted with leprosy, who became cured as she lived by herself on the sea shore by a concoction of plants and shell-fish. Sycamores and stunted mountain pines are the trees of the neighbourhood; and no tree looks more stark when withered than the latter. The strands of shell sand are the conspicuous feature of the western coasts of all the Hebrides.

327 iv. 201 and 203.
Certain well-waters had properties conducive to fertility; the plants valerian and water-cress were also used for childlessness. Such wells were visited at dawn. Sufferers from cancers of the lip or the breast exposed their affected places to the sun on a rock on hot days. A well-prayer for children, being incomplete, has been slightly implemented with the dawn fragment of a cancer-sunning rune.

328 iv. 188-9. *Ann O'Henley, cottar, North Boisdale, South Uist.*
Cf. 218, 226f, 311, 329, 355. Erysipelas of the breast is highly infectious and gives rise sometimes to the spread of a puerperal fever of virulent character. The infecting organism (the Highlander was right in blaming and attacking the *grid*) is *streptococcus pyogenes*. A very fatal kind of the disease attacks new-born infants. The rose charms are accompanied by a lunge of a pointed instrument (knife, needle, or brooch pin) at the spot. Erysipelas (the rose or St Anthony's Fire) is of three sorts—simple, affecting only the skin; phlegomonous, which goes deeper and may become malignant or gangrenous erysipelas; and the oedematous or internal variety which attacks places where the skin-covering is absent. In the last two cases incisions should be made before pus forms, and perchloride of iron is prescribed.

329 iv. 190-1. *Duncan Maceachainn, crofter, Stilligarry, South Uist.*
This charm, also for rose, is incomplete, the second couplet of the third stanza being interpolated. The last two stanzas are variants. It has obscurities also. Erysipelas was sometimes confused with ergot poisoning, of which there were terrible continental epidemics in the Middle Ages, and which recently reappeared in

France; it comes from eating bread made of diseased rye; it causes gradual gangrene in the extremities and is a fatal illness.

330 ii. 10-11. *Margaret Macdonald, cottar, Howgarry, North Uist.*
Cf. 222. There were both toothache charms and toothache wells. This charm is not quite complete, the line invoking Christ being added. The second stanza contains variants of the couplet that precedes it. Poultices and counter-irritants seem indicated. A charm of threads bound round the thumb was resorted to for many ailments.

331 iv. 214-17.
Cf. 80, 97, 224. This sort of charm was accompanied by thread-binding, which would tend to act as a splint.

332 iv. 254-5. *Ewen Maclennan, farmer, Achadh an Tobair, Resolis, the Black Isle.*
Cf. 81, 154, 333ff, 480. Consumption is a disease called by the Greeks φθίσις (phthisis), a decline or decay, the Romans retaining the name and adding another of their own, *consumptio*. They are now distinct medically, and there are various forms of *phthisis* or wasting as of consumption. In these poems the disease (*glacach*) is either a form of *phthisis pulmonalis* or of pulmonary consumption. In the latter the *bacillus tuberculosis* is invariably present. There are three main types of the disease, the acute, the chronic, and the latent. The method of healing in this poem is transference pure and simple; it must have involved some special attractive power over the *bacillus*. The charm was handed down from man to woman and from woman to man. The two palms must be placed on the floor or ground before beginning, and must be washed in running water afterwards. Violent massage was practised.

333 iv. 258-61. *Isabel Calder, crofter, Tulloch, Bonar Bridge.*

334 iv. 262-3.
This trampling charm indicates an alternative to transference; it would be accompanied by appropriate action or symbolism. The following specifics were used: unmelted hog's lard, oil for smearing wool, drawn seal oil, heron or crane oil, the oil of deer's horns, neat's-foot oil, strong spirits and foreshot; these may be compared with the modern cod-liver oil, iron and tonics, especially quinine. *Glac* is the gripping, seizure, or spasm used of consumption or wasting. The tubercle appears at the apex of a lung, causing a dry cough and affecting the breathing. Expectoration follows with sympathetic fever.

333 iv. 258-61. *Isabel Calder, crofter, Tulloch, Bonar Bridge.*
Trampling and transference are here combined. There are, however, many obscurities. The old death-king, Geigean, is depicted as a bowman, like the fairies. St Patrick is introduced in the same way as Fionn sometimes appears, the incident being legendary.

336 iv. 306-7.
Consumption had many names and many charms, showing how prevalent it was and how seriously taken. It was called the Macdonalds' disease, or seizure, chest-struggle or constriction, chest spasms, and the hollow disease.

337   iv. 274-5. *Ian Mackay, crofter, Kinlochewe.*
King's evil or scrofula, known also as *struma* and *tabes-glandularis,* is a disease of anaemic and feeble condition; it is liable to suppurative and ulcerative states of the skin and other parts of the body, the glands of the neck and jaw being particularly susceptible to it. The principal remedies are iron and cod-liver oil. Seventh sons were the gifted ones for healing this disease, which was performed with the rune and well-water.

338   iv. 278-9. *Mary Macrae, cottar, Camas Luinge, Kintail.*
Swelling from rupture or hernia is both painful and dangerous. The final line of the charm is incomplete, nor is any indication given of the treatment, though the rune is straightforward enough.

339   iv. 283-4. *Mary Gordon (of 103 years), spinster, Crask of Aigas, Kilmorack, from a man in Strath Spey.*
Certain persons had the power to stop the bleeding of people and animals. Usually a plant such as the crowfoot was worn, but it was not essential.

340   iii. 200-1.

341   ii. 158-9. *Catherine Mackintosh, cottar, Baleloch, North Uist.*
Highland "second-sight" (really the "two sights") is well known, and there are numerous attested instances. The Augury of Mary, as it is called, of which this poem is an example, is a special application of this faculty, the name deriving from the incident of the young Christ in the Temple with the doctors. Certain augurers and diviners were reputed to see into the unseen; the divination was performed fasting before sunrise on the first Monday of the quarter.

342   iv. 162-5. *Kate Cameron, cottar, Killtarlity, the Aird.*
The evil eye is a belief as curious as that of the second-sight; it was a similar characteristic over which the possessor had not always control. Its effects, when laid on a person or an animal, were distressing—yawning, vomiting, and a general physical disturbance together with a repulsive appearance. In the counter-action, consecrated water (with precious metal in it), and in the case of an animal a thread-binding and an anointing between the horns, were used, the water being given as a draught and also sprinkled over the subject. The remains of the water had to be poured on a stone. The bear (the handed-stirk) was once common in Scotland. Cf. 82, 139, 150, 155, 216, 220f, 420.

343   ii. 44-7. *Isabel Chisholm, tinker, temporarily of Lochmaddy, North Uist.*

344   iv. 170-1. *Dugal Macaulay, cottar, Creagorry, South Hacklett, Benbecula.*
In the case of an animal the evil eye seems to have had a definite association with covetousness, appraising being countered by greater praise on the part of the owner. Thread charms were the normal antidote to the effects (the binding being round the tail). A three-ply was used, black for God's condemnation, red for the crucifixion, and white for the Holy Spirit. The rune was said in conjunction with the Creed and the Paternoster.

345   iv. 158-61.
This incantation is of cattle. There is an attempt to divine the

cause of the trouble (the grey man's eye); some exorcists were able to tell whether it was a man or a woman. *Locha Leargain* is the loch of the place exposed to sun and sea, probably symbolical of health. The significance of the back-head joints and back-leg sinews is the whole length of the frame from the top of the spinal cord to the foot of the Achilles tendon.

346 iv. 176-7.
The "nine" stanza is of uncertain meaning; it was a mystical number and proverbial. The general sense is of a complete confusion of life—perhaps a scattered and frightened herd, an echo of a stampede or of the reiver. Some practitioners of these charms were always ill after a successful performance.

347 iv. 236-9. *William Maclean, gillie, Alness.*
One of the most strange and most widely attested practices is the removal of particles from the eye, even at considerable distances; and not only were they removed, but they were transferred to the tongue or to the hand of the operator. A small basinful of water, an invocation of the Trinity, and the drawing up of the water into the mouth formed the basis of the ritual. Cf. 103.

348 iv. 240-1.

349 iv. 242-3. *Isabel Calder, crofter, Tulloch, Bonar Bridge.*

350 iv. 246-7.

351 ii. 62-3. *Sarah Macphie, crofter's daughter, Balgarva, Iochdar, South Uist.*
This is an incantation of the eye, probably for the "sight".

352 iii. 210-11.

353 ii. 303.
Through constant exposure some Highland cattle were liable to diseases of climate and environment. They suffered sometimes from a throat complaint, and their gulping or coughing could be heard at a distance in the mist. Rueval (the red hill) is the ben of the fords which gives its name to the whole island of Benbecula. It rises only to 409 feet above the sea, but being by far the highest point commands an extensive view.

354 iv. 304-5. *Mary Macmillan, crofter's daughter, Liniquie, Iochdar, South Uist.*

355 ii. 6-7. *Catherine Maccuithean, cottar, Fernilea, Skye.*
This udder charm is the only erysipelas poem that directly invokes transference.

356 ii. 122-3. *Donald John Mackenzie, gamekeeper, Amhuinn-suidhe, Harris.*
Murrain has both red and black stages. It is caused by cattle eating the young leaves of certain shrubs, or in the Isles the sundew (*drosera rotundifolia*). The red pleura (*haematuria* or blood in the urine) can be active or chronic; the first is preceded by dysentery followed by costiveness, caused by a kidney inflammation. After the red water comes fever and heavy breathing and the

beast soon succumbs. In the chronic form (more usual) the water is brown or dark-yellowish and a natural diarrhoea clears the complaint (which springs from the liver) in a few days. The cure of the charm was done by the exorcist (a woman) catching the affected urine in her hands and throwing it into running water; after washing, she formed her palms into a trumpet and intoned the rune to the rising sun as loudly as possible. Manann is an old Gaelic sea-god (the Isle of Man is his), son of King Lir (Neptune) or Lear of the sea; his nine wells are a symbol of the total cleansing power of the sea.

357 ii. 124-5. *Donald Macphie, crofter, Carnan, South Uist.*
Gravel or gravel-stone is caused by small particles or concretions in the urine, so that sometimes blood appears in the water. The charm is similar to those for red water.

358 ii. 140-1. *Archibald Currie, crofter, South Lochboisdale, South Uist.*
An animal suffering from surfeit through over-eating or drinking must chew the cud to reduce the swelling. Other methods must be applied if this is not done.

359 iv. 294-5.
The overfeeding which causes the surfeit comes from too rich a pasture; in the last resort it must be cured by a knife-thrust into the swollen belly, which must be done with accuracy about four inches from the hip-bone and four inches from the back-bone. This is called "tapping" in Ireland. In the charm the Christ has taken the place of St Columba, Loch Scridain suddenly becoming a Sea of Galilee, and Ardmeanach a country of the Gergesenes, with a hint of the walking on the water. The poem is incomplete, the lacuna coming after the couplet of the veins. The name of endearment, *Prugag*, seems to derive from a Mull and Argyllshire cattle-call, *pruidh*. Cf. 83, 245f, 315.

360 iv. 300-1. *John Sinclair, Thurso.*
Foot disease or bruised soles of cattle is a complaint of the hoof caused by rough walking; it is troublesome and obstinate. No method of treatment is indicated here. In the last line there is an unusual hint of fatalism, but v. below.

361 iv. 308-9.
Black spaul or black quarter (scientifically but inaccurately known as *symptomatic anthrax*) is very swift and fatal; it is almost impossible to cure, though it may be prevented. This accounts for the note of fatalism. It comes from a virus; the muscles beneath the skin, usually at the head of a quarter, are darkened and a sour odour is emitted. No indication of the method of treatment is given here, although it would accord with the modern practice of destroying the carcass completely and keeping livestock away from any elements of contact. Once the disease has taken hold, even the slashing of the side and the injection of disinfectants are seldom successful. The charm is similar to that above for the bruise.

362 iv. 310-11. *Mary Macdonald, crofter, Toscaig, Applecross.*
Hide-binding affects cattle, especially cows. If a herb concoction failed to cure, the back was scarified till blood flowed; this was

done by teasel, card comb, or cat pulled by the tail. They were drawn against the hair to the lunges of the tethered animal.

363   iv. 312-13.
It was a custom at Beltane to lustrate cattle with fire, ammonia, water and salt, accompanied by incantations.

364   i. 158-9. *Ann Morrison (Ross, from Skye), mason's wife, Trumisgarry, North Uist.*

365   i. 148-9. *Alexander Macdonald, shoemaker, Baleloch, North Uist.*
At Hogmanay the custom in the Outer Isles was for guisers to run round the outer wall-top of the black house, one being clothed in a bull's hide, and the others beating him. After this, meat, meal, butter, cheese, crowdie, eggs, and other things were provided by the inmates for the Hogmanay bag.

366   i. 150-1 and 152-5. *Archibald Mackinnon, shoemaker, Ersary, Barra, and Patrick Morrison, crofter, Monkstown, Benbecula.*
Two similar versions are here conflated. A sheepskin, lit at the head, was passed round from hand to hand and the smoke inhaled within the house.

367   i. 156-7. *Neill Morrison, bard-shepherd, Island of Pabbay, Harris.*
With this poem the guisers came to the door and sang for their entrance; after their entertainment they circuited the fire, blessing the house. If they were inhospitably treated they went round widdershins and raised a cairn outside. (Two lines are interpolated to represent this.) Of the vermin here, the buzzard (*buteo vulgaris*), and the hen-harrier, ringtail, or white hawk (*circus cyaneus*) are still found; neither the wild-cat (*felis catus*) nor the badger (*meles taxus*) is of the Isles; the wild boar was of the oak woods; the marten is either the polecat or foumart (*mustela putoria*) or the pine marten (*martes foina*); the latter still exists, but the former has left Scotland.

368   ii. 288.
The Wolf-month was usually the last fortnight of winter and the first of spring, corresponding roughly with February, when of old the wolf would approach houses. The Garron was normally the nine days following. The Whistle or Pipe was the third week of February; the Old-Woman was the week after the Garron or the Whistle (but sometimes mid-April); the Little Broom was three days (7-9 April).

369   i. 171-3.
A number of St Bride's (1 February) and St Patrick's Day (17 March) lines are here combined. Flocks were checked and counted on St Bride's Day in Uist and dedicated to her. The raven is the first bird to nest, the mallard and rook following. St Bride's page is the pyet or oyster-catcher (*haematopus ostralegus*).

370   i 182-5. *Donald Wilson, crofter, Ardmore, Iochdar, South Uist.*
Beltane Day (Hallowmas and May Day) was 1 May and a great occasion. All fires were put out and rekindled from the dual heaps of the neid-fire lit on the knoll. Lustration and fumigation were practised for households and stock, which passed between the fires.

371 i. 186-9. *Flora Macniven (Beaton), crofter's wife, South Hacklett, Benbecula.*
May Day, additionally to the above, began one of the most important seasons of the year; it was the day of migration to the summer shielings or hill pastures, the whole household living in huts while the stock fed in the uplands, the lowland pastures being allowed to grow. A procession or trek was made, commencing with a hymn of this sort. The first two lines are missing in the seventh stanza. The Rock of Eager (cf. 113) is in South Uist, named after the Norse king or god of the sea.

372 ii. 190-3. *Alexander Macdonald, crofter, Borvu, Barra.*
In this century it was only in Lewis that the people still went to the shielings. The most distant pastures of all were those of Lochalsh and Kintail, which lay in the uplands east of Loch Monar.

373 i. 212-15. *Ewen Wilson, crofter, Griminish, Benbecula.*
The two main home tasks of Michaelmas Eve were the preparation of the lamb and the baking of the cake (*struan*). This latter was made of all the cereals grown on the farm, thus representing the fruit of the field. In the poem the three beloved apostles are probably the usual combination of St Peter, St Paul, and St John. The dandelion is the "little notched of St Bride"; the three carle-doddies are flower-stalks of rib-grass (*plantago lanceolata*). The grey ox- or cow-plant and the "seven-pronged" are unidentified. Cf. 151, 182, 288, 504.

374 i. 216-21. *Janet Macisaac (Currie), crofter's wife, Stoneybridge, South Uist.*
Sunday poems represent one of the oldest purely Christian traditions of the Celt. It is easily forgotten what a social revolution the introduction of the Sunday's rest would be. The poem is ancient, and exceedingly unclear in parts, particularly in the variants which have been worked into the version. For Sunday travelling cf. 412.

375 i. 222-3. *Ian Pearson, cottar, Kenntangaval, Barra.*

376 i. 294-9. *Mary Macdonald, weaver, Locheport, North Uist.*
The Highlander's clothes were normally entirely home-made; the cloth was almost always. The preparation, spinning, weaving, and manufacture of the cloth was known as *calanas*. The song (a weaver's) is suited to the action involved. One hundred and fifty strands is about average for a tartan sett; the Macdonald has one hundred and thirty, whereas the Ogilvie (the most complicated) has eight hundred and sixty-two. The blue, white, scarlet (red), and madder sett is not one of the usual clan plaids.

377 i. 300-1. *Mary Wilson, weaver, Torlum, Benbecula.*

378 i. 302-3. *Christine Macinnes, cottar, South Hacklett, Benbecula.*
Iomairt is cloth with stripes longwise only. The web was formed on St Columba's Thursday. The chant has lost the second couplet of the third stanza.

379 i. 304-5. *Donald Macintyre, catechist, Aird, Benbecula.*
Cf. 132.

380   i. 306-7.
When the web of cloth has been woven it is waulked (or fulled)
for thickening, strengthening, and brightening it. It is a long task
performed by a team of women. Many songs of all sorts are
sung during the process, nor must one be repeated. This refers to
Prince Charlie, disguised as Morag. Waulking consists of the fol-
lowing stages—thickening, cleansing, folding, giving tension, and
consecrating. All are done meticulously.

381   iv. 94-5.

382   i. 306-9. *Duncan Cameron, constable, Lochaline, Morvern.*
Begged cloth is a reference to "thigging", newly-wedded couples
being allowed to beg from friends and acquaintances to help
themselves to set up house; but they would not necessarily get
the best. The last stanza is obscure, but almost certainly of good-
wish attributes.

383   iv. 96-7. *Duncan Cameron, constable, Lochaline, Morvern.*
There are three female celebrants in this ritual, and the prayer is
a trio.

384   iv. 100-1.
This poem was sung or intoned as a shoe of laced raw-hide was
stitched into a brogue.

385   iii. 378-9.
These are some of the lines of a song to a Lewis funeral air; they
would keep alive the proscribed costume. "The universal Dress
here is a striped Plad, which serves them as a Covering by Night
and a Cloak by Day. The Gentry wear Trousings, which are
Breeches and Stockings of one piece of the same striped Stuff;
and the common People have a short Hose, which reaches to
the Calf of the Leg, and all above is bare." (*A Journey thro'
Scotland*, iii, pp. 126-7, London, 1723).

386   ii. 166-7. *Euphemia Maccrimmon, cottar, Island of St Kilda.*
Cf. 36.

387   iv. 106-11. *Euphemia Maccrimmon, cottar, Island of St Kilda, and
Roderick Macdonald, Clachanagluip, North Uist, from a St Kilda
woman.*
Martin (the great authority on St Kilda) explains the theme of
this love duet, which is called a *iorram* or rowing song. "It is
ordinary with a fowler, after he has got his purchase of fowls, to
pluck the fattest, and carry it home to his wife as a mark of his
affection; and this is called the rock-fowl. The bachelors do in
like manner carry this rock-fowl to their sweethearts, and it is
the greatest present they can make, considering the danger they
run in acquiring it." (pp. 316-17). The poem was composed by the
reciter's own father and mother before their marriage. There is
a huge colony of gannets or solan geese (*sola bassana*) in the St
Kilda group of islands—"one-fifth of all the 167,000 breeding adult
gannets in the world, in 1939" (J. Fisher, *The New Naturalist*,
pp. 99-102). The fulmar petrel (*fulmarus glacialis glacialis*) "was,
once, entirely St Kilda's bird, for until 1878 it nested nowhere
else in Britain" (ibid., pp. 97-9). The turtle dove (*turtur communis*)
and the mavis or redwing (*turdus musicus*) are migrants; but the
St Kilda wren (*troglodytes troglodytes hirtensis*), which lives no-

where else in the world, is not included in the song. The little auk (*alle alle*) is a frequent winter visitor; the last known great auk (*alca impennis*) in the world was destroyed by St Kildans in 1840 in mistake for a witch. The commonest bird is the puffin or coulter-neb (*fratercula arctica*); next to this come the guillemots (*uria aalge aalge*) with the ringed variety (*uria cline* or *lacrimans*) —which is of the song— and a few of the black variety or tystie (*uria grylle*), and also artic fulmars (*fulmarus glacialis*). With all these and more come the predators, the skuas, and the black-backed gulls (*larus marinus*), while the barnacle (*branta leucopsis*) and other geese are visitants. The common or broad sun-fish (*orthagoriscus mola*) is often taken in British waters in the summer as it basks on the surface. The mountain of mist is proper to St Kilda, a home and maker of clouds—hills "often covered with ambient white mists". (Martin, pp. 409-10).

388 iv. 114-15. *Euphemia Maccrimmon, cottar, Island of St Kilda.*
This is a St Kilda waulking song.

389 ii. 319. Composed by *Marion Gillies, a St Kilda maiden.*

390 ii. 252-3. From the *Banais Ioirteach, St Kilda Wedding.*
With the exception of Village Bay or Loch Hirta, the main island of St Kilda is entirely bounded by cliffs that are for the most part terrific. The Clett of Gàdag is one of these; cletts are the name also of the unique drying huts of the island.

391 ii. 225. *Euphemia Maccrimmon, cottar, Island of St Kilda.*

392 iv. 112-13. *Euphemia Maccrimmon, cottar, Island of St Kilda.*
Absence of the men was always a source of anxiety in St Kilda; the occasion of this song was the storm-staying for eighteen weeks of a whole crew of eighteen in North Uist Boreray, where they had gone for sheep.

393 ii. 102-3. *Kirsty Macleod, cottar, Island of St Kilda.*
St Kilda has about 140 species of flowering plants, a number considerably less than a corresponding area of the mainland. The strange title, "yellow swan" (the normal Gaelic name for the plant), perhaps alludes to St Columba's connection with the bird. Cf. 232, 238, 242, 249f, 495.

394 iii. 202-3.
Clearing stones from the road was sometimes done for persons of importance (v. Johnson, p. 335). Cf. the pilgrimage prayers *supra*, 65ff.

395 i. 316-17. *Flora Macleod, cottar, Island of Baleshare, North Uist.*

396 iii. 172-3.
The extent of Highland travelling even in the eighteenth century was considerable. At the Crieff Fair, for example, at least thirty thousand cattle were sold. The "Attendance" of the Highland gentlemen "were very numerous . . . these poor Creatures hir'd themselves out for a Shilling a Day, to drive the Cattle to *England*, and to return home at their own Charge" (*A Journey thro' Scotland*, iii, p. 194, London, 1723).

472

397   iii. 180-1. *Dugal Macaulay, cottar, Creagorry, South Hacklett, Benbecula.*
There is a tremendous and original name for the Deity in this prayer—*A Re nan re,* thou Evermore of evermore; *re* is the moon and the time measured by her, but moon of moons is difficult in English for God, even when coupled with night rest.

398   iv. 120-1.
Cf. 235. The fir club-moss or snake moss (*lycopodium selago*) is only a moss in appearance; its Latin genus-name means wolf's foot.

399   iii. 190-1. *Ann Mackinnon, crofter, Sorisdale, Coll.*
The favourite travelling charm in some districts was a Gospel text on parchment or paper, sometimes in illuminated script, and kept in a linen bag which was sewn into the waistcoat or bodice and worn under the arm. Cf. also 438, 480.

400   iii. 192-3. *Mary Maclean, crofter, Manal, Tiree.*

401   iii. 196-9.
There are two lacunae, both the oaktree line, and the two centre lines of the penultimate stanza being interpolated.

402   iii. 318-19.

403   iii. 208-9.

404   ii. 170-1. *Margaret Macleod, crofter's wife, South Hacklett, Benbecula.*
In a farewell poem of this sort, all departing would be named. Presents, too, would be brought by neighbours. Cf. 69, 108.

405   iii. 246-9.

406   iii. 252-3.

407   i. 285. *Clara Macdonald, of Canada, crofter woman, Ormacleit, South Uist.*
This farewell was made in Canada to Donald Maclean who was returning for a visit to the Small Isles of his origin by an old woman of the Isles of 102 years.

408   iii. 208-9.
In the Highlands, roads went no further than Inverness until the advent of General Wade.

409   i. 50-1. *Gilleonain Macneill, cottar, Castlebay, Barra.*

410   i. 52-3 and 54-5. *Catherine Mackintosh, cottar, Stilligarry, South Uist, and Janet Currie, crofter's daughter, Iochdar, South Uist.*
Two similar South Uist poems are here conflated. Justice anciently was Columban. Under the Lords of the Isles it was administered by hereditary brehons or brieves. The ritual is a dawn purification; the washing is the purification, the meeting of three streams is the Holy Trinity, the rays of the morning sun, divine grace. The deer symbolizes wariness, the horse strength, the serpent wisdom, the king dignity. The white swan is innocence. Cf. 69, 469.

411 i. *56-7. Rachel Maclean (Ferguson), crofter's wife, Balmartin, North Uist.*
Although a litigious poem, this might be applied with more sublimated sense to the last enemy or to the evil one. St Columba was famed for both his voice (clear right across the Sound of Iona to the Ross of Mull) and his eloquence.

412 i. *58-9. Mary Macinnes, cottar, South Hacklett, Benbecula.*
The basic principle of the old Gaelic laws of Scotland, administered by such brieves as the Morrisons of Ness, but difficult of modern interpretation, was compensation for injury. The brieves were more law-experts than judges. The "Sunday King" is possibly a reference to one of the "four chief Laws of Ireland" which prohibited Sunday travelling.

413 iv. *144-5. Catherine Macneill, cottar, Breivig, Barra.*

414 iv. *146-7.*

415 iv. *140-3. Una Macdonald, crofter, Buail Uachdrach, Iochdar, South Uist.*
A number of personages, Christian and pre-Christian rubbing shoulders, are invoked in this rune, particularly from Arthurian and other romance. Fite, a sort of personified spirit of magic, is discussed below (472). Cf. 468.

416 iii. *136-7.*
This poem is only a fragment.

417 i. *64-5. Janet Macisaac (Currie), crofter's wife, Stoneybridge, South Uist.*
The "Visiting One of the Temple" can also mean accessible to visitors and suppliants.

418 iii. *202-3.*
Cf. the "cockman" of Kishmul Castle in Barra (Martin, p. 157).

419 ii. *26-31. Duncan Cameron, constable, Lochaline, Morvern.*
Dornghil or Whitehand was the vesturer and armourer of the Irish hero, Murdoch MacBrian.

420 ii. *54-5. Mary Mackintosh (Smith), tailor's wife, Garrynamonie, South Boisdale, South Uist.*
This is an eye spell (cf. 82, 139, 150, 155, 216, 220f, 342ff). There are at least seventeen St Ciarans (Kieran); the two most likely here are St Ciaran of Saighir (earth from his grave was reputed to have saved his friend St Columba in the whirlpool of Corrievrechan; he is the Cornish St Piran), or St Ciaran of Clonmacnoise (a visitor to Kintyre and the west, one of the twelve apostles of Ireland, in whose honour St Columba composed a hymn). Cf. 281.

421 ii. *36-7. Dugal Macaulay, cottar, Creagorry, South Hacklett, Benbecula.*
In this prayer each of the seven Paternosters is counted out in full and not telescoped as in the version.

422 iii. *174-5.*

423   iii. 202-3.

424   ii. 354.
A chief or chieftain did not usually move about without his "fighting tail", of which his piper was a member. The Mac-Crimmons of Bororaig, the most famous pipers, hereditary to Macleod of Macleod, had a silver chanter of fairy origin.

425   ii. 359.
Two variants are compounded here. The places are in Benderloch, Glenorchy, and Lochaber. Dunkeld, for a period the seat of the Argyll bishopric, was famed for "honey, beeswax, and silk". Clan Paterson were the best sword-makers; their forge was in Benderloch. The arrow-makers were MacLeisters or Fletchers and attached to different clans. The greatest yew (*taxus baccata*) in Scotland is in Glen Lyon at Fortingall. The birch, both the common silver variety (*betula alba*) and the drooping or weeping sort (*betula pendens*), is Scotland's most numerous tree. The golden eagle (*aquila chrysaëtus*), now much reduced, is traditionally of Loch Treig on the Lochaber bounds.

426   ii. 299-300. *An old woman in Uist.*
Auldearn (9 May 1645) was one of the Marquis of Montrose's famous victories, when 1,750 Highlanders routed nearly 4,000 Covenanters. The song was composed by a lady for one of the Clanranalds in Montrose's army. The war-doublet was a short jacket of scarlet or of tartan cloth, with a short cut-away tail. The final line in error refers properly to Charles II; it has been modified to the historical situation of Charles I.

427   iv. 360-3, and ii. 362.
The weakness of all Highland military movements was the predilection for raids, usually for cattle. This pipe-tune and song gives the spirit of this land and sea reiving, and it would, and was meant to, provoke a vigorous reaction and reprisal. Here probably the men of Clan Çhattan were out, though the Cat-men was applied to others as well. Highland chiefs, wrote Pennant, "conducted their plundering excursions with the utmost policy, and reduced the whole art of theft into a regular system" (p. 399). From these activities arose the pleasant custom of black meal or blackmail—a kind of Danegeld.

428   ii. 279-80.
The mantle of this song is the arasaid; Johnson and Boswell heard a version of it as they were rowed to Raasay (p. 354). It was in honour of Allan, Captain of Clanranald, who fell at Sherrifmuir, From internal evidence it must belong to South Uist. Balmeanach (Balvanich) is Monkstown of Benbecula; the Isle of Beagram is in Loch an Eilein by Dremisdale, Kilphedar (St Patrick's Church) being away in the south of the island.

429   ii. 351, 290, 292, and 349.
"The son of my king" cannot but be Prince Charlie. The poem is of five pieces. Raven-knowledge is proverbial of those who arrive at an opportune moment. All the elements are let loose on a night of the seven. Few Hebrideans were not Jacobites.

430   i. 112-13. *Allan Macphie, tailor, Stoneybridge, South Uist.*
St Michael is here in his duel capacity of chief of the heavenly host and of soul-meeter.

431 iii. 236-7.

432 iii. 92-3.
The last line is added to complete the prayer. Another sea prayer is 205.

433 iii. 204-5.
This is a general and a coxswain's or pilot's blessing.

434 i. 32-3. *A. B., lightkeeper, Island of Heisgir nam Manach, North Uist.*
Only St Kilda and Rockall are further west than Monks' Heiskir.

435 ii. 348. *Kenneth Morrison, cottar, Treen, Minginish, Skye.*
The herring's (*clupeo harengus*) main predators of the shallow are the coalfish and the hake, of the deep the porpoise and the common rorqual. The salmon family (salmon, trout, turbot, sturgeon) both preys and is preyed upon. Seals, whether common (*phoca vitulina*) or Atlantic grey (*halichoerus gryphus*), breed largely in British waters. There are many Scottish whales; but the little whale is the killer (*orca orca*), largest of the dolphins. The kraken is fabulous.

436 ii. 260-1.
The only *sirenia* or sea-cows now existing are the manatees of American and the dugongs of Indian waters. The *rhytina stelleri*, or northern sea-cow, became extinct in the eighteenth century; from it originate all tales of sirens and mermaids. The old Caledonian cattle were reputed to be of this stock. This is a song of a sea-maiden tending sea-cows at Obbe in Harris. The Sea of Canna is the Minch; the cow-names correspond rather roughly to the Gaelic diminutive appellations.

437 ii. 257-8. From *Alexander Macdonald and Ian Lom (John Macdonald).*
The poem is two stanzas combined from two famous Gaelic seannachies—MacMhaighstir Alastair, laureate to Prince Charles Edward Stewart, and Iain Lom, laureate to King Charles II. The shell-drake or red goose (*tadorna tadorna*) is a common visitant of the machairs; "Uist of the shell-drakes" is traditional. The two stanzas are of farewell and welcome.

438 iii. 182-9. *Malcolm Sinclair, fisherman-cottar, Balephuil, Tiree.*
"The woman of the seven blessings" is the consecrating mother of the recipient, or some other wise woman; unless it be St Mary Magdalene with her first vision of the Resurrection. The swan on the miry lake refers to its nest; Tiree is the breeding home of the whooper and of Bewick's swan. Rowan berries are a universal charm. Cf. 399f, 480.

439 i. 322-7. *John Maccormick, crofter, Torlum, Benbecula.*
This is a steersman's prayer of the ocean—a consecration of his vocation, more than a voyage petition. For the opening cf. 46, and for other St Bride snake customs cf. 474. The second half is a sort of nautical calendar with an ecclesiastical flavour. *Daingnibh*, establish, is of a fortress, beside which quays, slipways, and moorings were often constructed. The Rock of rocks is possibly a great sea-cliff of nesting birds (cf. 117).

476

440   iii. 72-3.   *Roderick Macdonald, Manal, Tiree.*
The Prayer of Distress is the technical name of a sea-prayer of protection (v. 101).

441   i. 328-9.   *Malcolm Macleod, shipmaster, Lochmaddy, North Uist.*
This poem, which has lost two lines in the Sea of Galilee stanza, is one of the few of Old Testament references. The most celebrated whirlpool of the Highlands is that of Corrievrechan, between Jura and Scarba; it was negotiated by St Columba, although his whirlpool is more usually set in the Antrim waters of Rathlin Island.

442   i. 330-1.   *Alexander Matheson, shipmaster, Lornie, Lochalsh.*
The final line of this poem is added from the Gaelic title. The craft is technically later than the curachs, biorlins, and lymphads of the cians; it is the *iubhrach*, a wherry or barge, and usually a two-oared boat. In Barra, however, it denotes a cutter, or a "good sailing vessel of tidy build", and is used in song of a vessel under sail.

443   i. 332-5.   *Archibald Maclellan, shipmaster, North Lochboisdale, South Uist.*
A form of this prayer was printed in Bishop John Carswell's Gaelic Prayer Book of 1567, and it is copied by Martin (pp. 186-9). The final prayer for the steersman is translated by Martin in terms which have a close affinity to the preceding shipmaster's prayers.

444   ii. 348-9.

445   iv. 356-9.   *Archibald Maclellan, shipmaster, North Lochboisdale, South Uist, Ian and Catherine Pearson, cottars, Kenntangaval, Barra, and others in Kintail.*

446   i. 208; ii. 284, 265, and 363.   *A woman, Liniquie, Iochdar, South Uist, and a girl in Barra.*
There are four portions in this poem. "Torrarnis of the bere" is Hornish Point (cf. 113). The Land of the Bent Grass (more correctly marram grass, *ammophila arenaria*) is South Uist. The last stanza is part of a song composed by a girl carried away captive from Barra by the Norsemen, whose power was not finally broken till the Battle of Largs in 1263.

447   iii. 150-1.   Cf. 72, 163.

448   iii. 280-1.
This is a little new moon thanksgiving prayer.

449   ii. 216-17.   *Alexander Macneill, fish salter, Kenntangaval, Barra.*
This short poem seems to have been ascribed in error to Lismore in Dr Carmichael's original work.

450   iii. 270-3.

451   iii. 306-7.   *An old man in southerly South Uist, and an old man in the Island of Mingulay, Barra.*
These fragments are an adapted survival of sun-worship.

452   iii. 310-11.   *John Macneill, cottar, Balnabodach, Barra.*
This insular poem is of the dawn after the night's sea-fishing. In

many parts of the Highlands a right-handed or sun-wise (it is disputed whether it has anything to do with sun-worship) turn was always made by a boat setting out. The most celebrated disaster from neglect of this (in Loch Spelve) was the fatal campaign of Sir Lachlan Mor Maclean in Islay.

453   iii. 308-9. *An old man called Ian, in Arasaig.*

454   iii. 278-9. *An old man surnamed Robertson, Eigg.*
More of moon-worship has survived than of the sun, but the approach is usually Christianized. Sometimes a little obeisance or curtsey was made to the new moon with a prayer of this sort. Many tasks could only be performed under a waxing moon.

455   iii. 274-7. *Marion Macneill, cottar, Castlebay, Barra.*

456   iii. 284-5.

457   iii. 280-3.
Moonless nights were not welcome to sea-fishermen. Cf. 448.

458   iii. 286-7. *Isabel Macneill, cottar, Kenntangaval, Barra.*
Two words are used for moon in this prayer; hence the moonstar.

459   iii. 288-9. *Ann Maclellan, crofter, Mallaigmore, Morar.*
This poem comes from the shores of Loch Nevis (of heaven), which is not so far from Loch Hourn, known as the lake of hell ("the black river of the abyss").

460   iii. 290-1.

461   iii. 292-5. *Una Macdonald, crofter, Buaile Dhubh, Iochdar, South Uist.*

462   iii. 296-7.

463   iii. 298-9.

464   iii. 300-1.
Certain types of ancient Celtic brooches—much reproduced today—are recognizably lunar in form.

465   iii. 302-3. *Mary Mackintosh (Smith), tailor's wife, Garrynamonie, South Uist.*

466   iii. 304-5.   .

467   i. 122-3. *Neill Macneill, herdsman, Eoligarry, Barry.*

468   i. 310-13. *Angus Mackintosh, crofter, Dungannachy, Benbecula.*
Anciently a young hunter was consecrated and dedicated before he was permitted to try his skill. He was anointed with oil, a bow was set in his hand, and he stood with bare feet. There were certain rules which he must follow; normally he must show consideration for animal motherhood. St Columba preached and St Adamnan enacted that women should not fight in battle. Fite is discussed below (472). The cormorant here is the shag or green-crested cormorant (*phalacrocorax graculus*), in Scots the scart; it is the most plentiful of the waterfowl of the Hebrides. The

mallard (*anas platyrhyncha*) is Mary's duck, reputed the swiftest in flight.

469 i. 314-15. *Sarah Gillies, cottar, Moor of Aird, Benbecula.*
This was said at the outset of a hunting expedition. The ritual is similar to that of pilgrimage and of going to court (cf. 69, 410ff). The badger, which used to be eaten, is indicated in this poem; the heath-hen is the mate of the black-grouse or black-cock (*tetrao tetrix*), a bird of ill omen.

470 ii. 136-7. *Finlay Maccormick, cowherd, Grogarry, South Uist.*
In the Highlands deer-calves are usually born in June; the hind suckles her calf well on into the winter.

471 ii. 23-5. *Effie MacIain (of the Macdonalds of Glencoe), crofter's wife, Locheport, North Uist.*
Fionn's wife was set under a fairy *fith-fāth* spell, in the form of a hind; her son was born after this and was called Ossian from his patch of fawn's hair. While out hunting he met his deer-mother; when he left her he made this song, his first, warning her against the huntsmen and hounds of the Fiann.

472 ii. 22-5. *Effie MacIain (of the Macdonalds of Glencoe), crofter's wife, Locheport, North Uist.*
Fāth-fith and *fith-fāth* are interchangeable; they confer invisibility and metamorphosis. Invisibility and camouflage are in any case closely related. The background to the belief is mythological and magical. Whether Fite, who has already appeared (415, 468), be the spirit or druid of this is, however, a nice question. There are two possibilities; he was perhaps a tree or yew divinity—Fer hI, the man of yew, fosterson of Manannan and tutelary of Iona (W. J. Watson, *The History of the Celtic Place-Names of Scotland*, pp. 88-9). In the Book of Leinster it is stated that, "Fer Fith was found in his yew". There seems to be a definite druidic connection with Fite and *fāth-fith*. Another identification is as follows. When St Patrick had his contest at Tara with the druids, he was compelled to escape by turning his companions and himself into deer. "And the hymn or charm which he recited in his flight was the *Lorica S. Patricii*, commonly called, as the Preface informs us, *Faeth Fiada*, or 'The Deer's Cry'. . . . The title *Faeth Fiada* is perplexing. *Feth fia* is found in the *Book of Ballymote* . . . in a gloss on the word *druid* . . .", with the meaning of magical darkness (O'Donovan) and as a spell peculiar to druids and poets who by pronouncing certain verses made themselves invisible (O'Curry). "And thus our *Lorica* may have gained its title, not from any tradition about St Patrick and the deer at Tara, but from its use as a charm or incantation to ensure invisibility" (Bernard and Atkinson, ii, pp. 208-9). The striking parallels here indicate a Celtic belief in a Patrician Merlin of some sort, conjured up by the famous invocation of the Trinity-binding. This spirit of invisibility and metamorphosis—a magical hangover from a former (and defeated) world—may well be Fite, the personification of *fāth-fith*, fortified by the tradition of the deer of both Ossian and St Patrick. Cf. 415, 468, 504.

473 ii. 128-9. *Donald Maccoll, foxhunter, Glencrearan, Appin.*
Although at one time a considerable plague, later evidence is that the fox (*canis vulpes*) was not numerous in the Highlands. He is not found in Lismore and Appin according to the old

Statistical Account, and only in Skye among the Isles (Johnson, and Pennant), with a few in Mull.

474 i. 169-71.
Versions of similar sayings are set together here. It was the introduction of sheep-farming with land clearance and drainage that reduced the Highland serpent. The viper or adder (*vipera berus*) had a number of names, including that of daughter of Ivor. On St Bride's Day a serpent-effigy was pounded (the bruising of the serpent's head), and, as already seen in 439, a serpent was drowned in the sea.

475 ii. 192-3. *Annie Mackay, crofter's daughter, Melness, Sutherland.* Cf. 217.

476 ii. 184-5. *Isabel Macgrigor, cottar, Bailegarbh, Lismore.*
The barn or white owl (*strix flammea*) is not frequent in the Highlands, as is the long-eared owl (*asio otus*) of the woodland and the short-eared (*asio flammeus*) of the moorland and woodland. The snipe or little goat bird (*capella gallinago*) with its weird cry is a dormant bird in winter. The cuckoo (*cuculus canorus*) is very common and tame, the meadow pipit being its fosterparent. The wheatear (*oenanthe oenanthe*) is sained like the snipe and also dormant.

477 ii. 180-1. *Hector Macphie, crofter, Eilean Cuithe nam fiadh, South Uist.*
The duck and the swan together are the swan and the teal (*anas crecea*), the latter, "the page of the swan" attending the larger bird. The three on the wing are perhaps magpies as in Ireland.

478 iv. 26-7.
The British white swans are three in number, Bewick's (*cygnus bewickii*), the whooper (*cygnus cygnus*) and the mute swan (*cygnus olor*). The second is the normal wild swan and its call is the loudest. Bewick's swan is less common and more quiet, and does not normally breed in the British Isles (except Tiree). The mute swan is vocal (in spite of its name), but quieter still; it is the normal swan seen in England. Instances are recorded of wounded swans, attended by a mate, remaining the year round in Tiree, and becoming very tame. Cf. 20, 239.

479 ii. 182-3. *Malcolm Maclellan, crofter, Griminish, Benbecula.*

480 iv. 264-5. *Malcolm Sinclair, fisherman-cottar, Balephuil, Tiree.*
Other consumption charms are 81, 154, 332ff; other Gospel charms are 399f, 438.

481 iv. 20-3.
The mavis, throstle, or song-thrush (*turdus musicus* or *turdus ericetorum*) has a beautiful song, here set to words. The many snails in the machair provide plenty of food for it. MacLucas in this case refers to the lugworm.

482 iv. 22-3.
The corncrake or land-rail (*crex pratensis*) is a migratory wader frequently heard but seldom seen.

483 iv. 22-3.
There are three species of Highland crow. The red-billed chough

480

or red-legged crow (*pyrrhocorax graculus*) is a beautiful bird, and used to nest in Iona tower with the jackdaws. The hoodie crow (*corvus cornix*) is one of the pests, destructive of other bird life. But here the bird is the carrion crow (*corvus corone*)—a good scavenger.

484 iv. 22-3.
The columba, which gave its name to the Apostle of the Hebrides, is of three main varieties in Britain; *columba palumbus*, the ring-dove or wood-pigeon (in great numbers in wooded areas); *columba oenas*, the stock-dove (from its habit of nesting in tree stumps); and *columba livia*, the rock-dove, which is the one which normally extends to the littoral and the Outer Isles. It frequents the caves of the shore.

485 ii. 313-15. Attributed to *Sir Norman Macleod of Berneray, Harris.*
The long-tailed or ice-duck (*fuligina glacialis* or *clangula hyemalis*) comes every winter to the Sound of Harris and the Sound of Barra. "They arrive with the first frown of winter, and depart with the earliest blink of summer sun" (H. D. Graham, *The Birds of Iona and Mull*, p. 66). Their call is most remarkable. In Berneray of Harris there was a sept of people called Clan Macandy; the inhabitants in general regarded the long-tailed ducks as the enchanted sea-branch of the clan. The poem is twofold—the cries of the birds to their kinsfolk of Berneray; the reply of human affection back to these birds which revel in the roughness of the ocean.

486 ii. 336.
The nest by the mouth of the water occurs in 469 above; it is of the black-throated diver (*colymbus arcticus*), also known as the rain goose, the loon and the ember goose. It is rare or unknown in Britain apart from the Hebrides; but it is hardly ever seen in its beautiful breeding feathers. If drought occurs, the water's edge subsides out of reach and the bird is very distressed; the mother generates great heat in the hatching weeks, but it makes her very thirsty. Hence her anxiety. The first stanza is a rendering of her cries as current in North and South Uist, the second as in Harris and Lewis.

487 ii. 336-7.
When the water rises too much and threatens to flood her nest, the black-throat is equally concerned.

488 iii. 134-5. *Ann Macdonald, widow, Lochaber, and Catherine Macneill, cottar, Breivig, Barra.*
For other Lochaber poems v. 157ff, 251, 322; for other poems of the Blessed Virgin v. 146ff, 160, 215.

489 ii. 94-5. *Mary Stewart (from Skye), dairywoman, Malacleit, North Uist, and Ann Macisaac (Maclellan), cottar's wife, Ceannlangavat, South Uist.*
Two lines from a South Uist version have been incorporated into this North Uist poem. Yarrow or milfoil (*Achillea millefolium*) is common in the lower altitudes of the Highland deer forest of the north-west in dry places. It is an astringent plant, much used as a purge and for checking bleeding, as well as having a dairy connection. Cf. 221.

490 ii. 74-5. *Peggy Maclean, cottar, Trumisgarry, North Uist.*
The plant is not identified.

491 ii. 76-7. *Catherine Macpharlan (Pearson), soldier's wife, Kenntan-gaval, Barra.*
This plant is unidentified also; it does not at first sight call to mind the dandelion or notched one of St Bride (*taraxacum officinale*).

492 ii. 86-9. *Flora Macleod, cottar, Island of Baleshare, North Uist.*
The figwort (*scrophularia*) is the plant of Taranis, a thunder god, or of St Ternan, a sailor Saint. The water figwort (*scrophularia aquatica*) is the most likely species of these poems, with a stem of three or four feet, and a flower sometimes all white, though usually brown and green. It was once considered a remedy for scrofula, hence its generic name. Cf. 215, 275.

493 ii. 90-1. *Margaret Morrison, cottar, Moor of Griminish, Benbecula.*
St Ternan (12 June) is an apostle of Uist. He landed in a little bay in Benbecula at Calligeo to convert, or reconvert, the population, having been rejected in Ireland. His plant is popularly supposed to grow only near the sea which he loved. The site of his cell is in Loch Chaluimchille (St Columba's Loch).

494 ii. 92-3. *Gormul Mackinnon (from Skye), servant woman, Loch-maddy, North Uist.*
The plant of this charm (*an earnaid shith*) is not identified; but it might be fairy barley (*eorna* or *earna*).

495 ii. 97.
St John's wort (*hypericum perforatum*), like some other herbs, was considered effective only when found by accident. It was worn, like the Gospel texts, in a package or little bag in the armpit. It was used medically both as a tonic and as an astringent. Cf. 232, 238, 242, 249f, 393.

496 ii. 110-11. *Christine Macvicar, cottar, Moor of Aird, Benbecula.*
The *mothan* is uncertain, or it may vary according to district. Dr Carmichael inclined first of all to the bog-violet (*viola palustris*) which grows amongst the sphagnum with lilac or white scentless flowers. But it was identified apparently later for him in Mull as the pearlwort. It was in any case particularly prized. Cf. 86, 230, 269, 497f.

497 ii. 112-13. *Christine Macvicar, cottar, Moor of Aird, Benbecula.*
Dr Carmichael's original alternative for the *mothan* was the thyme-leaved sandwort (*arenaria serpyllifolia*). Used as a love philtre, nine roots of the plant were twined into a circle and placed in the mouth of the suppliant girl. Like St John's wort it might be worn beneath the arm for travelling, and it was used also for childbearing.

498 iv. 134-5. *From the Reverend Dr Kenneth Macleod.*
There are five or six species of the pearlwort (*sagina*) which seems to have been the final choice for the *mothan*. It belongs to the pink family, and has five or six pointed leaves and red roots; but it is rare. The species is probably the heath pearlwort (*sagina subulata*), although the common pearlwort (*sagina procumbens*) occurs in the islands. There are two further identifica-

482

tions. The butterwort (*pinguicula vulgaris*), sometimes called the bog-violet, is given and illustrated as the *mothan* in Dwelly's Dictionary; while the purging flax (*linum catharticum*) was claimed by Annie Johnstone of Barra (A. A. MacGregor, *The Western Isles*, p. 170).

499 ii. 118-19. *Angus Macleod, gamekeeper, Ceann Resort, Lewis.*
Cf. 298.

500 iv. 118.
The silverweed (*potentilla anserina*) preceded and was used as a substitute for the potato. Cf. 304.

501 iv. 124-5.
Both the primrose (*primula vulgaris*) and the wood-sorrel (*oxalis acetosolia*) with its oxalic acid were favourites with children. Wine and plovers mean good fare; the golden plover (*charadrius pluvialis*) is the largest species; it is of the moorland, but comes to the shores in severe weather, when it is very tame.

502 iv. 128-9.
The mountain-yew or juniper (*juniperus communis*) usually spreads laterally, but it can rise to about ten feet. It was much worn, and was an ingredient of the Michaelmas cake as well as making gin-spirits.

503 iv. 136-7.
The bog-myrtle or sweet gale (*myrica gale*) thrives in wet ground; its leaves could be used for brewing ale, and in Islay provided scent for clothes. The shrub also made bedding; the candle berries, coated with an aromatic wax could become small perfumed candles.

504 iii. 139-40.
The Michaelmas carrot was gathered by women on Carrot Sunday preceding the festival. A good store was required for the evening of the dance. The double carrot (*carduus benedictus*) was especially prized. Bunches of them were given to the young men by their girl friends. Cf. 151ff, 182, 288, 373. The identification of Fite is made with *Fàth-Fìth*, who is here Fite Fith. Cf. 415, 468, 472.

505 ii. 108-9. *Norman Macphaire, cottar, Island of Berneray, Harris.*
If found accidentally, the shamrock was "an invincible talisman".
Cf. 143, 236.

506 i. 234-5. *Archibald Morrison, crofter, Stoneybridge, South Uist.*
Smooring must be done with care because of danger from fire at night and because the peat must continue to smoulder. Cf. 9, 175.

507 iii. 324-5.
In smooring, the embers were spread evenly on the hearth in a circle, which was then divided by peats into three sections—one for each Person of the Trinity—and then covered over with sufficient ashes to preserve the fire.

508 iii. 326-7.
Embers were sometimes kept in a pit or a hole in the clay floor or under the dresser at night. There was a flagstone covering for this, with a hole in the centre.

509 i. 72-3. *Donald Maccormick, crofter, Killpheadair, South Uist.*

510 i. 78-9. *Patrick Smith, crofter, Lethmeanach, Stoneybridge, South Uist.*
This poem is incomplete, a gap coming after the third stanza.

511 i. 84-5. *Donald Macdonald, crofter, Griminish, Benbecula.*

512 i. 74-5. *Mary Macmillan, crofter's daughter, Liniquie, South Uist.*

513 i. 86-7. *Donald Macdonald, crofter, Griminish, Benbecula.*
Cf. 13, 50, 256, 516f.

514 i. 94-5. *Christine Macinnes, cottar, South Hacklett, Benbecula.*
The four archangels are parallel to the four evangelists of English nursery and folk lore, often confused with angels ("Four angels round my bed", etc.).

515 iii. 328-31. *Peggy Maccormick (Macdonald), crofter and nurse, Ard Buidhe, Loch Boisdale, South Uist.*

516 iii. 334-5.

517 iii. 332-3.

518 iii. 342-3. *Mary Macrae, cottar, Camas Luinge, Kintail.*
This prayer may be the second part of the ritual of 105. It is for putting out the light.

519 iii. 340-1.
Other evening prayers are 9ff, 50, 105f, 163ff, 175f, 214, 255f, 287.

520 iv. 4-5.
The golden or yellow butterfly was known as the fire or lightning of God; it represented the angel who came to bear the soul to heaven; sometimes a fiery-stick was twirled to imitate this butter- fly and encourage its beneficent function. The true yellow butter- fly was reputed to have emerged from the Holy Tomb. The lines were said by children.

521 ii. 246.
The mountain-ash or rowan-tree (*pyrus aucuparia*) was sacred and prized; it was used as a protective influence for livestock and for milking; fires of its wood were made for baking festival cakes. It was especially good to have a coffin or bier of this timber. Dwarf rowans grow in the Outer Isles. Dundealgan, the dun or castle of gold, has a literary parallel; in the Irish *Liber Hymnorum* at the end of a scribe's additions to the Amra of St Columba occurs the line (perhaps the fragment of a hymn) *Dundelga maith an t-inad oir,* "Dundelga, good the gold place" (Bernard and At- kinson, i, p. 188 and ii, p. 86). Although it is the name of Dundalk in Ireland, Dundealgan cannot be a real place—perhaps an ethereal fortress or palace of the Aurora Borealis.

522 iii. 368-9.
Good weather (to accord with peace) was much desired for passings and burials. Bad weather meant the black, and snowy the white wrath of God.

523 iii. 394-5.
The Saints were the natural counterpoise to the sinister spirits. The poem is not quite complete, with a lacuna after the disappearance of the body in light.

524 iii. 202-3.

525 i. 116-17. *Clara Macphie, tailor's wife, Stoneybridge, South Uist.*
This is the poem of the soul-friend who chanted it gently over a dying person—as in baptism the sign of the cross was made (in this case) over the lips. The soul-friend, who was like a godparent and, though an outsider, ever afterwards had a place in the family, was akin to the confessor of the Celtic Church; or possibly this Celtic term became attached to the priestly function in medieval times. But the office declined into that of professional mourning-women.

526 i. 118-19. *Donald Macdonald, crofter, Stoneybridge, South Uist.*

527 i. 120-1. *Mary Macisaac, crofter's wife, Stoneybridge, South Uist.*

528 i. 117.
Watchers by the dying said this sort of verse as the soul was seen to ascend "like a bright ball of light".

529 iii. 371. *From the people of Barra.*
This is a Barra view of Purgatory.

530 iii. 378-81. *Four or five versions from Lewis.*
These are words for a pipe-tune used at funerals. Other words to the same tune have already been given (385).

531 iii. 382-5.
This is a hymn for the professional mourning-women at a burial.

532 iii. 202-3.
Paths were sometimes cleared for funerals, and on the mainland also strown with birch and sycamore branches. Other death poems are 22, 51ff, 167, 259.

533 ii. 338-40.
St Oran was the monk related to St Columba after whom the burial-ground of Iona (Reilig Oran) is named. The story of his interment for three days and the reopening of his grave is well known. The poem is a version of the incident which caused his reburial. It has occasioned much heart-burning at different times. The conflicting elements of self-sacrifice and unbridled inquiry were resolved with St Columba's decision and his grief for St Oran; but the daring shown removed some of the sting of death and was therefore consecrated. It is a remarkable sublimation of what may have been a voluntary human sacrifice, or at least a courageous experiment. But there is a defect here—the absence of reference to the Easter joy and the Resurrection in the death poems. Psychologically the story is sound—admiration of a great failure and disappointment at what the Greeks might call ὕβρις (hubris). But cf. 64.

534 i. 224-7. *Roderick Macdonald, farmer, Suenish, North Uist.*
This dramatic poem has affinities with the R stanza of St

Columba's *Altus Prosator*, and to the *Dies Irae*, a fiercely appropriate six days of uncreation, watery, stormy, Hebridean. The lost Atlantis and the undersea remains which are sometimes visible on the western shores have left their echoes, together with such proverbs as that "the Macleans had an ark of their own at the time of the Flood". Grass and fish beneath the same flagstone denote a foundation where land and sea have become confused. "A red cross on each right shoulder" (cf. 32) is of uncertain meaning; but it must be of absolution and redemption here.

535 ii. 348.
This verse is a rendering of an ancient prophecy. It connects perhaps with a somewhat obscure line in the Amra (hymn in honour) of St Columba,. *Cét cell custói tond fo ógi offrinn,* "hundred churches' guardian of waves; under completeness of offering", explained in the gloss as "guardian of waves is he over seas of a hundred churches . . ." (Bernard and Atkinson, i, p. 177 and ii. p. 73). The prophecy witnesses to the greater permanence and strength of St Columba's Iona than of royal Ireland or chiefly Islay. Another tradition said that Iona's doom stones also would continue to move until the Day of Judgement.

INDEX OF FIRST LINES

488

493

498

AUTHORITIES

Only the chief works consulted are stated.

ADAM, Frank (ed. Sir Thomas Innes of Learney)
  The Clans, Septs and Regiments of the Scottish Highlands, 4th edition   Edinburgh 1952

ANONYMOUS
  A Journey Thro' Scotland   London 1723

BERNARD, John Henry, and ATKINSON, R., editors
  The Irish Liber Hymnorum, 2 volumes   London 1898

CARMICHAEL, Alexander
  Carmina Gadelica, 2 volumes, 1st edition   Edinburgh 1900
  2nd edition, Elizabeth Catherine Carmichael (Mrs W. J. Watson), editor   Edinburgh 1928
  volume 3, James Carmichael Watson, editor   Edinburgh 1941
  volume 4, James Carmichael Watson, editor   Edinburgh 1942
  volume 5, Angus Matheson, editor   Edinburgh 1954

Poems from the final volume of this are not included in this work.

DARLING, F. Fraser
  Natural History in the Highlands and Islands   London 1947

DWELLY, Edward
  The Illustrated Gaelic-English Dictionary, 5th edition   Glasgow 1949

FRAZER, Sir James
  The Golden Bough, abridged edition   London 1949

HYDE, Douglas
  The Religious Songs of Connacht, 2 volumes   Dublin 1906

JOHNSON, Samuel (ed. R. W. Chapman)
  A Journey to the Western Islands of Scotland (London 1775), with James Boswell, *The Journal of a Tour etc.*   London 1924

KENNEDY-FRASER, Marjorie, and MacLEOD,
    Kenneth
    Songs of the Hebrides   London 1909 etc.

MacALPINE, Neil
    A Pronouncing Gaelic-English Dictionary,
    new edition   Glasgow 1948

MARTIN, Martin (ed. Donald J. Macleod)
    *A Description of the Western Islands of
    Scotland* circa 1695 (London 1703) with
    A Late Voyage to St Kilda (London
    1698) and with Sir Donald Monro, *A
    Description of the Western Isles of
    Scotland Called Hybrides* (Edinburgh
    1774)   Stirling 1934

PENNANT, Thomas
    *A Tour in Scotland and Voyage to the
    Hebrides; MDCCLXXII*, 2nd edition   London 1776

REEVES, William, editor
    *Adamnan, Ninth Abbot of Hy, The Life
    of St Columba, Founder of Hy*   Dublin 1857

SHAW, Margaret Fay (Mrs John Lorne Camp-
    bell)
    Folksongs and Folklore of South Uist London 1955

WATSON, W. J.
    *The History of the Celtic Place-Names
    of Scotland*   Edinburgh 1926